Politics of Fear, Practices of Hope

Continuum Studies in Religion and Political Culture
Series Editor: Graham Ward and Michael Hoelzl,
The University of Manchester, UK

Titles in this series look specifically at the relationship between religion and political culture. Drawing upon a broad range of religious perspectives the series is open for studies of historical as well as current phenomena in political culture. It seeks not only to inform but to provoke debate at a time when religion is gaining increasing prominence in the public realm.

A Grammar of the Common Good, Patrick Riordan
The New Visibility of Religion, Graham Ward and Michael Hoelzl
Politics of Fear, Practices of Hope, Stefan Skrimshire
The Politics to Come, Arthur Bradley and Paul Fletcher

Politics of Fear,
Practices of Hope

Stefan Skrimshire

continuum

Continuum International Publishing Group

The Tower Building
11 York Road
London SE1 7NX

80 Maiden Lane
Suite 704
New York, NY 10038

www.continuumbooks.com

British Library Cataloguing-in-Publication Data
A catalogue record for this book is available from the British Library.

ISBN: HB: 1-8470-6075-7
      978-1-8470-6075-4

Library of Congress Cataloging-in-Publication Data
A catalog record for this book is available from the Library of Congress.

Typeset by Newgen Imaging Systems Pvt Ltd, Chennai, India
Printed and bound in Great Britain by Biddles Ltd, King's Lynn, Norfolk

Dedicated to my mother, Pascale Skrimshire.
1950–2002

Mais l'espérance, dit Dieu, voilà ce qui m'étonne.
Moi-même.
Ça c'est étonnant.

(Charles Péguy)

Contents

Acknowledgements

My thanks:

To Lucy most of all, for reading, questioning and ultimately improving the final manuscript; for supporting me throughout its preparation; and for being such an inspiration to me. Peter Scott, for reading it more than once and whose critique and sound advice have played a big part in its final form. Graham Ward for inspiring and encouraging the whole process. Ursula Rothe for proofreading it. Steven Grimwood, Matt Gardner, Daniel Fitzpatrick and Ben Gilchrist for giving valuable feedback. Jai Redman, Richard Searle, Sharon, Laura and Rachel, whose stories gave life to my discussion of practices of hope, for their time and passion. To the series editors, Michael Hoelzl and Graham Ward, for their help in making this book a reality. To my family, for their support: my dad Chris, my brothers Ant and Ralph, my sister, Suzanne, my grandpa, Michael and grandmère, Jeanette. And finally to the many friends, fellow activists and dreamers who give me reason to hope.

Introduction

Crises of hope

At the end of his 2004 Peace Lecture in Manchester, Noam Chomsky was asked this question from the floor: 'do you live in hope, or despair?' Despite having spent the past hour divulging the recent crimes of the US government, his response to this question was perhaps the most controversial thing he had said that afternoon:

> It doesn't matter, I mean whether you have hope or despair is kind of like a personal matter between you and your wife and children or something, maybe not even that, it just doesn't matter, you do exactly the same thing, whether you're optimistic or pessimistic, really doesn't matter, it's a subjective question.[1]

Perhaps because it came right at the end, or perhaps because it stuck out as the *only* subjective question posed during the lecture, that response seemed at best hasty, at worst the reflection of long-standing political taboo. I couldn't help feeling at the time, moreover, that it resonated with a more general cultural attitude towards this illusive and somehow intangible subject of 'hope'. It might be summed up as an intellectual aversion to treat one's own vision of the future with as much urgency as a description of the present. But this attitude raises important questions for anybody concerned about the concept of meaningful political action or that notoriously ambiguous term 'activism'. To ignore hope on the theoretical level (What does it refer to? Where does it come from? Is it a thing that we can study?) is surely to jeopardize a potentially powerful understanding of its practice.

Are our political cultures undergoing a crisis in their understanding of hope? This question underpins the direction of this book. It is an attempt to understand what motivations or reasons lead people to take political action. And behind this search lies my suspicion that hoping and despairing are, in contrast to Chomsky's comment, of great importance. They are,

---

[1] Noam Chomsky, Lecture at University of Manchester, Department of Government, 22 May 2004. Souled Out Films [DVD].

perhaps, even definitive. Do not our beliefs and attitudes towards what is 'to come' go beyond hypothetical curiosities (that we only share with our loved ones, for example)? Do they not move and shape the conditions for acting politically? These are not *originally* specialist academic questions about the future, eschatology, Utopianism or any other intellectual theories about the future covered in this book. They are questions that, at root, affect everybody, since they address what it is that gives one reason to *be political* at all.

This search for our motivations for hope takes place within a critique of contemporary societies as marked by a 'politics of fear'. How does the notion of hope relate to that of fear? Today our fears derive no doubt from a range of sources, from terrorist threats to flu pandemics and fears of global warming. But to explore crises in human cultures' expressions of hope, I shall be arguing, involves looking at not only externalized fears (the threat from 'outside') but the production of the experience of a fearful 'everyday' existence itself. In reference to a 'politics', then, I am interested in the *management* of fear as an emerging political condition for government. Fear, I shall argue, has become an essential ingredient of a culture of acquiescence and non-participation intrinsic to post-modern social life. This is particularly pertinent to cultures caught up in the 'war on terror', the proliferation of heightened security measures and the militarization of societies under the pretext of anti-terror strategies. But as we shall see throughout the course of this book, it can also be more widely understood as the condition for a normalized state of anxiety in our societies. Fear has become an environment from which the subject of 'hope' perhaps simply appears out of place. It has been replaced by an obsession with levels of alarm and emergency – the management of how much we are to be scared.

The past decade, then, has generated many reasons to fear and modes of articulating it. What might it mean to give equal attention to the cultural ability to project the future, to be forward-thinking, to articulate hope in the future? The signs of such a trend have been emerging for some time. Protest cultures put increasing energy and time into constructing and disseminating narratives of resistance in an age of globalization. We are living in a cultural climate dominated by the competitive ideologies of the 'end of history' and 'there is no alternative' (TINA) to neo-liberal capitalism. And within that climate people are once again telling stories of a culture and legacy of precisely that – political alternatives and the restlessness of history.[2] Perhaps, indeed, they always have. A cursory glance at the

---

[2] A recent example of this is Rebecca Solnit's book, *Hope in the Dark: The Untold History of People Power* (Edinburgh: Cannongate, 2005).

still-growing sections on anti-capitalism or global protest movements in mainstream bookshops is perhaps only one superficial manifestation of this storytelling.

It is certainly not the intention of this book to contribute one more catalogue of discontent with the global world order. I want instead to look at the language and practice of resistance. In doing so I am trying to make a case for the role of *belief* in the prosecution of *action*. I argue that the concept of 'living in hope' might also be called a type of faith, or belief, in the future. Some people, in order to avoid the terminology of faith and belief, may want to call it an attitude or world-view. There is no obvious problem with this distinction. But whatever it is called, what *must* be avoided is equating the concept of hope with 'optimism' or a 'positive outlook'. Being optimistic describes a state of mind that says little about the cultural, philosophical and other backgrounds to which the decisive act of faith refers. Faith, in this sense, is about what motivates and makes sense of our actions. Hoping and despairing, to repeat, cannot be confined to the realm of the subject. They are not merely qualitatively different *experiences*. They are involved in a cultural and political matrix of production and dissemination in which everyday political engagement is unavoidably caught and to a large extent oriented.

Cultures of defeat

What new analysis is needed for critiquing a culture of despair? A primary motivation for this book was a belief that more needs to be said not only about a lack of hope, but also the failure of traditional, historically rooted ideas and beliefs that once grounded hope. As is written in a recent and fairly typical compendium on the subject, 'a symptom of the times is the decline in interest in hope as a philosophical concept.'[3] Another study, relating more specifically to the role of theological language, claims that 'optimism has given way to a sense of ambiguity, messianic and utopian modes of thought have capitulated before the drawing of apocalyptic scenarios.'[4] This is clearly nothing new. Fifty years ago the Marxist and Utopian thinker Ernst Bloch lamented the lack of conceptual resources with which

---

[3] Mary Zournazi, *Hope: New Philosophies for Change* (New York: Routledge, 2003), p. 14.

[4] Miroslav Volf and William Katerberg, 'Introduction: Retrieving Hope' in *The Future of Hope: Christian Tradition Amid Modernity and Postmodernity*, ed. Miroslav Volf and William Katerberg (Cambridge: William B. Eerdmans, 2004), pp. ix–xiv (p. ix).

to counteract the culture of despair that succeeded two world wars. What was missing, he thought, was an appreciation of the sense of unfolding possibility that actually lies at the heart of human experience: 'the Not-Yet-Conscious, Not-Yet-Become, although it fulfils the meaning of all men and the horizon of all being, has not even broken through as a word, let alone as a concept.'[5]

Bloch's comments are powerfully relevant to the task of this book, for they seem to presage the political pulse or 'mood' of contemporary political culture. How might we define this mood? It is clearly more than an observation that our societies today face unprecedented threats to their survival (through ecological collapse or nuclear war, for instance). It represents a suspicion towards the very narratives of faith that have, at least since the Enlightenment, defined modernity's relationship with these crises of the future. Categories of progress, revolution and evolution do not belong only to the sciences of economics, politics and biology. They describe the conceptual tools with which people can be 'forward-thinking' at all. Today, however, we must consider whether such unified narratives of the future have become redundant, replaced by superficial or ironic expressions of expectation, or, at best, of personal achievement. Consider, as an example, the concept of 'millennium' leading up to the year 2000. In the United Kingdom at least, the media seemed more preoccupied with the impending malfunction of computer systems, the so-called Millennium Bug, than with the idea of new opportunity and renewal. Even today the word sits most easily with projects that seem to continue a certain banal continuation of the past. As Christopher Schwöbel has put it,

> where the millennium was used as a key-word for our situation it did not refer to the advent of a surprising new reality, but served as a decorative phrase for our more or less reasonable projects. Otherwise, in much of our culture great expectations appear to have given way to grave concerns and small pleasures.[6]

Bloch is also important because of the centrality that fear plays to his thought. For Bloch, fear had represented a systematic silencing of the aspirations and hopes innate to each human being. Fear represented a more

---

[5] Ernst Bloch, *The Principle of Hope*, vol. 1, trans. Neville Plaice, Stephen Plaice and Paul Knight (Oxford: Basil Blackwell, 1986), pp. 5–6.

[6] Christopher Schwöbel, 'Last Things First?' in *The Future as God's Gift: Explorations in Christian Eschatology*, ed. David Ferguson and Marcel Sarot (Edinburgh: T&T Clark, 2000), pp. 217–241 (p. 236).

'definite' form of anxiety suffered by people denied a sense of direction or aspiration. It absolutely prevented forward-thinking. It paralysed action and creativity.[7] Is this still the case in contemporary political cultures? This book attempts to show that if despair describes a suppression of vision for change, the contemporary political and cultural uses of fear go further than simply this absence of hope or historical direction. If the successive campaigns of terror and counter-terror that fill our broadsheets today are anything to go by, it is clear that the meaning of a politics of fear is also a rationale for embracing a way of life. Perhaps fear represents the *embrace* of despairing situations through the pretence of being assured security. It would then represent also the perversion of hopes as the original desires of, as Bloch thought, our originally Utopian, autonomous and creative selves.

Faith in the future

How then can we make sense of hope in the current political climate? Today threats of a ubiquitous and untameable 'terror' cloud any political strategies of progress beyond the immediate imperative of security at all costs. In such a climate the language of Utopias and new possibilities appear to many people futile at best and dangerous at worst. Of fundamental importance is thus an investigation into an emerging debate over the nature of political Utopianism in political life. Those on the Utopian left such as Frederic Jameson[8] continue to defend its legacy as a necessary antidote to the ideological closure of late capitalism. 'Ideological closure', a concept that will become indispensible to my analysis, is Jameson's way of describing the limits of discourse (and thus the ability to think, speak and act) imposed by a given ideology. We can therefore think of an ideology of fear imposing closure on the imagination of the future. Those of an 'anti-Utopian' persuasion, meanwhile, such as John Gray,[9] claim that any Utopian faith in a perfect future recalls the religious roots of all forms of contemporary political violence. Apocalyptic faith that breaks out into this religious terror, runs one argument, represents only the thin end of a large wedge in the West's tradition of imagining the end. Its remnants in traditions of Utopianism or religious faith in the future are one and the same thing. It is also common

---

[7] Bloch, *The Principle*, vol. 1, p. 3.

[8] Frederic Jameson, *Archaeologies of the Future: Utopia and Other Science Fictions* (London: Verso, 2005).

[9] John Gray, *Black Mass: Apocalyptic Religion and the Death of Utopia* (London: Penguin, 2007).

to make a crude distinction between an overly optimistic Utopianism (every-thing is possible) on the one hand and an overly pessimistic apocalypticism (we're all doomed) on the other.

As is often the case, these distinctions are too simplistic. They deal in gen-eralizations of three key terms that have enjoyed a recent revival of popular interest: 'Utopia', 'eschatology' and 'apocalypse'. But the context for that sudden uptake of interest is frequently one swept along by a contemporary wave of hysteria. It is manifested in our fascination with predictions of global catastrophe that consistently inhabit the world of politics and reli-gion. Politics and religion are, after all, both discourses of *risk* in one way or another. They provide a rationale, that is, for anticipating future events (that can be either in hope or in despair in both cases) and orienting behav-iour according to that sense of anticipation. All the more reason, therefore, to give more space and reflection to these complex and important themes. They are some of the intellectual staples that continue to frame our atti-tudes to the future. They have, consequently, everything to do with hoping and fearing.

Imagination and fantasy

Throughout this book I intend to convince the reader of a distinction between two concepts normally associated with psychology: *fantasy* and *imagination.* How is this distinction justified? It is significant to note a tradi-tion, going back as far as Kant (but influential on thinkers more contemporary to this study such as Gilles Deleuze), that emphasizes the psychological function of imagination (or 'productive imagination', to use Kant's term) as synthesizing the many and various intuitions of everyday experience.[10] The imagination is here explicitly *not* defined as the act of replacing the 'real world' with one that is fabricated and detached from it. Instead, it is the act of making sense of our creative 'constructions' of reality itself. Imag-ination is the way in which we colour the world and make practical sense of it. By contrast, if we then define as 'fantasy' precisely a process of substitut-ing the present world with an illusory one, the usefulness in this distinction becomes apparent. For it is by placing an emphasis on the *active* role of per-ception in the construction of everyday life that imagination emerges as distinct from any form of escapism. Once again using Bloch's ideas we can see immediately how fantasy thus allies itself with fear. For fear is that which

---

[10] Immanuel Kant, *Critique of Pure Reason*, trans. J. M. D. Meiklejohn, www.marxists. org/reference/subject/ethics/kant/reason/critique-of-pure-reason.htm.

paralyses action and is 'passive', much as we might summarize the principle of fantasy: that which mesmerizes and takes us 'out of ourselves'. Thus, though there are undoubtedly many different understandings of the word, I use fantasy as descriptive of a style of political participation *removed* from the public domain. In the course of this study this diminished form of public life will be identified by the commodification of social engagement – its reduction to the consumption of images and atomized social participation. Imagination, on the other hand, I take to be essential in the active construction of social reality, something that moves us *towards* others and other social realities. It is therefore relevant to this exploration of practices of resistance and protest that reclaim the political for popular participation. The former *de*politicizes where the latter has the potential to *re*politicize. To pre-empt Castoriadis' contribution, it is the 'social imaginary' that opens up a construction and vision of what reality *can be*, quite the opposite to responding to the shortcomings of the 'real world' by positing a fantastic one.

How then do I proceed to explore the distinctions between a 'passive/ fantastical' and 'active/imaginative' representation of the future, and how do they enlighten our understanding of hope? In what follows I will draw attention to the influence of political life through Utopia's imaginative and fantastic manifestations – from literature and popular culture to religious narrative and media rhetoric. It emerges that concepts of the future are diffuse and unavoidable. From the quasi-religious themes of 'apocalyptic' fervour to the language of protest and messianic hope, to the rhetoric of global crisis and risk: in both liberal and conservative traditions world events and cultural transformations have attracted our attention to these ideas. And, if taken seriously, they can explode, multiply and deepen our often simplistic assumptions about what it means to live in hope.

Political theology

As an argument for an extended analysis of those thematics of Utopia, eschatology and apocalypse, therefore, this book makes a case for the continued relevance of 'political theology'. I understand political theology to refer to a conversation between two inseparable discourses (the political and the theological). They are inseparable because, if for nothing else, both are intimately concerned with the imagination of the future. As such they have a vested interest in listening carefully to each other and at times finding points of convergence in their respective understandings of the nature of political acts. Understandings of 'the political' inevitably involve acts of projection and anticipation – what it is that is believed and hoped *to come*. They produce, consequently, definitive responses to the status of risk and uncertainty in society. In the Western tradition more specifically, this has manifest itself through the notion of a trajectory of history or 'progress'. But many of these themes bear resemblances, and in some cases have their historic roots, in theological discourses. Theology in the Judaeo-Christian tradition has been traditionally associated with the articulation of beliefs in a personal future beyond the present state of existence. More recent theologies nevertheless approach the concept of the future in much wider political terms. Beliefs about the future of the world, the imagination of its end and the grounds for hoping in the midst of crisis are dominant themes in all of the major religions. In the Judaeo-Christian tradition the emphasis on a futural trajectory cast in messianic and apocalyptic tones becomes particularly acute. Both the political and the theological, there-fore, hold a tension between the 'now' and that which is 'to come'. The nature of their tension – or indeed resolution – is the subject of a philosophy of hope.

Methodologically, therefore, this book is certainly not confined to a dis-cursive *comparison* between political and theological approaches to the future. It asks, rather, whether the one discourse opens up a deeper and more creative understanding for the other. Charles Taylor has argued on this subject that in the secular world today there is no direct (institutional) passage from social reality to sacred reality. For this reason 'the modern world endlessly produces new forms of spirituality'.[11] I would agree with Taylor's sense of the fragmentation of sites of contemporary sacralization. I disagree, however, with the judgement that 'an impassable membrane separates the realm of the spirit – interior – from that of physical reality – exterior . . . reinforced by an attitude of disengagement and the discipline of modern rationality.'[12] As this book concludes, among the many ways in which such an 'impassable membrane' is being surpassed, at least one is happening through a transformation in political assumptions about the nature of temporal living.

Practices of hope reveal, directly or indirectly, a confluence of political and theological themes. They do this through an ambiguous relationship between the *immanence* of political ambitions (what we fight for 'here

---

[11] Charles Taylor, 'A Place for Transcendence?' in *Transcendence: Philosophy, Litera-ture, and Theology Approach the Beyond*, ed. Regina Schwarz (London: Routledge, 2004), pp. 1–11 (p. 4).

[12] *Ibid.* p. 10.

and now') and a kind of *transcendence* of its aspirations (what we believe is always on the horizon – the permanent 'not yet', as Bloch put it). Theology can play a role in sharpening a distinction between fantasizing and imagining the end. For example, in the language of theology we discover an appreciation of the power of apocalyptic imagination; the envisioning of the end; and the centrality of the concept of future in all reasoning. Theological discourse can claim to be itself 'before its time', to be untimely, to quicken political sensibility. It is able to unbalance the immanence of the *saeculum* by blurring the lines between the 'before' and 'after' of eschatological history. Apocalyptic is therefore one of those 'quasi-religious thematics' that John Milbank believes lies at the root of post-modernism.[13] The eclecticism of contemporary uses of the concept of apocalypse and eschatology shows that if the traditional philosophical language of hope is temporarily out of action, the inventiveness of the imagination of the future has simply found other paths.

Why focus on the Judaeo-Christian tradition? There is, without doubt, a wealth of resources to draw upon from the eschatologies of many other religious traditions. On top of other major world religious traditions, one finds a wealth of interpretations of eschatology in the ancient traditions from which Judaism arose, from Canaanite to Persian traditions. To do them justice, however, is far beyond the scope of one book. Further, the Judaeo-Christian tradition presents itself with acute historical and contextual relevance to the task of this book. A politics of fear emerges as inseparable from American and European cultures. Unsurprisingly, then, it is to a predominantly Western apocalyptic tradition that one finds most parallels in the adoption of a language of both hopes and fears of *the end* in contemporary political cultures. As we shall see it is a peculiarly Christian apocalyptic vision that guides, for instance, much of the White House rhetoric on counter-terror propaganda. It is thus pertinent to engage with alternative interpretations of that concept within the Christian tradition itself.

The eclecticism of contemporary uses of the concept of apocalypse and eschatology shows that even if the influence of these traditional, broadly Christian concepts of theological and philosophical language has diminished, the inventiveness of political movements to express the future has not done away with Christian themes entirely. In fact, as this book argues,

---

[13] John Milbank, 'Problematizing the Secular: The Post-Postmodern Agenda' in *Shadow of Spirit: Postmodernism and Religion*, ed. Philippa Berry and Andrew Wernick (London: Routledge, 1992), pp. 30–44 (p. 30).

political practices frequently play with the 'quasi-theological' concepts I explore. I should also add, by way of highlighting what *unites* these practices with the theoretical resources explored earlier in the book, that they all make contributions to my analysis by collectively constituting a necessarily broad definition of 'the political'. That is, the thinkers and practices I have invited all in some way point towards a critique or appraisal of the uses and effects of power in social life, or the ethics of particular ways of relating to others and to the world. The book gains a wider understanding of the *scope* of the political and its relation to the imagination.

What kind of argument am I attempting through this interdisciplinary exploration? I argue that it is the persistence of practices of hope themselves that gives life and meaning to those philosophical and theological traditions. It is the because of the fact that hope *persists* in the world that we should look again at the intellectual foundations of Western thought and reclaim what has been lost, perverted or misunderstood, of our resources for cultivating cultures of hope. Far from attempting to 'map' a logic or rationale for hope derived on philosophical or theological traditions onto social practices, I am perhaps operating in reverse. The dynamic interrelation of ideas such as hope, fear, imagination and time is poorer where it confines itself to the limits of any one isolated discourse. This is why the book fuses the exploration of different practical responses to fear with such diverse areas of thought as (to mention a few) Marxist philosophy, media analysis, deconstruction, systematic theology, sociology and graffiti art. Their usefulness lies in their capacity to clarify the diverse nature of 'experiments in hope'.

Summary of the argument

Part I: Politics of Fantasy outlines some principal features of the uses of fear in contemporary culture, and its impact on the 'collective imagination' of the future. In Chapter 1 the war on terror in particular tells us much about transformations in liberal democratic cultures: fear is manipulated not simply through government propaganda but through the production of everyday anxiety. In Chapter 2 Gilles Deleuze and Félix Guattari's introduction of a 'politics of desire' provides an important foundation for critiquing the tendency for capitalist culture to provide a rationale for *desiring* a culture of fear. Why do cultures seem so paralysed by the crisis of the present and so compelled by ideologies of the 'end of history'? To answer this question, the subject of Chapter 3, involves appreciating the crisis imminent to capitalism itself, that which generates, as Philip Goodchild points out, a false or heretical form of secular eschatology[14] (or, to put it simply, 'discourse about the end').

Part II: Politics of Imagination attempts to answer the question stated earlier, 'which categories, ideas or beliefs are able to restore hope as a serious philosophical concept?' These areas are proposed for consideration, and 'time' emerges as the crucial explanatory concept. In Chapter 4, I outline the notion of Utopian imagination and its critique. The most useful exponents are Ernst Bloch, Cornelius Castoriadis and Paul Ricoeur. Attempting to understand the conceptual resources introduced through the Utopian impulse leads to exploring theological discourses of faith in 'the end' from the Christian tradition in Chapter 5. A comparison between the respective eschatologies of Karl Rahner and Karl Barth allows us to see eschatology as the political expression of a hope without foundation but not without ground.[15] Their respective eschatologies orient the ethics of certain political practices according to a particular ontology of time. The recent work on St Paul by the Italian philosopher Giorgio Agamben introduces the importance of these ideas to contemporary notions of both the legalistic 'state of exception', and the radical notion of *kairòs*, or the time of (political) possibility. The argument then turns, in Chapter 6, to the radical potential of a much more ancient tradition: apocalyptic discourse. Because the term 'apocalyptic' has so many intonations and interpretations today, its meaning is easily polarized. There is resurgence, for example, of apocalyptic rhetoric in the form of millennial cults, popular entertainment and the treatment of disaster in the media. But apocalypse also surfaces equally in attempts to give shape to a language of political possibility. As with the discussion of eschatology, the radical potential of apocalyptic discourse reveals itself in its ability to generate an alternative orientation towards time. This will be argued through tracing the legacy of three philosophical developments of the concept of 'apocalyptic time': Martin Heidegger; Antonio Negri; Jacques Derrida.

Part III: Experiments in Hope, with this focus on the apocalyptic imagination in mind, the book turns to three modes of political protest that characterize, more than symbolically, contemporary responses to a politics of fear. These modes are: political art and street theatre (Chapter 7); mass mobilization and 'global protest' movements (Chapter 8); and the uses of the body in acts of non-violent direct action (Chapter 9). How *do* social and

---

[14] Philip Goodchild, 'Capital and Kingdom' in *Theology and the Political: The New Debate*, ed. Creston Davis, John Milbank and Slavoj Žižek (London: Duke University Press, (2005), pp. 127–159.

[15] I owe the expression of this distinction to Peter M. Scott.

political practices confront a culture of depoliticization? I answer this with a mixture of personal accounts, theoretical analyses of the concepts generated (the influence of such thinkers as Foucault, Scott, Hardt and Negri, and Paolo Virno, for instance) and my own analysis. Each tradition of protest is read as one would a literary source: as serious expressions of political and social desires. And each reveals alternative political imagination to the form of endist fantasy produced by an economy of fear.

Part I

Politics of Fantasy

La politique est l'art d'empêcher les gens de se mêler de ce qui les regarde.

Paul Valéry[1]

In the following three chapters I outline some principal features of a politics of fear in contemporary culture. While the close relationship between fear and political strategy reveals itself most obviously in the tactics of the war on terror, its wider implications both precede and reach beyond this development. It reveals, fundamentally, a transformation of the public sphere from a culture of participation into one of consumption. I explore this transformation as a 'fantastic' future projection. In reality this represents the inability to exercise an alternative political vision of the future.

---

[1] Paul Valéry, *Tel Quel 2* (Paris: Gallimard, 1943), p. 41, my emphasis. 'Politics is the art of preventing people from taking part in affairs which properly concern them' (my translation).

Chapter 1

Post-Democracy and the War on Terror

Introduction

Hermann Goering is making a timely comeback, and it isn't every day that the last words of a Nazi war criminal become required reading for political activists. But it is hard to browse websites or the latest publications on global politics or the 'war on terror' without finding his (in)famous words of 60 years ago on the political uses of fear.[1] They were recorded in an interview with Gustave Gilbert, a psychologist granted access to all the prison cells at Nuremberg in 1946. It is worth quoting Gilbert's written account at length:

We got around to the subject of war again and I said that, contrary to his attitude, I did not think that the common people are very thankful for leaders who bring them war and destruction. 'Why, of course, the *people* don't want war,' Goering shrugged. 'Why would some poor slob on a farm want to risk his life in a war when the best that he can get out of it is to come back to his farm in one piece. Naturally, the common people don't want war; neither in Russia nor in England nor in America, nor for that matter in Germany. That is understood. But, after all, it is the *leaders* of the country who determine the policy and it is always a simple matter to drag the people along, whether it is a democracy or a fascist dictatorship or a Parliament or a Communist dictatorship.' 'There is one difference,' I pointed out. 'In a democracy the people have some say in the matter through their elected representatives, and in the United States only Congress can declare wars.' 'Oh, that is all well and good, but, voice or no voice, the people can always be brought to the bidding of the leaders. That is easy. All you have to do is tell them they are being attacked and

---

[1] The *Google* search engine reveals 33,600 separate entries of Gilbert's exact quote. www.google.co.uk [accessed 2 February 2006].

denounce the pacifists for lack of patriotism and exposing the country to danger. It works the same way in any country.'[2]

Those who quote the latter part of Goering's comment no doubt read in it a chillingly prescient logic in the light of the war on terror's uses of fear propaganda. But this unease should also provoke a more difficult question: should we be surprised? Has the situation ever been different in the nationalistic production of public consent? The aim of the present chapter is to explore the concepts that sustain and legitimate both the silencing of dissent and the maintenance of a permanent global state of terror and anxiety. In doing so I pose the possibility that a culture of paranoia championed by the war on terror addresses, albeit within a different historical context, the question put by another psychologist of fascism, Wilhelm Reich: 'why do men fight for their servitude as stubbornly as though it were their servitude? How can people possibly reach the point of shouting: "More taxes! Less bread!"?'[3] It was Reich's integration of psychological, sexual, and socio-cultural influences in the successes of both Hitlerian and Stalinian totalitarianism that led him to be more interested in the processes leading to and sustaining their popular legitimation than simply their 'madness' in the first instance as fascist ideology. He was interested, following Erich Fromm, in the 'fear of freedom and the craving for authority'.[4] It was subsequently Deleuze and Guattari who recognized in this kind of study the foundations for thinking beyond psychoanalytic 'disorder' to the production and maintenance of precisely an order or rationality for remaining within a repressive system. I attempt to answer these concerns first by describing a transformation in democratic culture. I focus principally on the demise of the public sphere in its traditional enlightenment understanding as the site of rational critique. This leads inevitably to a critique of the conditions of consumer culture, in which an illusion of security is attached to acts of consumption and acquisition. A politics of fear is then understood to be capitalized or commodified within this climate.

---

[2] Gustave M. Gilbert, *Nuremberg Diary* (New York: Farrar, Straus and Company, 1947), pp. 278–279, italics in the original.
[3] Quoted in Gilles Deleuze and Félix Guattari, *Anti-Oedipus: Capitalism and Schizophrenia*, trans. Robert Hurley and others (London: Athlone Press, 1984), p. 29.
[4] Wilhelm Reich, *The Mass Psychology of Fascism*, trans. Vincent R. Carfagno (New York: Farrar, Straus and Giroux, 1970), p. 219.

Fear and propaganda

Should we see Goering as remaining faithful to a legacy of modern statecraft established by the likes of Machiavelli ('fear is strengthened by a dread of punishment which is always effective'[5]) and Hobbes ('of all Passions, that which enclineth men least to break the Lawes, is fear. Nay, [. . .] it is the only thing that makes them keep them'[6])? What comes across in these thinkers is an almost banal awareness of the social utility of fear. Certainly for Hobbes, a seminal figure in the history of the 'production' of political fear, it was the task of the state to educate and instil a culture of fear in its citizens if it was to control them. Through subsequent historical developments it went on to become a key component in legitimizing sovereign rule and containing popular dissent. From the 'terror' of the French revolutionaries to Second World War and Cold War propaganda, the shift in thinking about fear has been towards its strategic public use and away from the privatized domain of personal morality.[7] Fear, in this sense, is not only all pervasive but all-controlling. It is frequently the deciding factor in campaign strategies in times of war.

Could the same be said for the strategies emerging from the war on terror? In order to answer this question, it should be suggested that of greater interest to today's political environment is not Goering's comments but those of the interviewer Gilbert himself. In particular, his retort that 'there is one difference, [. . .]. In a democracy the people have some say in the matter through their elected representatives, and in the United States only Congress can declare wars.' It is not my intention to explore a psychology of fascism as Gilbert does. Nevertheless, the passage just quoted does provoke the need to re-evaluate the notion of political participation within recent changes to the 'democratic' world. Much like Gilbert, modern proponents of democracy do of course continue to demand that 'the people have some say in the matter'. But today this sentiment should be considered alongside, to take the most obvious recent example, the case of the invasion of Iraq in 2003, cited by some as the 'most unpopular war in history'.[8] The decision to invade Iraq, decided in secret long before a mandate

---

[5] Niccolo Machiavelli, *The Prince*, trans. George Bull, new edn (London: Penguin Books, 1999), p. 54.

[6] Thomas Hobbes, *Leviathan*, ed. Richard Tuck (Cambridge: Cambridge University Press, 1991), p. 206.

[7] Corey Robin, *Fear: The History of a Political Idea* (Oxford: Oxford University Press, 2004), p. 8.

[8] Edward Said, 'Who's in Charge?', *El Ahram*, 6 March 2003, http://weekly.ahram.org.eg/2003/628/op2.htm [accessed 24 March 2006].

was sought from either the House of Commons or the UN,[9] represents to
many people a changing face of liberal democracy. In particular, it is felt
that while more emphasis than ever is placed on the appearance of democratic participation, levels of participation and engagement with democratic
institutions is at an all-time low. What emerges is a critique of traditional
forms of democratic participation based on shifting cultural trends. The
decreasing tendency for people in liberal democracies, for example, to vote
or otherwise get involved in a political party, stands as a strong indicator.
Another is the reduction of opposing or varying political 'options', and the
dumbing down of political issues through the entertainment-focus of media
reporting.

The illusion of consent

The production of an illusory consent thus poses a disturbing twist to
Gilbert's distinction between fascism and democracy. Is it possible that
people have the impression of having 'some say in the matter', but accept
at the same time that their dissent signifies little more than a symbolic
performance of democracy? At least since the backlash to the terrorist attacks
on US soil in 2001, the domestic erosion of civil liberties suggests a situation
closer to Chomsky's summary of contemporary democracy:

> the role of the public, as the ignorant and meddlesome outsiders, is just
> to be spectators. If the general public, as it often does, seeks to organize
> and enter the political arena, to participate, to press its own concerns,
> that's a problem. It's not democracy; it's what's called 'a crisis of democ-
> racy' that has to be overcome.[10]

Why, then, should we interpret contemporary culture as in the grips of a
'politics of fear'? One of many recently emerging theorists of political fear,
Corey Robin, writes that the most important piece of deception that must
be uncovered in the history of fear is the belief that it represents a 'thought-
less or wholly affective passion'.[11] Fear has been popularly conceived to
stand in polar opposition to the practice of reason and the freedom of

---

[9] 'Blair Made Secret US Pact', *BBC News*, 3 February 2006 <http://news.bbc.
co.uk/1/hi/uk_politics/4675724.stm> [accessed 24 February 2006].

[10] Noam Chomsky, 'Control of Our Lives', Lecture in Kiva Auditorium,
Albuquerque, New Mexico, 26 February 2000 <www.zmag.org/chomskyalbaq.
htm> [accessed 14 January 2006].

[11] Corey Robin, 'Reason to Panic', *The Hedgehog Review*, vol. 5, no. 3 (2003), 62–80
(65). See also Robin, *Fear*.

subjects. Yet even the so-called pre-modern theorists on fear, from Aristotle and Augustine to Hobbes, understood not only that fear represented a dialectical tool in distinguishing between virtue and vice, but that it was indispensable to any political economy of sovereign rule.[12] In his responsibility to make the distinction on behalf of his citizens, the sovereign must use more than violent coercion in successfully wielding fear as an instrument of the social good. There must also be a rationalization of social fears through education, religious teaching and media communication. 'One man calleth wisdom, what another man calleth fear',[13] Hobbes presciently observed. George W. Bush's declaration, a week after the attack on New York that 'freedom and fear are at war'[14] represents a not dissimilar rhetorical tactic. By polarizing the affective and the rational dimensions of fear, the strategic communication and production of fears become effectively hidden from view.

Propaganda and the myth of the public sphere

The emergence of political tactics that constitute that elusive political strategy we now call 'the war on terror' is marked by a series of transformations of the public sphere. The run-up to the 2003 invasion of Iraq provides a telling example. Facing an historic show of opposition by public demonstration in February, Tony Blair had far more success in rallying public support for his war in the United Kingdom by patrolling 50 tanks and 1,500 armed troops and police around Heathrow Airport in response to a terrorist threat than he did trying to rationalize 'sexed-up' dossiers. George W. Bush had already done this the week before by 'advising Americans to prepare disaster kits for their homes, making sure they had at least three days worth of water, food and medicine'.[15] We observe continuity, therefore, from those pre-modern rationalizations of a politics of fear mentioned above to contemporary strategies of public propaganda. The USA PATRIOT Act (Uniting and Strengthening America by Providing Appropriate Tools Required to Intercept and Obstruct Terrorism) was passed by Congress in October 2001 and authorized much more than just the power of incarceration and

---

[12] Robin, *Fear*, p. 34.
[13] Quoted in Robin, 'Reason to Panic', p. 67.
[14] George W. Bush, Address to a Joint Session of Congress, *September 11 News*, 20 September 2001, www.september11news.com/PresidentBushSpeech.htm [accessed 17 December 2005].
[15] Esther Addley, 'High Anxiety', *The Guardian*, 13 February 2003.

surveillance. It gave provisions that targeted people, 'simply for engaging in classes of political speech that are expressly protected by the US constitution'.[16] That act was followed by an executive order that allowed Bush to try any non-citizen he designates in a military court without a right of appeal or the protection of the Bill of Rights. What proceeded in the years to follow was an increasingly stratified process of cultural production, enlisting, most importantly, the help of media institutions. Looking at the history of government propaganda in the lead-up to war reveals considerable consistency on this point. Chomsky points out, for instance, that the first 'coordinated propaganda ministry' was set up by the British government during the First World War to try and convince American intellectuals of the 'nobility of the British war' and draw the nation into it.[17]

In December 2005 the Pentagon reported keeping records on citizens and officials who opposed the invasion of Iraq.[18] The 'new' context inaugurated by the war on terror therefore has done more than follow the pattern by which, for example, anti-communism became, in Chomsky's words, the 'national religion' during the Red Scares since 1919.[19] Contemporary forms of paranoia directed at the elusive, polymorphous and omnipresent figure of 'terror' has constituted a threat far more ambiguous than even the American understanding of communism was. A threatening 'other' in the form of 'radical Islam' may well have become a useful scapegoat. But it did not prevent people from generalizing its *sign* not in the form of 'clash of civilizations' but 'clash within each civilization',[20] the realization that a terrorist attack could come from within. What is threatening goes beyond America and can come from within America, and *that* is the point about terror. As Brian Massumi puts it: 'An unspecified enemy threatens to rise up at any time at any point in society or geographical space. From the welfare state to the warfare state: a permanent state of emergency against a multifarious threat as much in us as outside.'[21] We have gone

---

[16] Sheldon Rampton and John Stauber, 'Trading on Fear', *The Guardian*, 12 July 2003.

[17] Noam Chomsky, 'Collateral Damage', interview by David Barsamian, *Arts and Opinion*, vol. 2, no. 4, 2003, www.artsandopinion.com/2003_v2_n4/chomsky-2. htm [accessed 13 March 2006].

[18] 'Pentagon in Global Propaganda Drive', *The Guardian*, 15 December 2005.

[19] Edward S. Herman and Noam Chomsky, *Manufacturing Consent: The Political Economy of the Mass Media* (London: Vintage, 1994), p. 29.

[20] Žižek, *Welcome to the Desert of the Real!* (London: Verso, 2002), p. 44.

[21] Brian Massumi, 'Everywhere You Want to Be' in *The Politics of Everyday Fear*, ed. Brian Massumi (Minneapolis: University of Minnesota Press, 1993), pp. 3–37 (p. 11).

beyond the 'clash of civilizations', therefore, as the end-game of the current crisis of world order, to a hyperpolitical identification of 'terror' as universal signifier. As Žižek puts it, 'terror is thus gradually elevated into the hidden universal equivalent of all social evils'.[22]

Another facet of a politics of fear conditioning the new transformations of the public sphere reveals itself in military technology and the capacity for 'instant war'. The American strategic aim of being able to drop out of the sky upon the enemy even before it is able to pull the trigger has become a fantasy that erodes spatial difference. It does this through the technological desire for acceleration, that 'hidden side of wealth and accumulation, or capitalization'[23] as the French 'philosopher of speed' Paul Virilio puts it. But contained within this desire for speed is the production of paranoia and permanent anxiety. Deterrence, in fact, because it represents the inde-terminate face of disaster (because it remains as potential, not instance), crystallizes what is peculiar about the social production of fear. Integral to maintaining the illusion of *order* through a logic of MADness (Mutually Assured Destruction[24]) is the institution of boundaries by which any form of institutionalized violence (military invasions, economic sanctions, extraju-dicial internment, torture etc.) becomes order itself. This 'order' brings with it, understandably, a precondition of extreme paranoia such as no totalitarian regime, perhaps, has rivalled. Instant war capability or 'rapid deployment force' represents, then, in Brian Massumi's words, 'the virtual-ization of state violence, its becoming immanent to every coordinate of the social field, as unbounded space of fear'.[25]

How does this brief exposition of the birth of the war on terror shed light on the manipulation of public consent? We must take a closer look at its relation to the use of traditional tactics of domestic propaganda. By which mechanisms do ordinary people accommodate the kinds of militarization of social space and the silencing of dissent listed above? Has it only been made possible through the complete manipulation of 'public consent'? Hannah Arendt once suggested that the only people at risk of 'complete manipulation' of information are, ironically, presidents and prime ministers. For it is they who, more than any other social actor, are required to

---

[22] Žižek, *Welcome to the Desert*, p. 111.

[23] Paul Virilio, *Politics of the Very Worst*, trans. Michael Cavaliere, ed. Sylvère Lotringer (New York: Semiotext(e), 1999), p. 60.

[24] 'Mutually Assured Destruction', *Wikipedia*, http://en.wikipedia.org/wiki/Mutually_assured_destruction [accessed 24 February 2006].

[25] Massumi, 'Everywhere You Want to Be', p. 29.

surround themselves with advisors, lobbyists, spin doctors and other interpreters of outside reality.

If this is true, how then does it apply to a social entity like that of a critically engaged 'public'? Has it become able to simultaneously oppose and endorse policies that compromise its own freedom? How might it become caught within this snare of 'complete manipulation'?[26] Commenting on the Pentagon Papers, a 47-volume document detailing the US government use of public deception in order to secure support for war in Vietnam, Arendt was observing that, 'the psychological premise of human manipulability has become one of the chief wares that are sold on the market of common and learned opinion'.[27] The history of propaganda clearly predates the advice of Macchiavelli, yet it was only three decades ago that, as Arendt observed, 'democratic' governments attempted cultural manipulation on a grand psychological scale. They had been awakened to the knowledge that waging unpopular wars would demand a professional engagement with the then recent invention of 'public psychology'. Originally associated with market advertising, public psychology boasted the ability to predict, with some precision, what it would take for any product to attain public acceptance.

How has the use of public psychology in the war on terror directed the shape of the public sphere today? The globalization of media images may have created the problem for governments of their international exposition (consider, for example, the prominence of photojournalism initiated by the infamous photos of fleeing Vietnamese children burning with Napalm[28]). But that same development has certainly also provided a solution: namely, through the stratification of myriad levels of public psychological deception. Today many critics of the war on terror argue that the sensationalization of journalism continues to be an indispensable marketing

---

[26] See Michael Rosen, *On Voluntary Servitude: False Consciousness and the Theory of Ideology* (Cambridge: Polity Press, 1996); James C. Scott, *Domination and the Arts of Resistance: Hidden Transcripts* (London: Yale University Press, 1990); Don Herzog, *Happy Slaves: A Critique of Consent Theory* (London: University of Chicago Press, 1989).

[27] Hannah Arendt, *Crises of the Republic* (New York: Harcourt Brace Jovanovich, 1972), p. 8.

[28] See, for instance, Michael Browning, 'War Photos That Changed History', *Palm Beach Post*, 12 May 2004, www.palmbeachpost.com/news/content/news/special_reports/war_photos/history.html [accessed 24 February 2006]. See also Susan Sontag, 'Regarding the Torture of Others', *The New York Times*, reproduced in *Truthout*, www.truthout.org/cgi-bin/artman/exec/view.cgi/9/4592 [accessed 24 February 2006]; Susan Sontag, *Regarding the Pain of Others* (*New York: Farrar, Straus and Giroux, 2003*).

tool of propaganda.[29] They point, for instance, to the overwhelming pro-American bias of 'embedded' journalists in Iraq[30] and its doctored reporting by Hollywood producers.[31] After the highly orchestrated toppling of Saddam's statue in Baghdad, opinion polls were said to have finally swung in Blair's favour in a 'patriotic surge'. They symbolized 'a sweet political moment for Blair' in which bitter anti-war feeling was replaced by flowers on Blair's doorstep.[32] ICM polls showed that after the fall of Baghdad,

> the proportion of those who disapprove of military action has dropped to an all-time low of only 23% – less than half the level of eight weeks ago. In contrast, support for the war has risen from a low of 29% in mid-February to 63% . . . one of the most dramatic shifts in public opinion in recent British political history.[33]

Critics of mainstream journalism like John Pilger point out that these media tactics of collusion with power simply confirm a much wider and systematic strategy – namely, that by which political leadership in any country, whether democratic or totalitarian, address a vested political and economic interest in controlling what does and does not pass as newsworthy: 'democratic accountability and vision are replaced by a specious gloss, the work of fixers known as "spin-doctors", and assorted marketing and public relations experts and their fellow travellers, notably journalists. A false "consensus" is their invention.'[34] In the defence of a given political or economic order, in other words, 'normality' can be produced by the repetition of 'the definitions of the powerful'.[35] This suggests, moreover, that whatever the best

---

[29] See Sheldon Rampton and John Stauber, *Weapons of Mass Deception: The Uses of Propaganda in Bush's War on Iraq* (London: Constable and Robinson, 2003).

[30] See Robert Fisk, 'Telling It Like It Isn't', *Znet*, 31 December 2005 www.zmag.org/content/showarticle.cfm?ItemID=9432 [accessed 13 March 2006].

[31] For an account of the Hollywood style of war reporting of the 2003 Iraq war, see John Kampfner, 'Saving Private Lynch Story "flawed"', *BBC News*, 15 May 2003, http://news.bbc.co.uk/1/hi/programmes/correspondent/3028585.stm [accessed 13 March 2006].

[32] London Reuters, 10 April 2003, http://uk.news.yahoo.com/030410/80/dxgz4.html [accessed 10 January 2006].

[33] Alan Travis, 'Surge in war support confirms dramatic shift in public opinion', *The Guardian*, 15 April 2003.

[34] John Pilger, *Hidden Agendas* (London: Vintage, 1998), p. 5.

[35] S. Hall, C. Chritcher, T. Jefferson, J. Clarke and B. Roberts, 'The Social Production of News: Mugging in the Media' in *The Manufacture of News: Social Problems, Deviance, and Mass Media*, ed. S. Cohen and J. Young (London: Constable, 1981), pp. 335–367 (p. 351).

intentions of journalists, the *process* of manufacturing news inescapably attempts to voice a 'common opinion' alongside that of a dominant ideology. There is therefore a silent allegiance to power that greatly diminishes the critical intentions of a news-consuming public.

What does this critique of media propaganda lend to my search for the conditions of public manipulation in a politics of fear? It demonstrates that we can no longer locate the source of propaganda solely with specific agencies such as government intelligence. A manipulation of the public arises from a general cultural shift towards the consumption of the image as source of truth. As a consequence, the relationship between fear and fantasy is brought closer together. This idea parallels a critique frequently levelled at the televised representation of terror itself. Consider, as an example, the televised repetition of the burning Twin Towers in New York in 2001.[36] This media technique confirms what has already been identified by Guy Debord as the 'logic of the spectacle'.[37] It is a celebration of the spectacular as the triumph of the virtual over the real. It maintains distance between the image and the reality of the image. The power of the image of an ultimate fear (such as a terrorist attack on the heartland) can be argued to contain an element of post-modern 'jouissance'. This is a pleasure that has no recourse to universal standards of taste or judgement, an enjoyment of visual excess. The celebration of the image, the ability to draw and maintain attention into the fetishization of war, highlights the close relationship between fear and excitement. When Bush swooped down onto USS Lincoln in his fighter jet, clad in flight suit, helmet tucked under his arm to declare 'mission accomplished' to a background of sailors and heavy-duty military equipment (essentially a live commercial for the Republican Party estimated to have cost $1 million tax-money to orchestrate[38]) he wasn't just fulfilling a boyhood fantasy. He was providing a rationale by which a terrorized public is able to embrace prejudice and violence as the necessary answer to its crises. The ubiquity of this stance throughout mainstream media reporting of that symbolic event was also highly significant. As Robin points out, the conservative journalist Christopher Hitchens demonstrated this well on the first anniversary of 9/11 when he wrote:

> I should perhaps confess that on September 11 last, once I had experienced all the usual mammalian gamut of emotions, from rage to nausea, I also discovered that another sensation was contending for mastery. On examination, and to my own pleasure, it turned out to be exhilaration.

---

[36] See Žižek, *Welcome to the Desert*, p. 12.

[37] See in particular Guy Debord, *La société du spectacle* (Paris: Gallimard, 1992).

[38] Rampton and Stauber, 'Trading on Fear'.

> Here was the most frightful enemy – theocratic barbarism – in plain view
> . . . I realized that if the battle went on until the last day of my life, I would
> never get bored in prosecuting it to the utmost.[39]

The refusal to 'get bored' is important here since it confirms a common element of what we understand today as post-modern spectatorship. It is, as Žižek calls it, 'obscene enjoyment, or horrific *jouissance*'.[40]

The spectacle of terror goes some way to explaining how the desires of a public come to be subverted against their own interests. In the manner of the genre of horror, the image of an untouchable and ubiquitous terror is lifted to the level of horrific fantasy. It leaves the public as spectator engaged only on the level of the mesmeric, and thus also of social paralysis. Repelled and attracted in the same movement, terror has become an inescapable public fantasy of its own immanent insecurity and uncertainty. But before exploring in greater depth the function of terror as horror, a more precise understanding of the notion of 'the public' itself is needed. Who is it we refer to by ascribing affections or beliefs to the public? It is clearly not the same as other social agents. 'Public consent' cannot simply be defined as the convergence of many individually reached conclusions, as if people were isolated from social life in order to reach their views. For even if we grant John Pilger the right (and it isn't obvious that we should) to say that despite the huge bias of corporate-driven media there is yet 'a critical intelligence and common sense in the way most people arrive at their values',[41] this 'critical intelligence' must still be placed within the context of the emergence of specific tools and social sites that condition that process of conviction. A brief overview of the historical roots of a concept of the public is therefore instructive. It is inseparable from a history of public information and its collusion with a certain social and economic order.

The thing we now call the public did not arise outside of social privilege and domination (despite its etymological distinction to that which is 'private'). As Jürgen Habermas says, the emergence of the concept within the organization of the Greek Polis was bound to that of citizens (in distinction to women and slaves, for instance) participating in the state. They were defined by an ability to express 'freedom and permanence . . . an open field for honourable distinction' through the instituted public sphere.[42] It seems

---

[39] Christopher Hitchins, quoted in Robin, 'Reason to Panic', p. 75.

[40] Quoted in Terry Eagleton, *Holy Terror* (Oxford: Oxford University Press, 2005), p. 3.

[41] Pilger, *Hidden Agendas*, p. 11.

[42] Jürgen Habermas, *The Structural Transformation of the Public Sphere*, trans. Thomas Burger (Cambridge: Polity Press, 1989), p. 4.

that since those times the concept of public has always had something to do with an hierarchical distinction. Habermas considers, for instance, the way fifteenth-century European royals symbolically represented the public body, or again how the bourgeois public sphere of 'civil society' in the eighteenth century where 'publicity' was still restricted to the reading classes and practices such as literary discussions, the publicizing of letters and secret societies and lodges.[43] Indeed, published 'news' reporting only emerged as an aide to the 'commercial traffic' of trade between regions.[44] It only became 'public' news when capitalist expansion took on a public dimension. But simply because the role of the press expanded to include a critical interest in political issues does not mean that it became independent of those originally economic concerns. The common interest of businesses and state authorities to be in control of what the press says can be traced, according to Habermas, as far back as the seventeenth century. Figures such as Cardinal Richelieu used the new 'Gazette' as an 'intelligence agency' in the service of court ordinances.[45] Subsequently, it is true that press groups fought for independence of state authorities. It is also true that journals and pamphlets played important roles in the Chartist and anti-absolutist movements. Nevertheless, interpretations of a public voice in media bodies have overwhelmingly been associated with property ownership. The attempts at democratic representation of the will of the 'people' since the French revolution were held within an inherent contradiction. The public was then both the realm of universal rights alongside a bourgeois intellectual view that it was property-owning (male) individuals alone that had the right to direct that sphere. Following suit, the institutions that turned private concerns into public ones (the rise of the welfare state) have always been held in tension within the conditions of free-market capitalism. The political element of a critical public in a democracy depended on the freely competing reasoning of autonomous beings (in the Kantian understanding). This notion was, however, in the nineteenth century, an autonomy that meant self-sufficiency. This in turn meant someone with property or land.[46]

What does this glance at a history of the concept of public reveal? It demonstrates that the emergence of liberal democracy as the dominant ideology in modern European thought grounds our inherited notion of the public in the notion of a crisis of participation. In places of early socialist experimentation, public life may well have been synonymous with political life.

---

[43] *Ibid.* p. 35.
[44] *Ibid.* p. 16.
[45] *Ibid.* p. 22.
[46] *Ibid.* p. 109.

Their citizens may well have expressed the right to share in the universal rational capacity of social contribution.[47] Yet, turning to the laissez-faire ideology represented by such thinkers as J. S. Mill and Alex de Tocqueville, we see that the embrace of free-market capitalism *necessitated* a rejection of the notion of a public sphere as a rationalized political domain. Political engagement, to these thinkers, was subsumed within a philosophy of history that presupposed a 'natural order'. This order assumed that the will of the people need not define other than to affirm the principle in general: 'there was to be a natural basis for the public sphere that would in principle guarantee an autonomous and basically harmonious course of social reproduction.'[48]

This latter point highlights the birth of a hegemonic process by which a public has come to endorse or consent to the conditions of its own enslavement. This condition of acquiescence can be seen as a foundation to the contemporary crisis of participation in the political sphere. It adds significantly to a critique of those conditions that make possible the manipulation of consent in the war on terror. And it describes a paradox that has led some to talk of the *end* of the public sphere, or of 'post-democracy'.

Depoliticization and post-democracy

To understand why people consent is to ask not simply why people are only told certain things (the hegemony of a communications industry); it is also to ask why they are unable to say things to the contrary (the disciplining of discourse). Today the hallmarks of the transition described by Habermas from a critical public to a pacified, acquiescent one are a gradual decline in traditional sites of citizen participation. That transition can also be witnessed in the increasing association of the role of the autonomous citizen (i.e. one without the traditional ties to political parties or ideological adherence) with that of the consumer. The public *influence* of the autonomous citizen on policy is replaced by that of the markets. As Colin Crouch puts it, the 'commercialization of citizenship' simply fits into a logical progression of the specific model of liberal democracy whose first truly global marketing strategy came out of cold war ideology. In the new post-democratic model of citizen participation,

> while elections certainly exist and can change governments, public electoral debate is a tightly controlled spectacle, managed by rival teams of professionals expert in the techniques of persuasion, and considering a

---

[47] *Ibid.* p. 129.
[48] *Ibid.* p. 130.

small range of issues selected by those teams. The mass of citizens plays a passive, quiescent, even apathetic part, responding only to the signals given them. Behind this spectacle of the electoral game, politics is really shaped in private by the interaction between elected government and elites that overwhelmingly represent business interests.[49]

Crouch's point is that people's private lives do not today contribute to the creation of a public domain because they are cut off from it. The power of (particularly non-literary) mass media in contemporary society is certainly making sure this rift widens. The consumption of certain images associated with the outside world could be seen to replace the engagement of a public 'switched on' to current affairs and capable of responding to it. This was a process, as Habermas was well aware, that began a long while ago: 'a pseudo-public sphere of a no longer literary public was patched together to create a sort of super-familial zone of familiarity.'[50]

The depoliticization of public life is therefore intimately related to the capitalization of traditional modes of popular communication and the dissemination of public truths. Media institutions are now owned by an alarmingly small number of corporations and are profoundly rooted in private interests, whether through sponsorship, advertisements or the entertainment business. In this sense, the original role of the newspaper as aide to mercantilist trade has come full circle. Today 'the news' is big business because it is the bearer of commercial interests through advertising. Information is thus the servant of profit. Pilger has already succinctly shown that this marrying of news and capital has a profound effect on the everyday perception of political reality. The TV stations are directed by their ratings and are therefore concerned with keeping people's attention, of sensationalizing current affairs. There has been a shift, in Habermas' words, from a 'Culture-Debating to a Culture-Consuming Public'.[51] Communication, sociability and political debate of group activities has been substituted by the non-participation of mass-media forms, most notably television. Critical analysis has been replaced by the marketization of debate through talk shows, 'reality television' or panels of 'experts'. It is not simply that the marriage of 'public information' and 'state agenda' has increased. It is that the function of social life has itself become incorporated into this acquiescence.

In the light of these observations, perhaps the most useful description of the 'condition' of post-modernity is the ability to turn the intolerable and

---

[49] Colin Crouch, *Post-Democracy* (Cambridge: Polity Press, 2004), p. 4.
[50] Habermas, *Structural Transformation*, p. 162.
[51] *Ibid.* p. 159.

the shocking into the hyperreal. Political reality may be left on the harmless level of TV images. It may be packaged for individualized consumer needs, sanitized beyond recognition. Whatever else this trend implies, it clarifies a rationale for the invitation of a politics of fear and paranoia as a *normal* mode of engagement. In place of seeking the 'high' solutions and enquiries of a particular discourse of truth, the embarrassed reaction of ordinary citizens to the tragedy and the 'accident' of inevitable war is experienced with an obsession with the image. And it is embodied in the commodification of that image through media sensationalism.

Conclusion

It can now be argued that the only sense in which war with Iraq could possibly have become 'popular' is through an institutionalized acceptance of a pseudo-debate. Acquiescence was guaranteed by the establishment of staged discussions, expert panels, editorial letters and radio phone-ins. This was arguably done to assuage the anger of powerlessness that this might provoke.[52] Before the parliamentary speech that won a slim majority vote backing the US-led invasion, Tony Blair appeared on *Newsnight* to various citizen groups in an attempt to 'engage with the public'. While what he said has been severely condemned by experts of its content, what is remarkable is the fact that the structures of communication chosen to present these lies were taken to be a fulfilment of government's accountability and engagement of the public with the correct facts. The 'publicity' enjoyed by Blair before he declared war on Iraq thus only represented public debate in the sense that it was the discussion of a discussion. Despite the unprecedented amounts of people taking part in protests against the war all over the country, people also spectated the documentation of the parliamentary meeting. They viewed its myriad reporting, admired its deconstruction of spin, and judged who won and lost on points of rhetoric. With an irony only now being fully appreciated, Britain's newspapers were unanimous in describing Blair's speech to parliament as a defining moment in restoring the credibility and integrity of the prime minister and democracy. *The Daily Mirror*, for example, despite being in full swing of its anti-war 'phase', wrote:

> . . . we do not question [Blair's] belief in the rightness of what he is doing. It is one thing to have principles others disagree with, another altogether

---

[52] See *BBC News*, 5 February 2003, http://news.bbc.co.uk/1/hi/programmes/newsnight/2729297.stm [accessed 25 March 2006].

to have no principles. . . . Mr Blair and Robin Cook have helped to restore the integrity of parliament at this crucial stage in the nation's history.[53]

Such an illusion of publicity fulfils Guy Debord's perception that 'false choice' is manufactured by the appearance of diverse spectacles and the installation of 'trivial' oppositions.[54] Debord's paradigm is therefore an appropriate description of the conditions I have argued are likely to frame the politics of fear. That is, not only as a tool of coercion and propaganda, but of the normalization of acquiescence and the consumption of the fearful everyday. Debord described the masking of reality, the 'negation' of real life itself,[55] as the deceptive illusion of choice and participation. Disengagement from a pseudo-public realm is not threatened with a Hobbesian logic of terror but with social death, or disappearance. If the fabric of society is saturated by the logic of the markets and the imperative of consumption, the means of maintaining this 'order' are the concern of businesses no more than state authorities. The creation of a 'pseudo-public' realm of critique has proven to be the most sustainable guarantee of a compliant and unquestioning public. Just as governments sell off public services to private investment to be governed by the logic of profit, means of communication itself follow suit. At stake, therefore, are the very means of participation in the public realm and the possibility of criticizing it. This, and not the use of 'terror' traditionally conceived as a carrot and stick approach, is how to understand the interrelation of fear and desire as political strategy. This is why, for Hardt and Negri, 'communicative production and imperial legitimation march hand in hand and can no longer be separated. The machine is self-validating, autopoetic – that is, systemic.'[56]

---

[53] *The Daily Mirror*, quoted by David Edwards, 'Falling at the Feet of Power: Blair's Sincerity and the Media', *Media Lens*, 21 March 2003.
[54] Debord, *La société du spectacle*, p. 40.
[55] *Ibid.* p. 164.
[56] Michael Hardt and Antonio Negri, *Empire* (London: Harvard University Press, 2000), p. 34.

Chapter 2

From Fear to Desire

Introduction

The previous chapter's critique focused on the transformation of a critical public to one of passive consumers. This in turn enables me to pursue the contemporary meaning of a 'politics of fear' even further. I can now ask: how does this cultural climate give rise to an explicit complicity between fear and consumption? The kind of moral outrage or hysteria normally associated with a culture of insecurity was seen to be reinscribed as a kind of jouissance, a complicity with the thing feared. But what *positive* role is taken in this complicity by the masses? To answer this I turn to some recent observations, most notably by Brian Massumi, Frederic Jameson and Slavoj Žižek. These thinkers claim in various ways that the production of a *permanent* state of fear guarantees not only the acquiescence of 'civil society' but also the dominant mode of post-modern participation: consumption. Like Goerring's unsettling truth about war-time propaganda, this observation should not come as a great surprise. One of Hannah Arendt's most prescient observations was that people 'cannot be manipulated – though of course they can be forced by terror – to "buy" opinions and political views'.[1] Indeed, nowhere does the collusion between market interests and the production of political fear reveal itself more than in the reaction to a state of anxiety by 'advanced' capitalist nations themselves. Gilles Deleuze and Félix Guattari's introduction of a 'politics of desire' to this argument provides an important foundation here. For these men recognized powerfully the tendency for capitalist culture to deliver its desires to capital. In this way capitalism has provided the rationale for a fearful, self-perpetuated society of control.

Capitalizing fear

Two months after that great symbol of American wealth was destroyed in September 2001, President Bush was proud to announce publicly that

---

[1] Arendt, *Crises of the Republic*, p. 8.

terrorists would not stop America from shopping.[2] According to US citizens themselves, there was also an enormous sense of people returning to things that 'really mattered'. Spending more time with family and revising one's attachment to material possessions were frequently cited. Nevertheless it was also soon remembered that patterns of consumption were apparently the mark of an American identity that the terrorists detested. These were therefore seen to be the values to be defended at all costs. Bush's heart-warming response to the question 'what can be expected of us (Americans)?' was 'hug your children'.[3] Days later, attentions were turned to the 'victorious' return of the running of the stock market. The Iraq war also revealed an implicit assumption that war need no longer be a strain on lifestyles of *excess*. As Chomsky notes, during the Second World War, 'Americans conserved resources as never before. Rationing was imposed on petrol, tyres and even food. People collected waste such as paper and household cooking scraps so that it could be recycled and used for the war effort.'[4] War and consumption *today*, on the other hand, are often seen to go hand in hand. This view has been traditionally taken from the point of view of guaranteeing military spending, as well as encouraging consumer confidence as an act of patriotism. But to many critics it also features as a definitive stage in propaganda. It represents the development, as Chomsky puts it, of a 'philosophy of futility':

> The thought-control experts realized that you could not only have what was called on-job control but also off-job control. It's their phrase. Control them off job by inducing a philosophy of futility, focusing people on the superficial things of life, like fashionable consumption, and basically get them out of our hair. Let the people who are supposed to run the show do it without any interference from the mass of the population, who have no business in the public arena.[5]

---

[2] 'This great nation will never be intimidated. People are going about their daily lives, working and shopping and playing, worshipping at churches and synagogues and mosques, going to movies and to baseball games. Life in America is going forward' (George W. Bush, quoted in *September 11 News*, 8 November 2001), www.september11news.com/PresidentBushAtlanta.htm [accessed 17 December 2005].

[3] George W. Bush, 'Address to a Joint Session of Congress and the American People', September 2001, *The White House* www.whitehouse.gov/news/releases/2001/09/20010920–8.html [accessed 10 December 2005].

[4] Rampton and Stauber, 'Trading on Fear'.

[5] Chomsky, 'Collateral Damage'.

Scrutiny of a production of 'everyday' fears, explored in the first chapter, therefore reveals a simultaneous co-option of desire in *capitalizing* upon those fears. There are numerous concrete examples of this co-option, as detailed by Rampton and Stauber.[6] They include the aggressive marketing strategy for SUV cars after the televised images of the First Gulf War in 1991 had sensationalized the 'Humvee' armoured vehicle; the approval of drilling for oil in Alaska instead of relying on oil from the Middle East;[7] and the sale in America, after nuclear attacks on Hiroshima and Nagasaki, of atomic jewellery, the creation of the 'Atomic Undergarment Company' and atomic trinkets in cereal packets.[8] The logic at work here follows everything that has been argued above about the transformation of the public sphere. Consumption is expressed as the definitive act of continuing normal life in the face of disaster. Fear and desire also appear to be in particularly symbiotic relation in times of war. If proof were needed of the creation of new, marketable desires through the outpouring of violence, one only need think back to images of stalls around Ground Zero during the days after September 11. There vendors were, it seems, long before the dust had settled, selling catastrophe memorabilia and commemorative T-shirts.

> Produced within a matter of days by underground T-shirt suppliers and trinket manufacturers, most bore the words seen on televisions everywhere, 'America Under Attack,' above the silkscreen of a waving flag behind the Twin Towers. Several different messages appeared below the universal design, however, from 'I Can't Believe I Got Out,' to 'I Survive the Attack,' or just plainly stating many Americans' sentiment, 'Evil Will Be Punished.' . . . 'They are kind of funny. They appeal to my sick sense of humor,' said Greg Gomez, who purchased several for his relatives in Illinois at a bargain price of 4 for $10.

The author of this commentary, clearly shocked, called this a 'new sort of capitalism'. And yet might not the vendors in this story be simply reflecting the confluence of emotions involved in mourning, violence, anger and the entrepreneurial spirit? In the same anecdote one Air National Guardsman suggested that rather than sell commemorative T-shirts, 'They should start selling Iraqi flags. That way, people can take those out and burn them.'[9]

---

6 Rampton and Stauber, 'Trading on Fear'.

7 79 *Ibid.*

8 Mary Riddell, 'If in Doubt, Go Shopping', *The Observer*, 30 September 2001.

9 Adrian Brune, 'Terror and Response', *Columbia University Graduate School of Journalism,* 19 September 2001, www.jrn.columbia.edu/studentwork/terror/sep19/vendors.asp [accessed 17 December 2005].

   The notion that fear and terror can become commodified cultural norms themselves lifts Arendt's critique (that only terror can guarantee the complete co-option of public consent) to a new level. Instead of thinking of fear propaganda solely as the shocking, a politics of fear should today be identified as an unnoticed social condition. It is a 'background radiation saturating existence',[10] as Brian Massumi puts it. In addition to the carrot and stick model, in other words, we need to ask whether today people are able to isolate 'disastrous' political events from the concept of the everyday, or whether instead war and terror has *become* the everyday. Analysts of a culture of fear, like Massumi, suggest the latter. Ours is a culture where consumption of commodities defines a sense of 'who we are'. The production of fear through the propaganda of imminent threats and the 'necessity' of perpetual wars has therefore come to occupy the same privileged social space as those commodities. People may well, in this sense, understand themselves as having 'become' their own fears. They *buy* their own fears in the same way they buy 'themselves'. As Massumi puts it, 'if we cannot separate our selves from our fear, and if fear is a powerful mechanism for the perpetuation of domination, is our unavoidable participation in the capitalist culture of fear a complicity with our own and others' oppression?'[11]

   What are the implications of these observations about the power of commodification, and the role of the image in the society of the spectacle? They suggest that the most powerful strategic tools of public manipulation stem from the 'auto-productive' nature of paranoiac society. Whatever the nature of its origins, fear feeds and propagates itself. There is, as Massumi puts it, a 'collective complicity with fear'.[12] People are frequently able to say they are 'scared' while tacitly admitting that it is not enough to make them change their lifestyle. Asked how scared people felt by the risk of terrorist attacks in 2003, one response by a Londoner illustrates the point neatly:

I am getting home from work earlier because I don't feel like hanging around central London. My brother-in-law works in the City and I do worry a bit about him. When I go to Selfridges I carry on shopping, obviously, if there's a sale on, but it does cross your mind that something could go off. I suppose this is my generation's equivalent of living in fear of the Bomb.[13]

---

[10] Massumi, 'Everywhere You Want to Be', p. 24.

[11] *Ibid.* p. ix.

[12] *Ibid.* p. ix.

[13] Sara Cox, DJ, quoted by Lucy Mangan, Amy Fleming and Ian Katz, 'This Is My Generation's Equivalent of Living in Fear of the Bomb', *The Guardian*, G2 section, 13 February 2003.

To this effect, people may be justifiably said to be increasingly auto-productive of fear by constituting a way of 'being happy' with it. There are of course, many more ways in which the emotive capacity of fear could be widely held to be a desirable state of mind. The most obvious example is its capacity to quicken sensibilities and render people more productive in certain circumstances. Corey Robin, in fact, points out that for philosophers like John Locke, fear, as an 'uneasiness of the mind' constituted 'the chief, if not only spur to human industry and action' and was therefore one of the 'guiding spirits of liberalism'.[14] Perhaps, then, it is easier to understand contemporary politics of fear as a kind of perverted curiosity. Fear confronts a person with their absolute limit. Because that limit defines them, it also draws them to it out of sheer curiosity, like a horror film does.

Horror fear can be an almost imperceptible anxiety. It is provoked by the fascination, perhaps, of that which disturbs. As Alfonso Lingis describes it, a 'rapture of the deep'.[15] This is the will to 'lose oneself' in disorder only in order to test whether there *is* any identity and security to which we may return. Just as I have identified a sense of *jouissance* attached to the fantasy of the war on terror, the attraction of fear should also be understood as an initial curiosity that draws people to the spectacle of their own fears. The pre-eminence of television in our society can once again be seen to play a strong role here. We recall, for example, the helplessness and, more importantly, the *powerlessness*, with which the public watched the spectacular drama of the invasion of Baghdad. In the light of my critique of war reporting, we should add that this powerlessness is twofold. It is experienced not only in the sense of being unable to intervene, but also in being unable to distinguish fact from fiction, live coverage and statistical reports from Hollywood-style action shots. In reference to the subject of war reporting Thomas L. Dumm is able to conclude that 'fear is the political aesthetic of the medium of television'.[16] But this view also has overarching significance for the concept of fear as a transformation of the nature of political participation. The televised representation of war, we might sum up, represents the consumption of the fear image. It is the blurring between the self-perpetuation of fearfulness and the aestheticized form of distraction that is the mirror image of capital accumulation itself. The fearful happens, but in a form that doesn't *touch* so much as *lurks* in the background.

---

[14] Robin, *Fear*, p. 4.

[15] Quoted in Thomas L. Dumm, 'Telefear: Watching War News' in Massumi, *Politics of Everyday Fear*, pp. 307–321 (p. 312).

[16] *Ibid.* p. 313.

The purpose of analysing this 'capitalization' of fear is not to suggest that the power of hysteria has become superfluous. On the contrary, it has opened up a critique of how a public can be presumed to be *so easily* scared. When asked how scared he had become since the government's new wave of 'alerts' of possible terrorist attacks, one Londoner astutely answered, 'I'm very scared of how stupid the government thinks the people are. It's scare tactics to make us want to attack Saddam, a total double bluff.'[17] The point raised by my analysis, however, is that panic created by terror alerts does not simply constitute a judgement on public naïveté. It also relates to a sense of fear that permeates the economic and social fabric of capitalist culture. It therefore represents, as Massumi says, the 'saturation of social space by fear'.[18] What we are witnessing through the ongoing strategy of the war on terror is therefore a powerful awareness that the shocking and the banal can work hand in hand. They maintain a social *order* within the inherent *disorder* of a climate of imminent threat and apocalyptic anxiety. The production of permanent anxiety, which Massumi calls 'the media effect – fear-blur', means going beyond the realm of affectivity and emotion. This is why there is today a widespread interest in fear beyond the discourse of psychology and psycho-analysis. We must look also to those places in which fear is not only an experience but a socialized state, and hence a *condition* for experience.

Fear, we might tentatively conclude, may be an age-old philosophical and anthropological preoccupation, but today it takes on a peculiarly post-modern flavour. It colours social participation in ways that are inherently contradic-tory. It both binds together (we are all united in relation to the thing feared) and atomizes (it is our own fear that we are alone with) individuals. On the level of culture and socialization, fear can thus be understood within the collage of different texts. The deciphering of those texts comes not from any overarching theory or truth discourse, but from living out the text among many others. As Frederic Jameson has put it, 'political power becomes a "text" that you can read; daily life becomes a text to be activated and deciphered by walking or shopping; [. . .] war becomes a readable text'.[19]

The investment of desire

We should return once more to Willhelm Reich's question about the rise of fascism – how is it possible that people endorse and desire a system that

---

[17] Dinos Chapman, quoted by Mangan, Fleming and Katz, 'Fear of the Bomb'.

[18] Massumi, *Politics of Everyday Fear*, p. ix.

[19] Frederic Jameson, *Postmodernism, or, the Cultural Logic of Late Capitalism* (London: Verso, 1991), p. 186.

enslaves them? In posing this question again, we also return to Deleuze and Guattari's specific interest in the *operation* of desires within the wider context of 'social production'. The purpose of doing so is to understand not only how desire is co-opted into the type of capitalized fear-production described above. It is also to understand how desire might also be resistant to it.

In the 1980s Deleuze and Guattari applauded Reich for posing the question of social subservience in terms of a co-option of desire and not ignorance about the repressive mechanism itself. But they also distanced their own position from Reich's traditionalist (Freudian) polarization of rational and irrational elements of social desire. They rejected, that is, his obsession with 'negation' and 'inhibition' in the formulation of non-rational behaviour.[20] On the contrary, they thought, what is distinctive about capitalist society is not that it appeals to an inherent (or 'natural') sense of rational order but that it *defines* that order to us – it constitutes our world and all that is in it. Capitalist society organizes our desires, and thus our ability to aspire, to hope. Capitalism is a primal 'producer' of desire itself. But what then exactly is desire, and what can it tell us about the role of fear? Deleuze and Guattari understood desire to embrace every kind of force or flow that involves 'interested subjects'.[21] There is no use in looking for good and bad desires that might correspond to a more or less rational or ethical type of behaviour. There is only a flow of interested desires. It is thus possible that the thing one fears might also be believed to be the thing that one wants or even needs. According to Deleuze and Guattari's 'schizoid ontology' the action of desires comprises disembodied flows, bodily flows, perverted flows, ecological flows, conceptual flows, any type of flow by which different 'multiplicities' converge to form relationships.[22] These flows are also the basis for understanding culture itself, or the way in which we all interact with our surroundings. The idea of cultural production, with this view, is based on the criss-crossing of syntheses of 'desiring machines'. As a result, any imposition of laws, identities or segregations ('you are male'; 'you are black'; 'you are gay'; 'you are a socialist'; 'you are a fundamentalist' etc.) appear to Deleuze and Guattari as a repression of the flows of desire. They are false impositions of boundaries and definitions, of either/or. Desire is, for schizoanalysis, essentially anarchic. But in capitalist society it appears that this anarchic flow of desire becomes subverted through a kind of internal self-repression. By internalizing a sense of prohibition or law (you *must,*

---

[20] Deleuze and Guattari, *Anti-Oedipus*, p. 29.

[21] *Ibid.* p. 105.

[22] See Philip Goodchild, *Deleuze and Guattari: An Introduction to the Politics of Desire* (London: Sage, 1996), p. 4.

you *are*, you *are not*) we impose that repression on others. We live in a state in which any fluid, free movement (*across* boundaries) is a kind of illegal or 'abnormal'.[23] This might be seen in the way by which we, for instance, adhere to certain norms of behaviour bestowed us by class status (showing deference to those above our status) or sexual status (fulfilling macho stereotypes, fearing 'queer' behaviour). But it might also refer to a state closer to the concerns of this study: namely, the act of internalizing and promoting a state of paranoia and suspicion of others, perpetuating a state of hyper (in)security by imposing the illusory boundaries of the fearful other (terrorist, fundamentalist, radical) threatening 'outside' our own secure identities. The embrace of fear might in this way represent the perversion of otherwise fluid 'desiring-machines', in which we are all caught. If people are naturally predisposed to self-repression in the nature of an auto-productive fear, then perhaps it is because we become unwilling to recognize features of ourselves in that fearful outside. It is common for political rhetoric, for example, to portray the external terror as unable to identify with our own values, language and rationality. It is easier to reject them as abnormal, insane and entirely other, perhaps in order to reinforce a sense of our own boundaries – what we *are* and what we are *not*. In doing so the *affects* of unbounded schizoid flows are confronted with a social discourse that prohibits. In a sense, then, schizoanalysis boldly suggests that what is really feared in societies of control is freedom or the unbounded possibility of desires. Societies of control introduce 'lack' into the definition of desire, such as is embodied in Freudian psychoanalysis (the castration-complex: our primeval obsession with lacking something). The individual has become repressed by his/her own consciousness of being *this* rather than *that*. Hence, people desire their own repression because this is preferable, perhaps safer and more contained, to an awareness of their unbounded possibility.

How do Deleuze and Guattari's post-Freudian understanding of desire help us to analyse a politics of fear? They assume a social matrix in which both repression and liberation fight over common territory. There, a politics of fear is able to be simultaneously normal and outrageous. But they also urge us to appreciate how easily and logically political notions as choice, freedom and participation can become subsumed into a logic of passivity and consumption. Global capitalist society goes beyond modes of coercion and even of Foucauldian 'governmentality'.[24] It is able to direct and co-opt flows of desire. To understand how consent is produced is to recognize how

---

[23] Goodchild, *Deleuze and Guattari*, p. 87.
[24] Michel Foucault, *Histoire de la sexualité vol. 1: La volonté de savoir* (Paris: Gallimard, 1976).

in a capitalist society control is no longer located in one place. It is fluid and omnipresent, or, in Deleuze and Guattari's words 'deterritorialized'. Capitalist movement – the movement of money across borders (both physical and cultural) – now has 'no exterior limit'. It is perpetually overcoming barriers and becoming 'displaced' in its reproduction.[25] It is in this sense that liberal democracies are not only able, but *required* to incorporate a number of differing world-views, lifestyles, identities and resistances themselves. The historical rise of the state represents the saturation of the social sphere with capitalist logic. Even the apparent relenting of its claim over enslaved subjects (the forgiveness of debts, the redistribution of resources, election of a Labour government, etc.) are, in Deleuze and Guattari's radical view, a means to prevent uprising by allowing some concessions. Today, in a globally capitalist society, we are stitched into a cultural acceptance of capitalist logic *despite* these concessions. Today *everything* is commodifiable, even life itself. Flows of desire can become subverted to the production of the market, and therefore normalize consumer identity. One can participate in a radical, anti-establishment identity by buying the right clothes (Diesel's 'protest chic' clotheswear, for instance) or consuming the right symbols (the all-pervasive Che Guevara or Zapatista iconography). All is possible under the same roof: capitalism. This is precisely what is meant by the investment of desire: 'in this manner the system indeed holds together and functions, and perpetually fulfils its own immanence. In this manner it is indeed the global object of an investment of desire. The wage earner's desire, the capitalist's desire, everything moves to the rhythm of one and the same desire'.[26]

The illusions of Stockholm Syndrome

The last analysis would seem to cast a rather gloomy light on the possibility for resistance to undermine a politics of acquiescence and passivity in a consumer society. What, for instance, is this 'schizoanalysis' to make of practices in which a state of permanent fear is seen as a radically diminished form of existence, not at all 'desirable'? Perhaps Deleuze and Guattari's analysis is analogous to the conclusions of the phenomenon known as Stockholm Syndrome,[27] named after an infamous bank robbery in Sweden in the 1970s. Three bank employees were taken hostage for 6 days and ended up forgiving, befriending and eventually marrying their captors.

---

[25] Deleuze and Guattari, *Anti-Oedipus*, p. 231.

[26] *Ibid.* p. 239.

[27] 'Stockholm Syndrome', *Wikipedia*, http://en.wikipedia.org/wiki/Stockholm_Syndrome [accessed 17 December 2005].

Psychologists subsequently concluded that a pattern of sympathizing for one's captor recurs in any form of emotionally and physically intense situations that involve: (1) perceived threat to survival and the belief that one's captor is willing to act on that threat; (2) the captive's perception of small kindnesses from the captor within a context of terror; (3) isolation from perspectives other than those of the captor; and (4) perceived inability to escape. Is this a similar observation to the production of public consent through a manipulation of fear in capitalist society?

However interesting the comparison, it is too simplistic to 'explain away' the reaction of embracing one's fear as a survival mechanism (as Stockholm Syndrome is invariably depicted). If this study has provided any insight into a politics of desire, it is that a cultural preference for self-repression need not imply that one comes to trust one's captors. It might simply imply a rejection of trust in *anything*. It might represent instead an embrace of insecurity, or a paradoxical desire for the certitude of fearfulness. That embrace, as I have tried to demonstrate, has a preferred place – or rather act – in the form of consumption and accumulation. It is the absorption of one's energies into a cyclical pattern of production/consumption. The interruption, or questioning, of that pattern, is not even brought about by the threat of destruction wrought by terrorist attack or all-out war. To continue in the face of those threats, moreover, is today seen as an act of resilience and fortitude: it is patriotism.

The war on terror has been found to operate much as Deleuze and Guattari critique the operation of 'sovereign power'. Sovereign power, they believe, will always try to hide the meaninglessness of its violence by bricking itself into an 'organic purpose', 'thereby converting the absurdity into spirituality. That is why it is so futile to distinguish what is rational and what is irrational in a society.'[28] That is also why it is futile to distinguish between a rational understanding of fear as an emotional response (as psychoanalysis might try to decipher) from an irrational one. But it is a distinction frequently misused in the popular media discussions of social opinions on the perception of global risks. Far greater attention needs to be paid instead to the fearful foundations of 'normal', everyday life. We should, indeed, 'listen', as urged by Deleuze and Guattari, 'to a secretary of state, a general, the boss of a firm, a technician. Listen to the great paranoiac din beneath the discourse of reason that speaks for others, in the name of a silent majority.'[29]

---

[28] Deleuze and Guattari, *Anti-Oedipus*, pp. 345–346.
[29] *Ibid.* p. 364.

The war on terror provides a poignant test-case for this idea that desires can become socially 'productive'. For here anarchic and resistant passions can be seen to be unendingly threatened. What are they threatened by? The paranoiac polarization between 'us' and 'them'; the domestication of intensities and desires. Deleuze and Guattari's recommendation is that psychoanalysis, and in a wider sense *all* analysis, therefore broaden its understanding of the role of desire in society. This recommendation acts as a warning of the extraordinary ability of people, then as now, to accept the unacceptable and to desire the undesirable. Public engagement has been privatized from a space of speaking (*parliament*) to one of consuming. Even when we are not actively policing ourselves, we seem to be very good at convincing ourselves of what is worth our time to watch and think about. As Dumm puts it, 'resistance is not crushed by power so much as it is made irrelevant by being made uninteresting'.[30] Societies of control are about keeping a public switched-on and tuned-in. In our aggressively surveilled and informationalized society the investment of desire comes hand in hand with the sense of *jouissance*, alluded to earlier. We, the police, watch, and restrict our own behaviour:

> We see the most disadvantaged, the most excluded members of society invest with passion the system that oppresses them [. . .]. Being the cop for others and for oneself – that is what arouses, and it is not ideology, it is economy. [. . .] A violence without purpose, a joy, a pure joy in feeling oneself a wheel in the machine, traversed by flows, broken by schizzes. Placing oneself in a position where one is thus traversed, broken, fucked by the socius, looking for the right place where, according to the aims and the interests assigned to us, one feels something moving that has neither an interest nor a purpose.[31]

It is capitalized fear, this investment of desire, that makes possible such a social vacuum. In capitalist societies people are not as often ruled as in the 'molar' authority of totalitarianism.[32] Instead, diverse identities and desires are welcomed under the pretext of free society. At the same time that free-dom is actualized in concert with the capitalist axiomatic and within a culture of non-participation. The logic of capital directs free, desiring subjects toward an all-pervasive discourse of self-interest. It is the voice of

---

[30] Dumm, 'Telefear', p. 314.
[31] Deleuze and Guattari, *Anti-Oedipus*, pp. 346–347.
[32] See Brian Massumi, *A User's Guide to Capitalism and Schizophrenia* (London: MIT Press, 1992), pp. 119–120.

acting respectably and within the law. It can also, of course, always rely on the prerogative of police and military force, where necessary, to enforce this style of freedom. This is the supreme irony of the introduction of de facto permanent suspensions of civil liberties currently witnessed in liberal democratic societies. Under the pretext of anti-terror legislation, in which all citizens are required to give up certain freedoms in the name of freedom itself, more than just social coercion becomes the norm. Society itself, its spaces and modes of movement become transformed, in the 'fight for freedom', into exclusion zones and virtual detention centres. As Massumi says, modern 'democratic' society 'is not moral, just managerial. What it demands of its bodies is a practical acceptance of certain parameters of action, rather than a principled conformity to an absolute idea.'[33] Massumi's insight sums up the challenge that faces an appraisal of 'practices of hope', for they must be active questioning precisely of those 'parameters of action'. As a way of concluding Deleuze and Guattari's contribution to this book, therefore, it can be suggested that the production of fear revealed in the war on terror can be seen as a repression of desire. But at the heart of this repression desire *knows* it is powerful enough to overcome those boundaries and divisions inscribed into a society of fear. Political desires have every opportunity to contest certain parameters of action. But the business of social control today is to 'code desire – and the fear, the anguish of decoded flows'.[34]

At the beginning of this chapter the paradox of the repulsion-attraction movement of fearfulness was posed in its 'surface level' terms. That is, as an emotionally unclear division of what people 'want' to see when they witness tragedy as unreal and spectacular (as the 9/11 attacks were). This ambiguity implies not an indifferent sense of tragedy (many people died and many people still grieve, *this much* is unambiguous). It signifies rather that tragedy was communicated within a social sphere already 'terrorized'. Perhaps conversely we might say that terror has become 'socialized'. In both cases is the ubiquity of a virtual enemy, ready to strike from any point in time and space. With the above analysis of the investment of desire we can therefore say that fear can become immediately capitalized, made productive. We can consider, as an example of this state of indistinction, the legitimized public 'participation' in the grief, shock, anger and other emotional responses to 9/11 and other terrorist attacks. How might these outpourings of grief, in terms of their social 'function', be interpreted? It may be argued that they demonstrate the paradoxical posture of intense

---

[33] *Ibid.* p. 123.
[34] *Ibid.* p. 139.

emotion alongside disengagement and the feeling of powerlessness. They signify an increasing emphasis in the *aesthetic* nature of participation in crisis and tragedy. There is an imperative to *watch* the tragic events repeated. And here a clear link can be detected between our image-oriented style of social communication and the aestheticization of the political sphere itself. As a consequence, it becomes much harder to recognize tragic or fearful events as generating any political response other than silence. David Harvey once made precisely this point in relation to the post-modern mode of communicating human tragedy. Images of destitution and poverty on city streets, like those of the injustices and atrocities of war, can today be viewed aesthetically. They become no longer subjects of a social aberration but more like 'a quaint and swirling backdrop [. . .], upon which no social commentary is to be made'.[35] In the same way it can be argued that the centrality of television in the mediatization of the war on terror has played a defining role in limiting and shaping the possibility of any truly 'political' responses to terror.

Publicity, then, as opposed to the *public sphere* as Habermas described it, has never disappeared. Now, however, wherever one would expect to find 'critical publicity' they find 'manipulative publicity'.[36] To similar effect, Deleuze and Guattari term this latest transformation of capitalism as the shift from an 'age of terror' (because cruelty of exploitative relations has become 'bricked into the system') to an 'age of cynicism'.[37] Public participation remains only in terms of the choices made by commodity owners. Even without authoritarian control people are, 'sufficiently filled with the floating images constantly produced by capital [. . .]. The whole world unfolds right at home, without one's having to leave the TV screen.'[38]

Conclusion

It is clear that violence still remains at the heart of authoritarian social control. The erosion of civil liberties under domestic anti-terror legislation is one example. The doctrine of unilateral pre-emptive military action championed by neo-conservatives is another. But these are only the most obvious visible manifestations of a new wave of the violence of 'democracy'

---

[35] David Harvey, *The Condition of Postmodernity: An Enquiry into the Origins of Cultural Change* (Oxford: Basil Blackwell, 1989), p. 336.

[36] Habermas, *Structural Transformation*, p. 178.

[37] *Ibid.* pp. 212, 225.

[38] Deleuze and Guattari, *Anti-Oedipus*, p. 251.

in the twenty–first century. Today violence is present no longer solely as a Hobbesian leviathan, the authoritarian state. It appears also under the name of freedom; liberalism; the necessity of the market itself, the 'leviathan in sheep's clothing',[39] or as Deleuze and Guattari put it, 'capitalism's true police'.[40] The global war on terrorism is intractable from the maintenance of a global economic hegemony. This means that for neo-liberal culture the violence of Iraq, Afghanistan, and any other imperial ambition in the name of freedom and progress must be internalized and normalized as an inevitable everyday (and largely 'foreign', even where it involves 'our boys' on foreign soil) terror. *Our* violence is one of wilful neglect of the consequences of capitalist domination as much as it is the active repression of dissent. 'There is no alternative' today means there is no way out of permanent war. Permanent war means war without end, a kind of apocalypse whose reality is placed just out of reach, almost in a cultural blind spot, present but somehow unreachable. Our cultural heritage is to encourage, as Jameson puts it, 'that form of repression which is oblivion and forgetfulness, a self-deception that does not want to know and tries to sink ever deeper into a wilful involuntary, a directed distraction'.[41] The connection between limitless commodification and the auto-production of fear as the 'new situation' from which to understand a crisis of hope now becomes clear. In a social 'order' that hands down values through the free movement of commodified signs (logos, advertisements, sponsorship, etc.) into every area of life, culture is no longer about a search for the new, a celebration of transition.[42]

What is the use of introducing this idea of a politics of desire? Is there any benefit beyond reinforcing a sense of the depth of social repression? Why speak of ideas as if they were bodies, desire in terms of machines? Why blur the distinctions of inside and outside by claiming that the schizophrenic is 'closest to the beating heart of reality'?[43] Deleuze and Guattari, I argue, are important because they open up the possibility of thinking of political acts as not *originally* circumscribed desires of relations of power. Rather, they account for the manner in which desire is delivered to power through the conditions of a dominant ideology. Society is systematically 'protected' from the dangerous anarchic chaos of resistant political desires. It is protected by guaranteeing the 'safe' existence of permanent anxiety, as demonstrated

---

[39] Jameson, *Postmodernism*, p. 273.

[40] Deleuze and Guattari, *Anti-Oedipus*, p. 239.

[41] Jameson, *Postmodernism*, p. 358.

[42] *Ibid.* p. 310.

[43] Deleuze and Guattari, *Anti-Oedipus*, p. 87.

through the propaganda of the *security* paradigm within anti-terror strategies. Desire's horizons are denied from the beginning in the form of ideological closure. But by its very nature desire contains the seed of rebellion. This is the tendency for *flight*, for *escaping*. Its subservience is never guaranteed. In Deleuze and Guattari's way of thinking, this very notion is what affirms the mechanisms of control in society in the first place: 'if desire is repressed, it is because every possibility of desire, no matter how small, is capable of calling into question the established order of a society.'[44] Such possibilities are, of course the subject of hope, to which I shall turn in due course. But before then, I need to explore in greater detail the effect that a politics of fear has had in generating discourses of 'the end'. For it is only by recognizing the attempt of this fear/desire matrix to create a monopoly on the imagination of the *future* that the need to create alternative discourses as imaginative practices will become apparent.

---

[44] *Ibid.* p. 116.

Chapter 3

Accidents Waiting to Happen

Introduction

I have identified a depoliticized public sphere as a primary agent in generating a crisis in our expressions of hope. A politics of fear within this context means a kind of paralysis of the political experience of the present. The task of the present chapter is to explain how this same process involves the deprivation of a means to *project*, or in other words, to think the future. It is only from this standpoint that a thoroughgoing search for practices of hope as contestation of the *new* will become possible. A critique of contemporary crisis rhetoric has already been introduced through my exploration of Massumi's notion of 'fear-blur'. It is the experience of impending disaster as a kind of background noise to everyday life. It is also implied in the critique of the society of the spectacle, by virtue of its sensationalization and mediatization of imminent threat. We experience today, as Jameson puts it,

> a cultural form of image addiction which, by transforming the past into visual mirages, stereotypes or texts, effectively abolishes any practical sense of the future and of the collective project, thereby abandoning the thinking of future change to fantasies of sheer catastrophe and inexplicable cataclysm, from visions of 'terrorism' on the social level to those of cancer on the personal.[1]

This emphasis on risk and insecurity is therefore a fundamental aspect of the mode of 'fantasy' that I want to describe. I want to argue, in other words, that a politics of fear is essentially a taking hold of a culture's ability to hope and therefore plan for a better future. Risk has of course been a major focus of research in the humanities since Ulrich Beck's *Risk Society*[2] and more recently in the writing of Paul Virilio. Beck identified risk society as a

---

[1] Jameson, *Postmodernism*, p. 46.
[2] Ulrich Beck, *Risk Society*, trans. Mark Ritter (London: Sage, 1992).

kind of transition from industrial societies to one dominated by the management of an explosion of ecological and industrial risks and uncertainties to which society suddenly became aware. Virilio identifies the pre-eminence of the 'accident' in social consciousness. He has claimed that the 'supreme accident', has become the 'absolute energetic foundation' for instituting the doctrine of 'national security'. People willingly renounce their freedom from a state of (officially 'dealt-with') permanent insecurity: '. . . the apocalyptic revelation of the public accident implicitly promotes the administration of civil fear, and thus indirectly the massive, conspicuous consumption of substitutes for and other fallout from the concept of security.'[3] From this perspective, disaster is never some unforeseen, unplanned event. It is programmed into the very same technological idea of progress and 'civilization' that people felt was under attack through the symbolism of the World Trade Centre. Fear as a strategy for crisis rhetoric is therefore a comment about the false 'futurism' of modernist projects. It reflects with greater symbolic force than ever that 'when you invent the ship, you also invent the shipwreck'.[4] Catastrophe lurks within the psyche of affluent society. But it does so both as a pacifying, spectacular portrayal of its deepest fears and as a shocking, disturbing confrontation with the limit of everyday reality. It captures the inevitability of its end in the form of permanent catastrophe. It will be the task of the present chapter to contrast this illusionary form of waiting (a secularized 'eschatology' or discourse about the end-times) with the possibility for alternative imaginations of the future. I will do this first by looking at the new context from which we can understand contemporary society as obsessed by risk and insecurity, and the impact this situation is having on the means of communicating future crises. Next, I will show how such discourses play a part within a wider constitution of capitalized and militarized society. To such a society the fatalist rhetoric and aesthetics of projecting the future is fundamental.

Talking about the end

In order to uncover contemporary culture's obsession with 'endist' discourse, the first step is to review the persistence of crisis rhetoric within the new conditions initiated by the war on terror. Some critical responses to

---

[3] Paul Virilio, 'The Primal Accident' in *The Politics of Everyday Fear*, ed. Brian Massumi, pp. 211–218 (p. 213).

[4] Paul Virilio, *Politics of the Very Worst*, interview by Phillipe Petit, trans. Michael Cavaliere, ed. Sylvère Lotringer (1996), p. 89.

the terrorist attacks on New York in 2001 generate some interesting starting points. Jean Baudrillard infamously argued that the fall of the World Trade Centre was an accident waiting to happen, a mode of anticipation of disaster in popular fantasy:

> the countless disaster movies bear witness to this fantasy, which they clearly attempt to exorcize with images, drowning out the whole thing with special effects. But the universal attraction they exert, which is on a par with pornography, shows that acting-out is never far away, the impulse to reject any system growing all the stronger as it approaches perfection or omnipotence.[5]

Baudrillard's reflections unite the aesthetic and symbolic energy of the accident-form to Western capitalist culture that Virilio had already introduced in his philosophy of the accident. Alongside these two thinkers, many critics of capitalism have understood crisis as a cultural discourse that underwrites the experience of late-capitalism itself. When John Gray, for instance, wrote that 'the natural counterpart of a free market economy is a politics of insecurity'[6] he was relating laissez-faire economics and free trade to the original emergence of capitalism itself. This emergence inevitably involved the systematic removal of any form of popular, democratic political intervention in the workings of the 'unfettered market'. Crisis, as the inevitable social backlash caused by economic disparity and a rising underclass, is written into a system that undermines itself because its expansion is dependent upon dispossession and exploitation. Marx described one aspect of this crisis in terms of cyclical popular resistance. In industrial capitalism, 'overpopulated' masses are drawn in to fill demands of labour and then periodically 'set free' when increased productivity replaced them. An increasing population tossed between the alternations of 'expansion and contraction'[7] of labour demand can therefore be read in every stage of capitalism's journey. And Baudrillard's point is, of course, that global capitalism brings with it its own self-destructive capacity to alienate and dispossess the very masses it claims to be able to liberate. But crisis is also, of course, written into post-industrial society in the ecological limit it attempts to transgress through the limitless exploitation of natural resources. The inevitability of

---

[5] *Ibid.* p. 7.
[6] John Gray, *False Dawn: The Delusions of Global Capitalism* (London: Granta Books, 1998), p. 17.
[7] Karl Marx, *Capital*, vol. 1, abridged edn, ed. David McClellan, trans. Samuel Moore and Edward Aveling [1887] (Oxford: Oxford University Press, 1995), p. 353.

climate chaos now inscribed into a market logic of expanding consumption and development is expressed precisely as a sense of futility. For example, politicians now beginning to talk tough on climate change still often seem incapable of legislating against the 'free choice' of air travel and the exploitation of natural resources.

Critiquing a politics of fear therefore involves recognizing crisis as a dominant discourse in the public domain. It is expressed through the production and dissemination of appropriate ways of speaking, announcing or digesting a politics of risk and insecurity. Conceived more in strategic terms, risk presents itself as, in Beck's words, 'an (institutionalized) attempt, a cognitive map, to colonize the future'.[8] Perhaps due to the nature of mass media communication, within this discourse many different particular disasters can be seen to be united: the imminence of terrorist attacks are connected to those that communicate ecological disaster, economic meltdown or flu epidemics. Some have argued that this sense of the interconnected or 'global' nature of this awareness of crisis is due in part to the *scale* by which disasters are now predicted. François Ewald, for example, has argued that the notion of risk historically emerged as a consideration of insurance and localizable 'responsible parties'. Today, however, risk takes on 'ecological' proportions. The most significant shift is that global crisis (especially wrought by climate change) can be communicated as something too extensive and irreparable to generate political responsibility.[9] While many crises are the result of human action (such as nuclear war or environmental disaster brought on by rapid global warming), they are of the same 'order' of natural disasters and evade the same logic of responsibility. These projected disasters can become accepted as 'acts of God' or mythologized into apocalyptic narrative. When Ewald speaks of 'the universalization of the notion of risk', therefore, he is speaking about two things. First, its proliferation in everyday speech (everybody fears risks to themselves and others, often obsessively, so that death is 'inscribed in life'). And second, its tendency to translate into either denial or to be clothed by the 'individual frenzy of self-protection'.[10] He goes on, however, to portray the proliferation of risk discourses as an ironically unifying trait of globalization:

We are all each other's risks. [. . .] We already knew that we were in solidarity in risk at the local, regional and national scale. Now we are

---

[8] Ulrich Beck, *World Risk Society* (Cambridge: Polity Press, 1999), p. 3.

[9] François Ewald, 'Two Infinities of Risk' in *The Politics of Everyday Fear*, ed. Brian Massumi, pp. 221–228 (p. 223).

[10] *Ibid.* p. 228.

in solidarity in risk on the international scale: we have industrial
solidarities, market solidarities, pollution solidarities, ecological solidarities. It is the age of international moral prediction, of the 'global
challenge' [. . .]. The Vatican has announced the end of the world and
promises redemption in the afterlife; the Club of Rome, an organization
that was non-religious like its time, has taught us to live the catastrophe
of everyday life.[11]

It is interesting to note the intimate relation that a writer like Ewald
detects between endist discourses promising 'redemption' and those promising the 'catastrophe of everyday life'. What could this relation be? Has an
internalization of permanent anxiety and paranoia become subsumed into
the popular notion of collective responsibility? Is this what 'solidarity'
means? The media projection of national and global disaster sheds some
light on this problem. For the mass communication of disaster today infuses
not only opinion making but lifestyles. It does this on a scale that usually
implies (in its mode of reporting) that it is already upon us and too big to
cope with, whether in reference to climate change, AIDS, nuclear war or
accident, viral epidemics, or terrorism. As Massumi puts it, 'the enemy is a
what *not* – an unspecifiable may-come-to-pass, in another dimension. In a
word, the enemy is the virtual.'[12] To repeat Deleuze and Guattari's
argument, discourses of a terrorized public cannot be judged psychologically as rational or irrational responses to a perceived threat. They rationalize
and normalize a condition of permanent anxiety in everyday life. We can
thus affirm with greater strength Massumi's description of this cultural
production of insecurity as the ultimate 'war machine':

> The war machine finds its new object in the 'absolute peace' of terror or
> deterrence. It is terrifying not as a function of a possible war that it prom-
> ises us, as by blackmail. On the contrary, it is terrifying as a function of
> the real, very special kind of peace or 'pacified' existence it promotes and
> has already installed. It no longer needs a qualified enemy but, in con-
> formity with the requirement of an axiomatic, operates against the
> 'unspecified enemy', domestic or foreign (an individual group, class,
> people, event, world). There arises from this a new conception of security
> as materialized war, as organized insecurity or molecularized, distributed,
> programmed catastrophe.[13]

---

[11] *Ibid.* p. 227.
[12] Massumi, 'Everywhere You Want to Be', p. 11, italics in the original.
[13] Massumi (ed.), *Politics of Everyday Fear*, p. 219.

What brings about this future orientation of a politics of fear? There are undoubtedly concrete causal social phenomena involved here in the creation of insecurity. Popular studies in the sociology of fear point to a range of factors, from increased life expectancy to the atomization of social life and the increased knowledge of crime rates and contagious diseases, as causes of an increased propensity to panic.[14] More recent studies place an emphasis on informational society and the role of the media. As David Altheide has observed, a popular 'Mass Media format' today dominates news reporting. In this format, invented risks become an integral aspect of both local and universal events (from serial killers to global warming), in order to maximize the market potential of public information. Dramatized to the level of personal threat, the narrative structure of news parallels traditional morality plays. In other words, it becomes productive of 'a discourse of fear that then becomes a resource on which the audience may draw when interpreting subsequent reports'. This in turn produces 'popular culture that celebrates danger and fear as entertainment organized with canned formats delivered through an expansive and invasive information technology'.[15]

The end of the end

An even deeper origin for this endist trend can be traced, in philosophical terms, from the European modernist obsession with 'telos' in political thought. The idea of historic movement and progress derives in part from an enlightenment appropriation of Hegelianism. History, according to Hegel's view, described a trajectory of successive ideological struggles that resulted in an ever improving synthesis. Hegel originally used the expression to highlight the significance of a specific period in history (Napoleon's victory over Prussia in 1806) as 'end' in two senses. First in the sense of the termination of history as it was known. And second as *telos*, the ushering in of the modern era as the *revelation* of its higher purpose.[16] Thus, from colonial imperialist conquest to the religious apocalyptic overtones of the coming kingdom, we can view the heritage of a distinctively European obsession with history's end: its function and its destination. The success of

---

[14] See Frank Furedi, *Culture of Fear: Risk Taking and the Morality of Low Expectation* (London: Cassell, 1997), pp. 55–70.

[15] David L. Altheide, *Creating Fear: News and the Construction of Crisis* (New York: Walter de Gruyter, 2002), p. 49.

[16] Gamble, *Politics*, p. 27.

that world-view was, of course, never confined to one ideology or another. It is as easily traceable, for instance, in the messianic strands of revolutionary Marxism as it is in Adam Smith's theological vision of the guidance of providence. More pertinently, its influence reappeared in force through the controversially triumphant 'end of history' thesis of then neo-conservative thinker Francis Fukuyama. Jacques Derrida's well-known critique of this propagandistic appraisal for democratic capitalism high-lights a need to go deeper into this endist preoccupation. In particular, Derrida urges to ask, what are the nature of these underlying beliefs that have conditioned Western philosophy since the mid-twentieth century? He writes, 'the eschatological themes of the "end of history", of the "end of Marxism", of the "end of philosophy", of the "ends of man", of the "last man", and so forth were, in the "50s . . . our daily bread"'.[17] Ulrich Beck also famously treated the emergence of a 'risk society' as a symptom of the birth of moder-nity itself. Modernity generated new knowledge and technological innovation that presented industrial society with the shocking predominance of uncer-tainty.[18] This came accompanied by a preoccupation with the prefix 'post', which, he says, 'hints at a "beyond" which it cannot name'.[19] More recently, Andrew Gamble notes that 'endism' is a defining trait of post-modernity's rejection (or mark of its passing) of narratives of history as 'project'. It there-fore implicitly redescribes politics as a fatalistic enterprise.[20]

What does this proliferation of endist discourses signify? Why is the end of history so problematic? Fukuyama had infamously conflated 'end of his-tory' with 'end of ideology'. This conflation implied that the suppression of an alternative political ideology can be read as evidence of the end/telos of a unifying rationale within history. Fukuyama calls this the evidence of 'directionality' in history, or the revival of (the Hegelian) belief in 'Universal Histories'.[21] As Stuart Sim has pointed out, endism has, since Fukuyama's thesis become overwhelmingly associated with an obsession with the end as terminus. It is manifest in human preoccupations with being at the 'edge of an age'. It is perhaps also a contemporary version of millennialism in its original sense: a fascination with the approaching millennium.[22] But there

---

[17] Jacques Derrida, *Specters of Marx*, trans. Peggy Kamuf (London: Routledge, 1994), p. 14.

[18] Beck, *Risk Society*, p. 10.

[19] *Ibid.* p. 9.

[20] Andrew Gamble, *Politics and Fate* (Cambridge: Polity Press, 2000).

[21] Francis Fukuyama, *The End of History and the Last Man* (London: Penguin Books, 1992), pp. 72, 69.

[22] Stuart Sim, *Derrida and the End of History* (Cambridge: Icon Books, 1999).

is also a case to be made that the endist legacy of liberal thinkers like Fukuyama is in fact a perversion of all of these historicist philosophies. As Jürgen Moltmann has put it, for instance, today the end of history is read as 'lack of alternative' to our dominant ideology (neo-liberal capitalism) as opposed to, in its originally Hegelian sense, 'freedom from contradiction'.[23] In the context of a fearful, crisis-obsessed cultural environment, we would do well to ask: why is the former interpretation so attractive? Why, as Derrida put it a decade ago, have Fukuyama's ideas become, 'all the rage in the ideological supermarkets of a worried west where it is bought up just as, at the first rumours of war, people buy sugar and oil, when there is any left'?[24] Must the end of one history lead to the search for another one? Or should the contemporary task be, suggested Derrida, that we be 'late to the end of history'[25] by refusing such a totalizing ideological conclusion to the future in the first place? The war on terror attaches an added urgency to this question; it becomes simultaneously a critique of a 'world order' that is defined in advance by the necessity of its own crises. It expects further conflicts, ecological catastrophes and military struggles as definitive in the projection of its historic goals. In 2004, for instance, the Pentagon published a report that predicted that, in the next 20 years,

> nuclear conflict, mega-droughts, famine and widespread rioting will erupt across the world [. . .]. Abrupt climate change could bring the planet to the edge of anarchy as countries develop a nuclear threat to defend and secure dwindling food, water and energy supplies. The threat to global stability vastly eclipses that of terrorism [. . .]. Disruption and conflict will be endemic features of life, [. . .]. Once again, warfare would define human life.[26]

This announcement was, significantly, issued as a national security document, and thus of military concern more than any other. It was not a recommendation for reversing, for instance, national policy on climate change. As a military document, it represented the new geopolitical demands, as well as the accepted global 'price' of an accepted world order.

---

[23] Jürgen Moltmann, 'Is the World Coming to an End or Has Its Future Already Begun?' in *The Future*, ed. Fergusson and Sarot, p. 135.

[24] Derrida, *Specters of Marx*, p. 68.

[25] *Ibid.* p. 15.

[26] Mark Townsend and Paul Harris, 'Now the Pentagon Tells Bush: Climate Change Will Destroy Us', *The Observer*, 22 February 2004.

Fantasies of the future

Thus we are brought to the wider question of crisis and response. How might our communication of the future as a series of inevitable catastrophes possibly correspond to the generation of 'appropriate' political responses? Where might we find a faithful response to our own postmodernist view of forward-marching to the crises of our own making? There is no lack of cynicism in this endeavour. John Gray, as I have already observed, epitomizes the wholesale rejection of modernity's illusions of progress. From religious apocalyptic narrative to communist Utopian enclave, eschatological reasoning is necessarily couched in terms of an anthropomorphic hubris about the ability for humans (whether divinely, or scientifically, inspired) to solve the world's problems. *Straw Dogs* infamously attempted to relativize any of these political positions. As some critics have argued[27] he does this by following through the neo-Malthusian conclusions of his evolutionary determinism: 'the destruction of the natural world is not the result of global capitalism, industrialisation, "western civilisation" or any flaw in human institutions. It is a consequence of the evolutionary success of an exceptionally rapacious primate.'[28] This attack is significant since it applies not only to the delusions of Western progress, but also those of political practice in general (at least in the Western tradition) as the choice between Utopian or dystopian future projection. His approach therefore represents a kind of accommodation with inevitable crises as a response to the political manipulation of fear of the future. It is a peculiarly European arrogance (more specifically, echoing his alliance with Nietzsche's critique, 'a Christian prejudice'[29]) to be obsessed with the notion of transcending the evolutionary process, and thus forestalling anything. For Gray, a staunch Darwinist, 'Epidemiology and microbiology are better guides to our future than any of our hopes or plans.'[30]

Gray's peculiarly conservative form of determinism is instructive to the present analysis of crisis rhetoric because it concludes, in its own ironically 'enlightened' manner, a certain impossibility of framing the very question of human destiny in terms of hope. *Straw Dogs* therefore could be seen to epitomize the language of crisis as a sign of the disappearance of hope as a 'philosophical concept'. But it also highlights the need to distinguish

---

[27] See, for example, Danny Postel, 'Gray's Anatomy', *The Nation*, 22 December 2003.

[28] John Gray, *Straw Dogs* (London: Granta Books, 2002), p. 7.

[29] *Ibid.* p. 47.

[30] *Ibid.* p. 9.

between human imagination and the fantasies of progress. How might this distinction affect our understanding of Gray's attack on Utopianism? Gray's unwillingness to distinguish between different levels of 'illusionary' human imagination leaves him unable to really critique specific 'endist' projects (within his overarching critique of humanity, 'genocide is as human as art or prayer'[31]), such as the war on terror. But what, then, are the 'fantastic' hallmarks of a politics of fear? Baudrillard provides a suggestion in his critique of the 'illusion of the end'. For Baudrillard, the truest sense in which history has 'ended' is that the meaning of progress has slipped entirely out of its trajectory. The replacement of modernity with an endless spectacle of events has taken away the capacity to imagine the future, to see an end. The 'dreaming' of catastrophe, or progress, or anything linear, is therefore pure fantasy:

> the perception and imagination of the future are beyond us [. . .]. History comes to an end here, not for want of actors, not for want of violence (there will always be more violence), not for want of events (there will always be more events, thanks be to the media and the news network!), but by deceleration, indifference, and stupefaction. It is no longer able to transcend itself, to envisage its own finality, to dream of its own end; it is being buried beneath its own immediate effect, worn out in special effects, imploding into current events.[32]

Alongside the erosion of the means for engagement in civic politics, it is inevitable that a means to envisage the possibilities of the future also disappear. Moreover, they disappear as the fantasies or 'ruins' of a failed modernity. Lamenting the 'success' of human achievements, Baudrillard thus expresses a cruel indictment of Fukuyama's original argument.

Unlike Gray's pessimism, Baudrillard's critique of a cultural inability to imagine the end is at least posed in terms of the failure of a moral impulse. It has at least as its target a contingent *cause* of this illusion (the emergence of a society of consumption, for example). Baudrillard's critique is therefore capable of provoking an analysis into the specific causes of some of those failures. As a result it is better equipped to distinguish between acts of fantasy and acts of the imagination. Fantasy represents an inability for the imaginative process to breach the walls of an accepted discourse. It is the inability to *transcend*: '[history] is no longer able to transcend itself, to

---

[31] *Ibid.* p. 91.

[32] Jean Baudrillard, *The Illusion of the End*, trans. Chris Turner (Cambridge: Polity Press, 1994), p. 4.

envisage its own finality, to dream of its own end; it is being buried beneath its own immediate effect, worn out in special effects, imploding into current events.'[33] The real end-desire that defines post-modernity is in fact the *never ending*. It is an inability even to conceive of one's inevitable termination through a drowning in simulation and effects. Baudrillard therefore pushes the logic of that highly revealing Hollywood production *The Day After Tomorrow*[34] to its limits. In Roland Emerich's film an accelerated pace of climate change plunges the planet into a new ice age, forcing the entire Northern Hemisphere to emigrate south. At the conclusion of the film, when the storm is over, an observer from a space shuttle looks on planet earth and says, 'have you ever seen the air so clear?'[35] The desire for a new Eden may well represent a powerful and enduring manipulation of political desires. Baudrillard's conclusion, however, is that the *real* fear-fantasy of future disaster is not one of a new Eden but rather, the interminable simulation of a paradise lost.

Saving time

The ability for a politics of fear to incorporate political desires themselves, began in Chapter 2, must now be transferred to the observations made here about fantasies of the end. For Baudrillard's emphasis on the inability to 'transcend' history does indeed introduce a principle that can be seen to lie at the heart of endism as the *perversion* of desires. In contemporary political culture future projection is deceived into seeing the present as its own end, a simulated and permanent apocalypse. How, to follow Deleuze and Guattari's approach, do people come to love insecurity and an incapacity for moving forward? Nietzsche, whom Derrida has called one of the 'classic' apocalyptic thinkers of modern times,[36] is well known for providing an interesting perspective on this problem. He offers us an appraisal of *amor fati*. Love of fate can represent the means to accept historical events without attaching an external intention to them:

> man is not the effect of some special purpose, of a will, and end; nor is he the object of an attempt to attain an 'ideal of humanity' or an 'ideal of happiness' or an 'ideal of morality.' It is absurd to devolve one's essence

---

[33] *Ibid.* p. 4.
[34] *The Day After Tomorrow*, Dir Roland Emmerich, 20th Century Fox, 2004.
[35] *Ibid.*
[36] Derrida, *Specters of Marx*, p. 15.

on some end or other. We have invented the concept of 'end': In reality, there is no end. One is necessary, one is a piece of fatefulness, one belongs to the whole, one is in the whole [. . .]. That nobody is held responsible any longer, that the mode of being may not be traced back to a *causa prima*, that the world does not form a unity either as a sensorium or as 'spirit' – that alone is the great liberation; with this alone is the innocence of becoming restored.[37]

On the face of it, therefore, Nietzsche's recommendation accurately pres-ages a twenty-first-century *Zeitgeist*. He foresees the pessimistic fallout from failed Utopian projects, and an accompanying sense of the inevitability of the present. Should Nietzsche therefore be seen as a fatalist? In his defence, Nietzsche's doctrine is not *quietist*. Elsewhere he describes *amor fati* as a positive quality (specifically applicable to Goethe, for whom Nietzsche reserved some of his greatest adulation):

> such a spirit who has *become free* stands amid the cosmos with a joyous and trusting fatalism, in the *faith* that only the particular is loathsome, and that all is redeemed and affirmed in the whole – *he does not negate any more*. Such a faith, however, is the highest of all possible faiths.[38]

Fate, seen in this light, is a call to action and life-affirming creativity, in spite of a determinist vision of history in which all are caught. But such a view appears at radical odds with the climate of non-participation described earlier. What then, can we say about a contemporary love of fate as the means to 'become free'? It is fitting at this point to expand Nietzsche's own recommendation of fatalism as an ultimate and superior form of 'faith'. We might suggest that today we are witnessing a dominant cultural mode of anticipating the future – a secularized eschatology. Eschatology simply means talk of the end-times, or the *eschaton*. It thus represents a cultural frame that goes beyond specifically religious traditions. At the same time, it serves to draw awareness to some unavoidably religious influences on many secular expressions of time, which are crucial for understanding our attitudes to hope and political action. Nietzsche's rhetoric can highlight a need to scrutinize the faith of cultural projections. It reminds us also that the adoption of attitudes towards the future has *political* ramifications. They

---

[37] Friedrich Nietzsche, *Twilight of the Idols: Or, How One Philosophizes with a Hammer* in *The Portable Nietzsche*, ed. and trans. Walter Kaufmann (New York: Penguin Books, 1976), pp. 463–563 (pp. 500–501), italics in the original.

[38] *Ibid.* p. 554, italics in the original.

do not simply guide social practices but undergird them with unquestioned metaphysical beliefs about what is to come.

The concept of a secularized eschatology has been used recently by Philip Goodchild. In his critique of the delusions of 'pious' attention to the narrative of capitalist progress, he affirms that an appropriate response to crisis must constitute a form of 'purified' reflection. To combat the self-destructive nature of capitalism we need a clearer way of thinking and directing attention.[39] Catastrophe is on the horizon only to the extent that human imagination continues to be forced into the mould that capital, the new god and source of piety, requires it to fit. Crisis must interpret the root of people's 'attention' as the symptom, in Deleuzian terms, of perverted desire.[40] Modern directions of piety are formed around the 'religion' of capitalism, its self-justifying logic and credibility, in a manner of passivity and consumption: 'embedded in the liturgical performance of symbols: we no longer believe, but the symbols (of capital) believe for us'.[41] We can trace an attachment to these symbols to the embedded desire generated by capital for putting off the 'finality' or end of the future. Goodchild argues that capitalism generates a relationship to the future founded on perpetual debt, or the guarantee of further credit from the certainty of future loans. There are at least three levels to Goodchild's understanding of capital as representing a secularized eschatology. The first concerns the ontological basis for a politics of money, centring on the principles of debt and credit. Goodchild's purpose in linking ontology to the political 'practices' of capital is to 'demystify' the metaphysical beliefs that legitimize a certain political order and to uncover the secret of how the one, theoretical, gives rise to the other, practical. The question of ontology is, therefore, a way of asking how 'real' money is, in the sense of its constitution in capitalist culture as 'objective reality', the 'non-human power' conditioning the means by which people relate and order society.[42] Repeating Marx's analysis, Goodchild reminds us that through the introduction of money as 'standard for deferred payments', a (now global) circulation of money came to be constituted principally by 'bills of exchange'. This paradoxically generates both the social demand of repayment and the impossibility of its (total) repayment due to circular and spiralling borrowing.[43] The notion of depoliticization

---

[39] Philip Goodchild, *Capitalism and Religion: The Price of Piety* (London: Routledge, 2002), p. 248.
[40] *Ibid.* p. 248.
[41] *Ibid.* p. 249.
[42] Goodchild, 'Capital and Kingdom', pp. 129, 139.
[43] *Ibid.* p. 133.

takes on new proportions within this description. Not only are desires co-opted into the logic of anxiety and insecurity but have, according to Goodchild, a metaphysical grounding: the necessity of money as debt constitutes its 'real' existence as constantly deferred payment.[44]

The second level is understanding money as 'effective demand'. In order to 'make money' through real production/trading, more money must be created in the first place through trust. Money is made by 'entering into a liability'.[45] A spiral of debt now defines economic life. The need to make money in order to make money is underwritten by its definition as 'both means of payment and unit of account'. Money is 'the universal, the supreme value, the means of access to all other virtues'.[46] Once again, we can see all previous critique about a politics of non-participation subsumed into this spiritualization of the demands of capital. But we are still essentially talking about a mode of future projection, and thus an eschatological frame. The desire for money, as the ground of all other desires, radically determines the scope of future action, relativizing its value to that of market needs.

On a third level, Goodchild notices that this increasing subsumption of social power and human life to the law of credit and debt acquires the quality of an 'imaginary' relationship with the future:

> financial value depends on an imagined future. This imagined future is transcendent to current reality, and, furthermore, the future never comes. For, even if there is a stock market crash, the value of any asset still depends on projections about its future. In this respect, financial value is essentially a degree of hope, expectation, or credibility.[47]

Here Goodchild critiques the conditions of late capitalism not only as containing imminent crisis but also generating a perpetual *deferral* of crisis. The political practices generated by the moral and political imperatives of capital can be seen as a kind of spiritualization of debt and the never approaching future.

In distinction to Goodchild, who is happy enough to use the terms interchangeably, I can now assert that capitalist practices represent a *fantasy* rather than *imaginary* future. A discourse of the 'end' as expression of hope in the future may be conceived as the positioning of society and ecology as

---

[44] *Ibid.* p. 133.

[45] *Ibid.* p. 135.

[46] Philip Goodchild, 'Debt, Epistemology and Ecotheology', *Ecotheology*, 9.2 (2004), 151–177 (168).

[47] Goodchild, 'Capital and Kingdom', p. 133.

expressions (and imaginations) of faith *in* the end. But its parallel in the realm of fantasy is certainly that which defers the responsibility of such an expression. This fantastic element to capital is well described by Massumi's reference to 'Timex-philosophy'. This idea treats capitalism as a warding off of death: 'capital appears as a time-form: a future (fulfilment) forever deferred (signified) buckling back with accelerating velocity into a "having been" (productive)'.[48] The point is not that capital's limit (death) promises any hope of liberation through a realization of death. On the contrary, the potency of consumer logic is that death, the crisis of annihilation, can be altogether transcended through 'buying into' an immortal, commodified existence:

> The inevitable. We all know our time will come. But if we follow the existential imperative of capitalism – don't crack under pressure (pick the right watch) – we don't have to worry about never having been. Even if we take a licking, our consumer heritage will keep on ticking. We will live in the sparkle of our great-great-grandchildren's fashion accessories. [. . .] The future perfect – or to translate the more suggestive French term, the 'future anterior' – is the fundamental tense of the time-form constitutive of the consuming subject [. . .]. 'Will have bought = will have been': the equation for capitalist salvation.[49]

Capitalist salvation is the act of deferral and of saving time. It is an immortalization of the present. Goodchild agrees, adding the new twist that this salvation looks increasingly like a perverse kind of piety, a new religion:

> not only as a Being transcendent to material and social reality, yet the pivot around which material and social reality is continually reconstructed, the value of money is essentially religious. To believe in the value of wealth is to believe in a promise that can never be realized; it is a religious faith. Yet one only has to act as though one believes in it, and by some miracle, it becomes true – for others may treat money in the same way, accepting it in exchange.[50]

This concept of 'secular eschatology' is not confined to a critique of consumer culture. It is also consonant with another recent argument, this time accusing the tactics of the war on terror as a kind of spiritual adherence to

---

[48] Massumi, 'Everywhere You Want to Be', p. 16.
[49] *Ibid.* p. 9.
[50] Goodchild, 'Capital and Kingdom', p. 133.

perverted faith in the future. As Paul Fletcher has put it, the war on terror, and in particular the erosion of civil liberties it has generated, represents the, 'martial aspect of eschatology . . . predicated on a metaphysical foundation in which juridical judgement is endlessly deferred'.[51] This concept of deferral as *legal* suspension is based primarily on Giorgio Agamben's analysis of the state of emergency in political life. Agamben's interest in the state of exception is derived principally from the German political scientist Carl Schmitt. Central to Schmitt's legal theory was the paradox that the sovereign is 'at the same time outside and inside the juridical order'.[52] Sovereign power in the European tradition has traditionally been expected to be able to indefinitely suspend the rights of its citizens in order to 'protect' them through the exercise of extra-legal power. Agamben's point is precisely that such a possibility has always been latent and inherent to the European model of sovereignty. Sovereignty represents both constitutive law and the existence outside that law. This is a contradiction with more pressing ethical consequences than logical ones, making as it does 'the sovereign [. . .], the point of indistinction between violence and the law, the threshold on which violence passes over into law and law passes over into violence'.[53] Today, runs the argument, we are witnessing the exercise of this principle of suspension as the rule and not the exception, to normal legality.

How does this relate to a secularized eschatology? Today's proliferation of permanent urban surveillance, detainment of terror suspects without trial and the new paranoiac 'security' paradigm of Western social culture can be seen to create a perverted faith in the future. It constantly and indefinitely defers the freedom of citizens in the present in the interest of an ambiguously defined future 'freedom'. This situation can, therefore, like the paradigmatic feature of capital as indefinite debt repayment, be seen as the false or illusionary guarantee of a future that is simply inscribed into an experience of the present. It is thus integral to a state of permanent insecurity and the hypermilitarization of social space descriptive of the political climate of the war on terror. Eschatological vision is perverted by moving from the undecidability of the future – a suspended judgement, a blindness of hope (or a trusting fatalism, to return to Nietzsche) – to the paralysis of fear. Fear, to put it simply, makes politics a constantly deferred

---

[51] *Ibid.* p. 59.
[52] Giorgio Agamben, *Homo Sacer*, trans. Daniel Heller-Rozen (Stanford: Stanford University Press, (1998), p. 15.
[53] *Ibid.* p. 38.

project. It is, as Fletcher puts it, a 'metaphysics of crisis': the suspension of normal time by which 'political time is terminated'.[54]

With Goodchild and Fletcher's description of currently operating secular eschatologies, Baudrillard's 'illusion of the end' is given a deeper significance. Both the money and security paradigms can be seen to function as acts of faith in the future. But what is the nature of this faith? The conditions of both debt and insecurity are self-perpetuating and indefinite. Hence, the future that is desired by them is defined by its failure to materialize. It is the establishment of a new permanent condition, the state of exception that becomes the rule. This indictment of an illusory or fantastic eschatology also gives greater sense to the concept of capitalized fear. A sanctified war without end becomes the foundation for internalizing insecurity. Limitless consumption becomes the secular salvation offered within a climate of fear and depoliticization. As Massumi puts it, 'capitalist power actualizes itself in a basically uninhabitable space of fear'.[55]

These expressions of secular eschatology epitomize what is politically *functional* in the cultural obsession with risk, security and endist rhetoric. They describe, that is, the political *rationale* behind the maintenance of an illusion of the end. That rationale is a political desire to perpetuate the state of the present, and a guarantee of the power of those who *define* the state of the present. In the interests of maintaining the militarization and capitalization of social space, therefore, it seems necessary to determine a certain control of the perception of crises. Crisis management has more to do with the management of the language of crisis. Within the tactics of a politics of fear, this mode of crisis rhetoric has been predominantly through the maintenance of an unknowable, unquantifiable and permanent threat: the ubiquity of 'terror'. One can even see this fantastic obsession with hastening the end expressed in *The Day After Tomorrow*. The principal reason, I suggest, that the film avoided any great criticism from climate sceptics within the US government was that such discourse is infused with an apocalyptic fantasy whose effect on many people may be simply a sense of disempowerment from political intervention *until* the system has been overhauled by an event as cataclysmic as the freezing of the northern hemisphere. Crisis fantasy includes, in other words, an aesthetic strategy. Whether through image or text, it is a vision that generates no *further* vision

---

[54] Paul Fletcher, 'The Political Theology of the Empire to Come', *Cambridge Review of International Affairs*, vol. 17, no. 1 (April 2004) 49–61 (59).

[55] Massumi, 'Everywhere You Want to Be', p. 23.

or imagination. And this occurs in the same way that debt and insecurity were seen to defer the responsibility to respond, to do something new. The intention of this fantasy may, whether consciously or unconsciously, desire to hasten the end-time with a view to being able to start again, the flood that must precede the rainbow, the catastrophe that necessitates new paradigms.

How, then, should one communicate the evidence of future crises, if not to expect catastrophic change and the ability for renewal or rebirth? *One* answer must surely lie with the manner in which the projected future necessitates new paradigms or lifestyles. People can and do demand political changes to the present, not a deferred fantasy of the future. For even at the conclusion of *The Day After Tomorrow*, the only hint we get from the repentant US government is that they were 'wrong' to assume that the world's resources could be consumed without consequences, and that the global reality is now 'changed', bringing nations together in solidarity and mutual dependence (in the film the survivors of the northern hemisphere are forced to take refuge in, as the president puts it, 'nations we once called the Third World'[56]). One suspects that a greater change in consciousness than can be imagined within these moral categories would be needed to overcome the challenges posed by such a radically altered world. The international 'unity' described here also recalls Ewald's ironic sense of the new 'solidarities of risk' that bind nations and communities together. While 'ecology' has become the great leveller of political crises – that which makes all life a political responsibility – the mode by which people actually face this reality is one of helplessness, not collective responsibility. The logic of the global financial market overpowers a sense of collective risk. Paradoxically, therefore, it creates an absurdity out of risk (perhaps currently being internalized as a self-destructive, sinking-ship form of post-modern irony), as opposed to a moral imperative. To stop using one's car or using planes has become a (middle class) eccentricity. But accepting a civil terrorism law (making yourself feel both scared and guilty) is a responsible act of self-preservation.

Does the rhetoric of waiting for future crisis always reveal a culture of helplessness, or an ironic detachment from the reality of the present? We have at least been able to see that the *communication* of that mode of waiting is of crucial significance. The question is still open for whether crisis is capable of generating a discourse of hope or not. Might it yet generate a qualitatively new orientation to political practices to those that have been

---

[56] *Ibid.*

assumed within a culture of fear? Introducing the notion of 'secular eschatology' has proved a useful conceptual tool in preparing an answer. For just as Goodchild locates the appropriate response to crisis in the act of a purified orientation towards future practices, or, as he puts it, 'right eschatological expectations',[57] the use of this concept in critiquing crisis fantasy indicates the next necessary step in my argument. This must be a search for alternative modes of imaginative engagement in the political sphere. These must be acts of 'faith' in the future that do more than brace believers for the shock of coming crises. Instead they should orient new political practices of the present in *light* of the coming crises.

Conclusion

In this chapter I have tried to show how a politics of fear is also a specific orientation towards future crisis. The philosophical and cultural roots of our approach to the future and to crisis in general make significant differences to how 'the political' itself may be conceived. John Gray, for instance, challenges the assumption that human *projection* of solutions is the appropriate response to crisis. He suggests in the place of 'moral hopes or mystical dreams' that the 'aim of life' might be 'simply to see'.[58] The Nietzschean overtones of this emphasis on the acceptance of fate do not, however, account for the political *effect* of certain modes of 'seeing' themselves. Baudrillard also challenged the illusions of the very foundation of endist rhetoric, that of a history, of a forward movement. But he has also showed that the perseverance of this illusion in contemporary rhetoric serves a political, or at least cultural, purpose – the perpetuation of war without having the 'reality' of war, for example.[59] Lastly, the analyses of Goodchild and Fletcher recognize effectively the political effects of the role of the 'end' in everyday life. Those effects confirm some of the conclusions of Chapter 1, with this added futural dimension: fear is both produced and producer of public belief and social discourse in neo-liberal democracies. It is able to frame the conditions for political responses towards the fate of humanity. The latter half of this chapter, however, showed that more than an awareness of human illusions of the end is needed to suggest the possibility for end-discourse that *repoliticizes* the public. By describing certain

---

[57] Goodchild, 'Capital and Kingdom', p. 148.

[58] Gray, *Straw Dogs*, p. 199.

[59] Baudrillard, *Illusion*, p. 62. See also Baudrillard, *The Gulf War Did Not Take Place*, trans. Paul Patton (Sydney: Power Publications, 1995).

tactics of a politics of fear in terms of a late-capitalist, secularized eschatology we can locate the places and methods by which a certain collective indebtedness to future catastrophe is perpetuated. Those aspects of contemporary life that are about putting off crisis by saving time, making money, accepting a state of insecurity and paranoia and being terrorized signal certain political practices whose rationale can be challenged.

An acquiescence and quietism in the face of inevitable crisis only has the power it does because it replaces desires that might transcend a historicist kind of fatalism. These desires thus appear as a kind of religion, a directed piety, to use Goodchild's idea. They simulate a fantasy of the future as the perpetuation of the present.

Reflections on Part I

Throughout the first three chapters I have tried to show that the contemporary concept of a politics of fear, popular among critics of war propaganda and governmental 'spin' on current affairs, should be viewed within a much wider critique of contemporary Western society: namely, a society increasingly depoliticized and detached from its desires for a radically alternative future. The presence in our midst of capitalized fear appears as an almost untouchable 'imminent crisis'. That means that it *disallows* taking 'the end' seriously as an act of the imagination. It is now time, therefore, to study those attentions, desires and actions that *do* take seriously the realm of human imagination. Imagination, in contrast to fantasy, will be seen as that which welcomes the new, that which breaks the cycle of inevitability.

Part II

Politics of Imagination

Imagination is not fantasy [. . .]. The imagination is a linguistic gesture, hence a common gesture; the gesture which throws a web over the to-come so as to know it, construct it, organize it with power.

Antonio Negri[1]

The task is now to examine those categories that engage the imaginative framing of the future: Utopian; eschatological; and apocalyptic attitudes and beliefs. This section therefore makes explicit the claim made in the introduction that both theological and political discourses are enterprises in generating appropriate gestures towards the future. How do they help people define the function of hoping? As a projection of collective values? As the promise of a revealed future? The following chapters explore in detail the complex relationship that emerges between the hope for a politically defined 'better world' and the hope for a radically 'other world'; one that transcends the conditions of the present altogether.

---

[1] Antonio Negri, *Time for Revolution* (London: Continuum, 2003), p. 156, my emphasis.

Chapter 4

Utopia: Radical Imagination

Introduction

The purpose of this chapter is to examine some of our Utopian intellectual heritage and make some suggestions for the contemporary direction of Utopian ideas in political life. Since Thomas More coined the term in 1515 the concept of Utopia has always been both ambiguous and controversial, quite independently of its literary incarnations. Today this controversy is most active where discussion of Utopianism becomes conflated with those concepts of the 'perfect', uncompromised society. Utopia is thus associated with a kind of ideological purism, or fundamentalism. 'Anti-Utopianism' seems to have emerged as a reaction to the failed Utopian experiments of the twentieth-century fascism and totalitarian communism.[2] Utopia as a *political destination*, and conceived originally by Thomas More as an imaginary state of (near) perfect society, appeared to many to represent some guide or blueprint to political 'purification'. It was thus felt to say too much about what might be politically imaginable. John Gray has also renewed a critique of Utopian thought. For Gray, Utopianism represents that remnant of liberal thought that carried through the Judaeo-Christian obsession with the evolution of human progress. Utopianism in any of its many different political and religious hues was at best ridiculous, at worst, as dangerous as the renewed apocalyptic sensibilities of fundamentalist sects.

But perhaps we can avoid some easy misunderstandings here by stressing the divergence between constructed or attempted Utopias and Utopianism. Since Thomas More's opening of the 'generic window', in fact, Jameson traces a split between the imagined *realization* of Utopia and the more ambiguous Utopianism as an omnipresent 'impulse'.[3] For it is within the

---

[2] See Stefan Skrimshire, 'What Is an Anti-Utopian? Gray, Jacoby, Jameson' forthcoming in *Cultural Politics: An International Journal*, vol. 4, no. 2 (July 2008), 231–247.

[3] Jameson, *Archaeologies of the Future*, p. 3.

deviations of the latter's development that we trace the evocation of Utopia itself as a paradox of human thought: can we imagine the unimaginable? Another way of putting this question is to ask: how do political practices *transcend* political limits?

In this chapter however I wish to argue that at very least Utopianism represents the desire to *transcend* ideological boundaries, to live as its outside. It thus presents an essential resource in responding to the ideological closure I have associated with a politics of fear. How does Utopia relate to ideology? Political thought in the Marxist tradition has produced the most fascinating exploration of these two ideas. I thus begin this chapter with some classic Marxist critiques of Utopian thought. The classic works on ideology theory by Karl Mannheim and Antonio Gramsci in particular are considered. Contesting the finality of these ideology theories, however, comes eventually from the ideas of Ernst Bloch, Cornelius Castoriadis and Paul Ricoeur. All of these thinkers are in some ways influenced by the Utopianism of Marx as one of the originators of the idea of a 'discursive break' in history. But Utopianism is a subject that has roots in many traditions of belief, both secular and religious and thus provides us with a rich basis for exploring further political expressions of hope.

The death of spontaneity?

Is Marxism a Utopian philosophy? On the one hand Marxist thinkers have stressed the structural conditions for political imagination. In their classic formulation of the 'dominant ideology thesis' Marx and Engels claimed that 'the ruling ideas of each age have ever been the ideas of its ruling class.'[4] They argued, in other words, that class relations and relations of production are naturalized and inserted as cultural truths. They are subsequently accepted and endorsed as *belief* by the subordinated class. On the other hand Marx himself has been considered a Utopian thinker. His critique pointed towards a state of universal liberation from oppression, envisaged principally as the classless society. How is this tension lived out? The Marxist sociologist Karl Mannheim explained Utopian imagination as in continual dialectical relationship with the existing order: 'the existing

---

[4] Karl Marx and Friedrich Engels, *The Communist Manifesto* ed. David McLellan, trans. Samuel Moore [1888] (Oxford: Oxford University Press, 1992), p. 24. See also Marx and Engels, *German Ideology*, quoted in Nicholas Abercrombie, Stephen Hill and Bryan S. Turner, *The Dominant Ideology Thesis* (London: George Allen and Unwin, 1980), p. 7.

order gives birth to utopias which in turn break the bonds of the existing order, leaving it free to develop in the direction of the next order of existence.'[5] Within Mannheim's sociology of knowledge, one is always 'bound into a system of relations which to a large extent hamper (one's) will'.[6] To think outside of this is to 'shatter, either partially or wholly, the order of things prevailing at the time'.[7] It is also to be able to think the unthinkable. In what sense is this possible? In Mannheim's words it means to think those ideas that 'can never be realised in the societies in which they exist, and because one could not live and act according to them within the limits of the existing order'.[8] Mannheim thus speaks of Utopia's capacity to 'transcend reality',[9] though it isn't clear what exactly is meant by this use of the category 'transcendence'. Is it something that points beyond the given material conditions, or which promises a suspension of material conditions altogether, and which would therefore seem closer to a theological sense of transcendence (as in the 'kingdom of God')? In general, Mannheim echoes a hallmark of traditional Marxist criticisms of those Utopias that substitute *applicable* transcendent ideas to those of mere fantasy because they come from 'another world' (as opposed to a rationally predicted historical process). This either/or approach to transcendence comes through in Mannheim's belief that once ideology is consonant with people's mastery of their own existence, thinking 'fantastically' simply becomes unnecessary. The need for Utopia disappears, in other words. Mannheim thus develops something of a sociology of Utopian evolution, always reflecting in the end the material social conflicts which give rise to ideological challengers. The chiliastic messianism of movements like Anabaptism or the Taborites in the sixteenth century represents the extreme manifestation of Utopia's original 'virtue'. Utopia is produced of a state of mind 'incongruous with the state of reality in which it occurs'.[10] The more recent manifestations of Utopia, however, those of socialism and communism, show, according to Mannheim, history to be closing the 'incongruence' gap. A realization of socialism therefore does away the need for Utopia itself in its original capacity to transcend history. This overtly Marxist approach to Utopia implies that the dialectic of Utopia and ideology has led human history out of the

---

[5] Karl Mannheim, *Ideology and Utopia*, trans. Louis Wirth and Edward Shils (London: Routledge, 1960), p. 179.

[6] *Ibid.* pp. 234–235.

[7] *Ibid.* p. 173.

[8] *Ibid.* p. 175.

[9] *Ibid.* p. 173.

[10] *Ibid.* p. 173.

need to transcend its own reality. The belief that the present age has 'achieved the highest degree of rational mastery of existence', is a 'heroic development' and 'at the highest state of awareness, when history is ceasing to be a blind fate'[11] suggests a critical assumption about where and when Utopian imagination arises as a social 'need'.

What are the implications of Mannheim's 'material' conditions for Utopian desire within the scheme of this book? The suggestion is that all attempts at 'transcending' (in the sense of imagining *beyond*) the given ideology of a politics of fear would be seen to succeed or fail on the basis of a congruence of Utopian desires and the new realities instituted by Utopian practices. The historical-social process is thus the resolution of a kind of Utopian pathology. Utopia here transforms itself, with the gradual 'mastery of the present situation', into (reality affirming) 'science'.[12]

We can trace some influence here in certain Marxist formulations of an aversion to the idea of *spontaneity* or the 'non-programmable' within a given ideological regime. To understand fully the consequences of this thinking 'outside' an ideological given, we can turn to the ideas of Antonio Gramsci. Gramsci proposed that spontaneity in popular political movements was essentially a *rhetorical* mechanism. 'Pure spontaneity does not exist in history', he wrote. Nevertheless, popular mobilization has need of the language of spontaneity to create, 'a stimulus, a tonic, an element of unification in depth. [. . . To give] the masses a 'theoretical' consciousness of being creators of *historical* and institutional *values*'.[13] The assumption is that either spontaneity represents a specific 'method' of directed leadership or that, once expressed, a spontaneous movement is brought into line: '*educated, directed, purged of extraneous contaminations* [. . . brought] into line with modern theory [i.e. Marxism].'[14] Gramsci is ready to admit that waiting for revolutions of 'one hundred percent consciousness' will be continually betrayed by historical reality, which 'produces a wealth of the most bizarre combinations'.[15] The point, however, is that collective activity always requires (ideological) leadership. There is always an 'intellectual' and 'cultural' mobilization of popular opinion and civil obedience. Furthermore these mobilizations always come *before* the possibility of resistance. Gramsci

---

[11] *Ibid.* p. 236.

[12] *Ibid.* p. 230.

[13] Antonio Gramsci, *Selections from the Prison Notebooks*, ed. and trans. Quenton Hoare and Geoffrey Newell-Smith (London: Lawrence and Wishart, 1971), pp. 196–198.

[14] *Ibid.* p. 198, italics in the original.

[15] *Ibid.* p. 200.

believed the oppressed would not be able to mobilize resistance and revolution without undermining the intellectual bases for their oppression through an 'organic intellectual'. The role of the organic intellectual was to 'give [a social group, or class] homogeneity and an awareness of its own function'.[16] Gramsci's contribution to a theory of Utopian imagination was therefore to avoid talk of escaping ideology outright. Instead he defined 'negative' ideologies from 'positive' ones. The former are, 'arbitrary, rationalistic, or "willed" [. . .], they only create individual "movements", polemics and so on'. The latter are, on the other hand, 'historically organic [. . .], they have a validity which is "psychological"; they "organise" human masses, and create the terrain on which men move, acquire consciousness of their position, struggle, etc'.[17]

How can ideologies be 'historically organic' except by affirming some sense in which *everybody*, not just the intellectual 'gatekeepers', have the potential to reimagine the historical process? This would seem to contradict Deleuze and Guattari's idea of a 'schizoid' element of social desires. Along with them, should we not allow social desire the permanent possibility for Utopian rupture before it becomes 'organized' by the control society? In his defence, Gramsci hinted at the possibility for human agency to break out of the more rigid interpretations of ideological closure. This was evident in those 'bizarre combinations' of social movements that never 'conform to the abstract schema' of the dominant ideology.

Nevertheless a view of the dominant ideology as the total co-option of belief, stands in contrast to 'thin' versions of false consciousness. According to James Scott, these claim that subordinated classes do not so much believe in as remain incapable of undermining the rationality of an ideology that maintains their own slavery: 'the thick theory maintains consent; the thin theory settles for resignation'.[18] A mistaken presumption in 'thick' versions is that 'ruling ideas' implies a saturation of culture within a single discourse (a logic of domination). This would imply that any 'subculture' of dissent has also likely internalized that logic of domination. Gramsci also picked up on this error. He observed that even where a class is most repressed and unable (or unwilling) to challenge their repression, people retain semi-autonomy as regards their ability to think differently. There is always 'common sense' formed through everyday experience that is able to reflect class interests not necessarily controlled by one group. A combination of

---

16 *Ibid.* p. 5.
17 *Ibid.* p. 377.
18 James Scott, *Domination and the Arts of Resistance*, p. 72.

'thick' and 'thin' theories of false consciousness therefore seems the more realistic. This combination amounts to, as Scott says, a 'culture of defeat and nonparticipation'[19] not unlike the climate of fear depicted earlier. It means that oppressed people, while not always incorporating a dominant ideology into their own scheme, are unwilling to attempt to completely tear themselves away from its influence on their lives. This is because people have an ingrained assumption about the parameters of political action – what can and cannot be done. Ideological closure, in other words, might simply mean a system of education and consciousness about what can and what can't be done about one's own situation.

A Gramscian view maintains that it is still ultimately *people* who lie waiting to manipulate the spontaneous intellect of dissenting masses towards their own ideology. This view is operative, therefore, in a production of 'what is realistic and what is not realistic and to drive certain aspirations and griev-ances into the realm of the impossible, of idle dreams'.[20] Scott's richly contextualized study goes on to argue precisely this point. It is the spaces left between these cultural assumptions of powerlessness and the fostering of 'dissident subcultures' that has threatened throughout history to break out in the form of material revolution. Hegemony is thus revealed in the success of ideology over violent state repression of dissidence. But emanci-pation from a *dominant* ideology still relies on the control of cultural discourse by one interested party or another. This is even true within an understanding of ideological indoctrination. As Habermas would say, there is a process of cultural 'legitimation'[21] through the (theatrical) enactment of our (post)democratic process.

Gramsci introduces a subtler and more nuanced approach to the seeming opposition between ideology and Utopia. He does this by appreciating the persistent element of uncertainty in the formation of subjects. Utopian imagination might still, within this understanding, be seen to play a founda-tional role in social transformation. It is not simply the privileged ability for one class to impose a system of ideas upon another. What goes unques-tioned among traditional Marxists is the belief that ideological production is the process of one class 'doing something' to another class, a one-way process.[22] Such a simplistic interpretation of ideology ignores, within our

---

[19] *Ibid.* p. 73.
[20] *Ibid.* p. 74.
[21] See Jürgen Habermas, *Legitimation Crisis*, trans. Thomas McCarthy (Cambridge: Polity Press, 1988).
[22] See Nicholas Abercrombie, Stephen Hill and Bryan S. Turner, *The Dominant Ideology Thesis* (London: George Allen and Unwin, 1980).

own context, the tendency for a politics of fear to inscribe itself into the fragmented cultural spaces of cultural production. That an ideology of fear comes to dominate cultural life in far more subtle ways has been demonstrated already through the complicity of media and educational institutions in perpetuating a 'culture of defeat and nonparticipation', for one gets exactly this sense of closure, of politics remaining 'out of bounds' buried within the rhetoric of security that emanates from the war on terror. In the wake of tragedies such as the London bomb in 2005 or the thwarted attack on Glasgow airport in 2007, mainstream political debate in the United Kingdom has focused almost entirely on the public's faith in the government's duty to tighten security and increase police powers. The ability of citizens to 'get on with life' is seen as a form of feigned ignorance of external threats as opposed to a vocal critique of its causes. This form of depoliticization is rightly recognized to oppose political practices that threaten the stability of a dominant political discourse (such as that of national security). And in the current climate it is easy to see how such an understanding of ideology becomes institutionalized across various social 'sites'. A significant contribution to ideology theory by another Marxist, Louis Althusser, defined such 'Ideological State Apparatuses'[23] (ISAs) to a similar effect. According to Althusser an ideology of domination can be handed down, reproduced, self-indoctrinated and mythologized from one ISA to another. In a slightly different way to Gramsci, therefore, Althusser like others in the Frankfurt school affirmed the appropriate mode of political struggle as the struggle for social *spaces* or modes of participation: 'ideologies are not "born" in the ISAs . . . but from the social classes at grips in the class struggle: from their conditions of existence, their practices, their experience of the struggle'.[24]

Everything that constitutes the new conditions of fear as I have described it therefore generates a corresponding imperative to resist. And this can only occur through *practices* that protest the 'illegitimacy' of a given ideological regime, breaking its hold on cultural consciousness. It has already become evident that the principle of ideological closure within a politics of fear only holds legitimacy through maintenance of the *illusion* or fantasy of participation in the depoliticized public sphere. To resist a culture of fear is to demand access to the political and economic process of everyday life, to *reclaim* those processes. This seems to be confirmed by the ways in which state legislation around the 'democratic world' has used terrorist threat as

---

[23] See Louis Althusser, *Lenin and Philosophy and Other Essays,* trans. Ben Brewster (New York: Monthly Review Press, 1971).

[24] Althusser, *Lenin and Philosophy*, p. 186.

the occasion for increasing its powers to criminalize and incarcerate its own dissident citizens.

Mannheim introduced the idea of the function of Utopia nevertheless as a necessary conceptual tool in achieving an harmonious, balanced world that is 'no longer in the making'.[25] It is not hard to see how such an outlook mirrors certain facets of the 'illusions' of endist discourses that were described earlier. The temptation of a simplistic Utopian lens is its polarization of the world into those whose strivings are satisfied and those whose strivings are historically determined. But this is to ignore a serious appraisal of political practices as states of permanent striving. Another way to put it would be the *refusal* to *cease* striving, contesting a world in which 'there is never anything new, in which all is finished and each movement is a repetition of the past.'[26] As Gramsci argued, the real obstacle to Utopian desire is simply the *common* inability of the majority of people to question a culture of non-participation. It is therefore incumbent upon us to supplement this 'thin' version of false consciousness for the contemporary culture of fear. It is something of a paradox that Mannheim admits, in his own systematic survey of Utopias, that something *essentially human* would be erased alongside the need to continue striving: 'with the relinquishment of utopias, man would lose his will to shape history and therewith his ability to understand it.'[27] It is precisely to this view of humanity as *fundamentally* concerned to shape history according to uncircumscribed visions of the future, that we are concerned.

All power to the imagination?

Mannheim's position generates a controversial test for how far a community might have 'achieved' Utopia: 'have we reached the stage where we can dispense with strivings?'[28] This relativist approach to Utopian function lies in sharp distinction to that of Ernst Bloch, his contemporary and critic. For Bloch, Utopia 'fulfils the meaning of all men and the horizon of all being'.[29] It was Bloch, indeed, whose writing of a similar period attempted to widen the understanding of Utopia to describe a condition of human existence itself.[30] One could thus talk not only of a Utopian function but also a

---

[25] *Ibid.* p. 231.

[26] *Ibid.* pp. 235–236.

[27] *Ibid.* p. 236.

[28] Mannheim, *Ideology and Utopia*, pp. 230–231.

[29] Bloch, *The Principle of Hope*, vol. 1, p. 6.

[30] Wayne Hudson, *The Marxist Philosophy of Ernst Bloch* (London: Macmillan Press, 1982), p. 21.

'Utopian subject'.[31] As such both Mannheim's and Bloch's positions represent a useful point of disagreement. For Bloch the very notion of Utopias failing or succeeding, according to Mannheim's conflict theory of social reality, was to misunderstand their function altogether. Utopian desire represented for Bloch a wider ontological condition of subjects who are 'not yet', who are always works in process. Bloch's inevitably broad conception of the concept 'Utopian' involves a complex (and often disorienting) mixture of mystical, cultural and philosophical sources as its foundation. But it can also be read as an anthropological study in the everyday practices of Utopian desire. His heritage can be seen in subsequent Utopian interpretations of protest cultures. The Belgian Situationist Raoul Vaneigem, for instance, once wrote of the resistances of 1968, in typically 'Utopian' fashion, that:

> The only forms of creativity that authority can deal with, or wishes to deal with, are those which the spectacle can co-opt. But what people do officially is nothing compared with what they do in secret . . . seething unsatisfied desires, daydreams in search of a foothold in reality, feelings at once confused and luminously clear, ideas and gestures presaging nameless upheavals [. . .]. All this energy, of course, is relegated to anonymity and deprived of adequate means of expression, imprisoned by survival and obliged to find outlets by sacrificing its qualitative richness and conforming to the spectacle's categories. Think of Cheval's palace, the Watts Towers, Fourier's inspired system, or the pictorial universe of Douanier Rousseau. Even more to the point, consider the incredible diversity of *anyone's* dreams – landscapes the brilliance of whose colours qualitatively surpass the finest canvases of a Van Gogh. Every individual is constantly building an ideal world within himself, even as his external motions bend to the requirements of a soulless routine.[32]

It was the Situationist International, indeed, who, through symbolic acts of theatre or subvertised street art, attempted to translate the means for social revolution into practices of everyday life. The Situationist International was a political artistic movement originating out of avant-garde trends in Italy and France, and who were influential in galvanizing and interpreting the protests in Paris occupations and barricades in May 1968. One of the

---

[31] *Ibid.* p. 22.
[32] Raoul Vaneigem, *The Revolution of Everyday Life*, trans. Donald Nicholson-Smith (London: Rebel Press, 2001), p. 191, italics in the original.

principle hallmarks of this movement was an active (and sometimes performative) critique of the 'society of the spectacle'.[33] The aim was to disempower a certain hegemony about what was and was not possible in society. And this aim resonates clearly with Bloch's thought. The imperative for anarchic creation lies at the heart of human consciousness: 'everybody's life is pervaded by daydreams: one part of this is just stale, even enervating escapism, even booty for swindlers, but another part is provocative, is not content just to accept the bad which exists, does not accept renunciation.'[34]

Bloch's view of Utopia as creative human function generates a critique of the ideological elements of Utopia itself that have been insinuated in the thought of Mannheim. In *The Principle of Hope* Utopia appears as a kind of cultural limit to ideological closure, a 'surplus' over false consciousness that seeks new things.[35] This Utopianism is constituted by diverse categories with which to colour his materialist reading of history. The principal of these is *Novum*, 'the new'. History should be read, Bloch believed, whether it was through a Marxist or religious world-view, first and foremost in terms of what it has not yet achieved: 'man everywhere is still living in prehistory, indeed all and everything still stands before the creation of the world, of a right world. *True genesis is not at the beginning but at the end*'.[36]

This view, of course, was also the foundation of Mannheim's criteria for 'successful' Utopian experiments. But unlike Mannheim's, Bloch's articulation of the forward direction of historic Utopianism is already present in the ontological quality of this act of anticipation. Bloch's Utopia is dialectical not in terms of a certain resolution from which striving will cease. It is dialectical, rather, in its transformation of concrete events according to an 'authentic' state of expectation. What makes Bloch a conceptually useful thinker over Mannheim is therefore his opposition to the very notions of progress and the end of history, identified earlier as instances of a heretical eschatology and an economy of fear. Bloch's project was to regain for Marxism as a science of the future its spiritual roots. Marxist hope represented the openness of culture towards dreams not defined in advance by a science of progress. Utopia is practical precisely in the sense that it locates transformative practice in the primal impulse that people have for disobedience, eccentricity and openness to an all-consuming idea. He does not simply repeat Marxism's reduction of consciousness, and therefore

---

[33] See Debord, *La société du spectacle*.
[34] Bloch, *The Principle of Hope*, vol. 1, p. 3.
[35] Bloch, *The Principle of Hope*, vol. 1, p. 156.
[36] *Ibid.* p. 1373, italics in the original.

spiritual consciousness, to their economic determinants.[37] Utopia's function, rather, is to reimagine social relations based on an imaginative and 'cosmic' resistance to the coercion of ideology:

> to shape a path from the lonely waking dream of the inner self-encounter to the dream that goes out to shape the external world at least to alleviate it [. . .]. For how could there be an inwardness, and how would it notice that it was one, whether as sorrow or as truly paradoxical joy, if it stopped being rebellious and desperate against everything given?[38]

Bloch's much broader use of the word Utopia clearly introduces a much more explicit engagement with its transcen*dent* element, though he is careful not to confuse this element with 'transcendence' itself: 'certainly everything, and above all human life, is a kind of transcendere, a venturing beyond the given, but this transcendere, as concrete-utopian, also certainly does not involve any transcendence.'[39] But as with Mannheim, it is not clear what understanding of transcendence is operative. How legitimate, for example, is to apply the concept of transcendence, normally reserved for the religious notion of a movement beyond the material sphere, to everyday material Utopian practices? As the suspicions of 'anti-Utopianism' by Jacoby attest, there are clearly dangers here, for to invite Utopian 'eccentricity', going 'outside' of oneself or one's material context can seem like the visionary pursuit of *nowhere*, an inherently escapist attitude. In defence of Bloch's position, and the value of Utopianism more generally, however, there are dangers on the flip side, for leaving out the concept of transcendence altogether. For it is precisely the historical-materialist Utopianism that *rejects* this notion of imagining 'beyond' one's material conditions that can be seen at the heart of totalitarian, 'blueprint' Utopians. Even Lenin, as Bloch notes, was wary of the tendency to translate too easily a Utopian dream into the state-form. He was anxious to give a freedom to the question 'what must we dream of?' not defined in advance by the rigidly strategic dreams of historical materialism, or the party. As he put it, paraphrasing 'Comrade Pisarev':

> The gulf between dream and reality is not harmful if only the dreamer seriously believes in his dream, if he observes life attentively, compares his

---

[37] Ernst Bloch, *The Spirit of Utopia*, trans. Anthony A. Nassar (Stanford: Stanford University Press, 2000), p. 243.

[38] *Ibid.* pp. 237–238.

[39] Bloch, *The Principle of Hope*, vol. 3, p. 1373.

observations with his castles in the air and generally works towards the realization of his dream-construct conscientiously. There only has to be some point of contact between dream and life for everything to be in the best order.[40]

The lessons from revolutionary history thus urge us to take this desire for dreaming seriously and to allow at very least a creative exploration of this category of *transcendere*, of moving *beyond*. For who is qualified to decide what it means for someone, following Lenin, to 'seriously believe' in their dream, and what permutations of transcendence may appear in the spaces of that belief? Another way to ask this question is to return to the question of the imagination in its Kantian sense as a tool by which people ordinarily constitute their reality. Doing so opens up a clearer basis for contesting the ideological closure inherent to a politics of fear. Cornelius Castoriadis' philosophical discussion of the 'social imaginary' addresses precisely this question. He goes, that is, to the root of the question of how our reality is normally 'ordered' through everyday representations. There is a logical and ontological prejudice, Castoriadis believes, in traditional philosophy for the 'determinacy' and predictability of rational thought. The processes of logic by which we assume our choices to be made denies the primary role that imagination has in formulating ideas: 'man's distinguishing trait is not logic but imagination and, more precisely, unbridled imagination, defunctionalized imagination'.[41] Castoriadis argues that the role of the imagination has been historically subordinated to the 'first cause' of reason. Imagination, in other words, is usually placed as an outside to rational processes and can be easily distinguished from it. The implication is that our imaginary worlds, like that of dreams, are wholly identified with illusory or pathological mental constructions about real existing relationships. But this view seems counter intuitive. For the experience of most people is surely that the processing of ideas and formulating beliefs relies on a host of 'imaginary' functions. And it seems reasonable also to maintain that these imaginary tools are not completely dictated by the 'instituted' imaginaries given by an ideological (and rational) system. The function of the imagination in ordering our own individual perception of the world would seem too fundamental. Marxist theory may have successfully critiqued those myths and fantasies that have indoctrinated the masses for so

---

[40] Lenin, 'What Is to Be Done?' quoted in Bloch, *The Principle of Hope*, vol. 1, p. 10.
[41] Cornelius Castoriadis, *World in Fragments: Writings on Politics, Society, Psychoanalysis, and the Imagination*, trans. and ed. David Ames Curtis (Stanford: Stanford University Press, 1997), p. 247.

long in feudal and religious society. But in order to do so it placed too much faith in an assumption that the imaginary impulse can be replaced by the transition to a secular, rationally motivated style of creating history. Perhaps, then, we should embrace instead a 'rediscovered' Marxist Utopianism. For clearly the Marxist emphasis on the power of the dominant ideology serves as a useful reminder that Utopian discourse cannot simply appear out of nowhere and easily transcend normal social discourse with the promise of a new world. On the contrary, we notice today an ambiguity to Utopian discourse. It is arguably as much present in the language of mass media culture and the status quo as it is of the radical political imagination. The urban saturation of advertisements and corporate sponsorship can also create an 'imaginary' world out of social spaces by which to 'transcend' reality. Are they therefore legitimate Utopian expressions? Perhaps the most we can say at this point is that Castoriadis' insistence on the subversive power of the imagination must be supplemented with the warning that it is not always clear who, or what, maintains control of that discursive power. Resistance can often be seen to be as much prey to the kind of logic of progress, success, consensus appeal and 'marketability' as the economic order it attempts to undermine. Often in anti-capitalist propaganda, as Michel de Certeau put it, 'refusal speaks the same language as seduction'.[42] This is partly to do with the nature of resistance as a parallel form of communication to the corporate image: in so far as it remains as 'writing on the wall', both the 'advert' and the 'subvert' speak of a world that isn't really there: 'The same writing on the wall announces happiness for sale and happiness for the taking [. . .]. In both cases, what is represented 'demonstrates' because it is not *given*.'[43]

Other experts in Utopian theory, notably Jameson[44] and Paul Ricoeur,[45] have supplemented the above warning with suggestions to the effect that there is both something ideological about Utopia and something Utopian about ideology. The former can be seen in the way political governance and the ordering of society requires a certain amount of imaginary institutions to generate a sense of legitimacy. Such, argues Benedict Anderson, would explain the success of the ideology of nationalism. Consider, he suggests, the tacit acceptance of the 'reality' of borders and sovereign states,

---

[42] Michel de Certeau, *La culture au pluriel* (Paris: Éditions du Seuil, 1993), p. 37 (my translation).

[43] *Ibid.* p. 37, my italics (my translation).

[44] See Jameson, *Political Unconscious*, pp. 271–290.

[45] See Paul Ricoeur, *Lectures on Ideology and Utopia* (New York: Columbia University Press, 1986).

the generation of 'imagined communities' through a 'vast pedagogical industry'.[46] All of this required simply in order to internalize a sense of rationality for any state of war against another. It is certainly reflected in my analysis of a politics of fear. For the creation of an illusory 'peaceful' order of productivity and consumption alongside that of permanent anxiety and *disorder* is also a manipulation of the imagination. In return for suspended liberties and a state of permanent anxiety, citizens are guaranteed the pursuit of a total, uncompromising war on terror, in which nothing less than freedom itself is pitted against the forces of unfreedom. This ideology of fear becomes 'Utopian' in the sense that it promises a world (elimination of the unseen enemy) just out of reach – to you and I – that is, nowhere, just beyond the present, deferred.

Ironically these examples only serve to emphasize the point made earlier by Castoriadis – of the primacy of the imagination in illuminating and artic-ulating social meaning. Imagination thus paradoxically becomes constitutive of what we mean by the phrase 'living in the real world' – that is, living in a world defined by a dominant imaginary, or the imaginary of a given ideology. How, then, can one distinguish the Utopia of a dominant ideology from the radical Utopian imagination? Can we apply here the distinction I have so far attempted between the imagination and *fantasy*? Castoriadis' analysis of the relationship between 'the institution' and 'the individual' would sug-gest that we can:

> through this social fabrication of the individual, the institution subjugates the singular imagination of the subject, and, as a general rule, lets it man-ifest itself in and through dreaming, phantasying, transgression, illness [. . .]. Everything occurs as if the institution had succeeded in cutting off communication between the subject's radical imagination and its 'thought'. What ever it might imagine (whether it knows it or not) the subject *will think* and will make/do only what it is socially obliged to think and make/do.[47]

So dreaming and 'phantasying' mean expressing one's imaginary self only in ways that do no harm to the dominance of the status quo. Fantasy, to repeat my distinction, like the effects of a politics of fear, is that which removes us from the political sphere, which *depoliticizes*. It is nowhere more prevalent than in a politics of fear. Fear as paralysis produces an endless

---

[46] Benedict Anderson, *Imagined Communities: Reflections on the Origin and Spread of Nationalism* (London: Verso, 1991), p. 201.
[47] *Ibid.* p. 264, italics in the original.

desire for the maintenance of present conditions, a state of anxious inertia that turn only inwards.

How have Bloch and Castoriadis helped this analysis of the Utopian imagination?

The transformation of a public sphere into one of passive consumers governed by a state of permanent anxiety is therefore also the practice of instituting boundaries to the imagination. And if the concept of Utopia holds any hope in resisting this transformation it must, as this chapter has shown, at least acknowledge the ambiguity of the transcendent element of Utopian imagination. Utopia, in other words, is simultaneously everywhere and a nowhere, radical and capitalized, eccentric and reactionary. In their worst 'dysfunctional' manifestations, Utopias display 'eccentricity', a 'taking outside' of normal discourse. They place singular demands upon what can be imagined. Both Bloch and Castoriadis suggest that any attempt to control or judge what a 'healthy' vision of Utopia might look like appears dangerously like ideological control itself, and could easily slip into the Utopia of totalitarian statecraft. Perhaps, then, we should concur with Ricoeur. He suggests that we try not to separate the two, but, rather, see Utopia and ideology as providing the cure to each other's pathologies, controlling their respective excesses. Utopianism, whether messianic-chiliastic or anarchist-libertarian, represents a necessary unstable element to our projects. Ideology, on the other hand, grants a community the sense of history, tradition and identity by which it can make judgements about escapist or reactionary Utopian thinking.[48] Utopia *retains* its social role alongside ideology, in other words, by insisting in a sense of 'incongruence' in every stage of history. It is an impulse, in other words, that keeps people striving, seeking better societies. However 'mastered' that state might be, it is possible for people's dreams to not become the tools of mastery over others. The need for a Utopia that appears (as it does to Marxists) irresponsible at times, is expressed not just as the need to take risks, but the need for madness. It is the need to encourage a permanent reconstitution of reality and sanity itself.[49]

Ricoeur's emphasis on Utopia's dual function effectively does away with the idea that ideology and Utopia are at war with each other. 'The function of utopia', writes Ricoeur, 'is finally the function of the nowhere. To be here, *da-sein*, I must also be able to be nowhere.'[50] Ironically this means that

---

[48] Paul Ricoeur, *Du texte à l'action* (Paris: Éditions du Seuil, 1986), p. 391.

[49] Ricoeur, *Lectures on Ideology and Utopia*, p. 303.

[50] *Ibid.* p. 310, italics in the original.

imagination is of first importance to practices of hope precisely because of its propensity for non-engagement. Ricoeur effectively celebrates the human capacity for suspending the real – for example, by questioning the received reality of an unjust social order: 'it is in this state of non-engagement that we try out new ideas, new values, new ways of being in the world.'[51] As we shall see in Part III, many practices of resistance today represent experiments in precisely this movement – of exercising the Utopian impulse by escaping, by refusing to acknowledge the legitimacy of the 'real world'.

Conclusion

What has this tentative exploration of Utopianism revealed? For one thing, that Utopian imagination need not be understood as either a dogmatic search for human perfection nor a naive claim to be suspending one's ideologically conditioned reality. More attention should be paid to the role of what Jacoby calls 'iconoclastic' Utopianism, of which Bloch's approach is exemplary. It means quite simply a Utopianism that does not depict a 'blueprint' for the exact shape of the Utopia it strives for, just as the religious iconoclasts taught against portraying the image of God. Within that concept we can see the act of striving as more of an imaginative basis for affirming politics as the 'art of the impossible'[52] than as a prescription for statecraft.

My second observation has been that ideological closure persists as a permanent antagonism to Utopian desire. In relation to a politics of fear, we could say that an ideology of non-participation and permanent anxiety may simply define which beliefs can be 'taken seriously' within our dominant political discourse, those 'appropriate' responses to terror; discourses that dominate social imagination today. In a review of the persistent function of ideology today, Žižek expressed precisely this awareness when he wrote, 'one can thus categorically assert the existence of ideology *qua* generative matrix that regulates the relationship between the visible and non-visible, between imaginable and non-imaginable, as well as the changes in this relationship.'[53]

---

[51] Ricoeur, *Du texte à l'action*, p. 20 (my translation).

[52] This concept is attributable both to Foucault, quoted in David Toole, *Waiting for Godot in Sarajevo: Theological Reflections on Nihilism, Tragedy and Apocalypse* (London: SCM Press, 1998), p. 210, and also to Vaclav Havel, *The Art of the Impossible: Politics as Morality in Practice*, trans. Paul Wilson (New York: Knopf, 1997).

[53] Slavoj Žižek, 'Introduction: The Spectre of Ideology' in *Mapping Ideology*, ed. Slavoj Žižek (London: Verso, 1994), pp. 1–33 (p. 1), italics in the original.

In one way this analysis simply reaffirms the persistent role of imagination within social life *in general*. But in another way it demands that we distinguish an imagination that opens up the future from a fantasy that closes it. In this chapter I have argued for this distinction by affirming a Utopianism as a qualitatively different form of looking forward to one dominated by fear. And in the sense that Utopianism represents a suspension of the conditions of fear, we should also see the imaginative capacity of Utopia in terms of movement as opposed to inertia. Utopian imagination can represent flight *to*, not *from*, the political. It does *not* necessarily represent the imagination of a perfect and normally idealized, 'colonial', fantasy society.[54] Utopia's insistence on non-engagement, therefore, should not be seen as a call to inaction. Rather it should encourage a search for the act of speaking prohibited speech and enacting prohibited acts in this detached (in the sense of requiring no adhesion or affiliation), and yet engaged, fashion. The ability, perhaps, to live 'as if' one's actions did not belong to this world. It is precisely this exploration of an *eschatological* sense of living that is to be explored next – the idea that political expectation might be an active state of suspension, the lived 'as if'.

---

[54] For a critique of the 'colonial' element of Eurocentric literary utopias see Terry Eagleton, *Figures of Dissent* (London: Verso, 2003), pp. 24–31.

Chapter 5

Eschatology: Radical Waiting

Introduction

The present chapter attempts to deepen my distinction between imaginative and fantastic political desires by looking at both traditional and contemporary interpretations of eschatology, the category adopted by Christian theologians to distinguish discourse about the end. Returning briefly to Deleuze and Guattari's critique goes some way to clarifying this transition to theological language. A principal aspect of their description of political culture was that it is 'no longer the age of cruelty or terror, but the age of cynicism, accompanied by a strange piety'.[1] What is this 'strange piety'? They go on to explain it as a principal strategic element of the capitalist axiomatic, 'the maintenance of a spiritual Urstaat [. . .], capital as God-capital'.[2] What this pseudo-religiosity of contemporary culture implies is that a politics of fear *already* implicitly involves a kind of belief system resembling religious adherence. And if there is a 'faith' involved to fear-production then one response is to search for alternative counter-faiths. Deleuze and Guattari's comments can be seen, to this effect, to inspire Philip Goodchild's call for an *alternative* piety to the religion of capital. The alternative that is sought must be, in Goodchild's terminology, a form of purified attention.[3] It should be stressed that adopting this approach will not provide an opportunity to apply religious beliefs *onto* secular political practices. Rather it will allow us to notice an overlap in their expression. An originally theological category can articulate a quintessentially human dilemma. We can properly call this anthropological dilemma – how do people give a meaning to their experience of the future – the domain of eschatology, or the study of the end. As Goodchild puts it, 'we become indebted to the future that we have created; life is determined by

---

[1] Deleuze and Guattari, *Anti-Oedipus*, p. 225.
[2] *Ibid.*
[3] Goodchild, *Capitalism and Religion*, pp. 177–199.

eschatology'.[4] This chapter therefore provides Christian eschatology with an opportunity to make its own case for an alternative discourse to that 'religious' adherence to a politics of fear. The latter, as we have already seen provides eschatological reasoning based only on an 'immortalized' and terrifying present.

Why draw upon only one religious interpretation of eschatology? In comparison to other traditions, the Judaeo-Christian eschatological vision offers a fascinating interpretation of the notion of 'crisis' and history. For the first communities inspired by the teachings of Jesus, an interpretation of the political and cultural world around them was arguably defined by the ostensible failure of his apocalyptic predictions of the coming kingdom. This view takes its cue from the Alsatian theologian Albert Schweitzer's *The Quest of the Historical Jesus*, written in 1907. Schweitzer famously asserted that the actions and convictions of Jesus recorded in the gospels only make sense in the light of his real eschatological belief in an immanent rupture of historical events precipitated by his death. As Gerhard Sauter notes, Schweitzer is therefore credited with establishing 'consistent eschatology'. The legacy of this idea is the emphasis on *continued crisis* in Christian hope.[5] The exact nature of Jesus' predictions – how literally they were to be interpreted; to what extent they presaged temporal transformation and how soon they were to be expected – continues of course to be the subject of possibly insoluble debate. But that debate is not fruitless if it considers the wider cultural and philosophical implications of living in the shadow of a paradoxical mixture of hope and crisis. John Gray concluded that the perseverance of Jesus' eschatological fervour is indicative of the very roots of our 'Utopian' political violence. It charts, in other words, the very history of the crisis of Utopia's non-realizability. In claiming that 'the history of Christianity is a series of attempts to cope with this founding experience of eschatological disappointment',[6] Gray is thus perhaps justified. What he ignores is that a legacy of crisis brings with it a multitude of traditions, practices, desires and values, some contradictory and certainly not all of them bent on violence. Indeed an originally Christian 'problematic' of the future might also be closely related to the crisis described in the introduction to this book; it highlights the redundancy of traditional modes of optimism in anticipating the future. As the theologian Harvey Cox demonstrated, the inherited crisis of the original delay of the *parousia* (the 'presence' or

---

[4] Goodchild, 'Debt, Epistemology and Ecotheology', p. 169.

[5] Gerhard Sauter, *What Dare We Hope? Reconsidering Eschatology* (Harrisburg: Trinity Press, 1999), pp. 32–33.

[6] John Gray, *Black Mass*, p. 7.

'arrival', or expected appearance of Christ[7]) to the first Christian community was an event that generated eschatology as a systematic tool for
interpreting crisis with its own historical narrative – of constructing stories
of hope and expectation. For Cox, Albert Schweitzer's ground-breaking
discovery at the turn of the twentieth century was that

> [the hope in the *parousia*] was replaced by an attempt to cope with the
> same problems of living by tracing their origins. Eschatology looked to
> the future for help in grappling with the present issues of life. Dogma
> looked to the past for the wisdom and revelation which was mediated
> through the church in the apostolic succession.[8]

The original emergence of dogma in theology itself can thus be said to
represent a product, or a condition, of 'de-eschatologization'. This essentially means a focus on the past as manifestation of the inability to deal with
the future. For all its variations and metamorphoses, teaching and research
on Christian eschatology therefore essentially have one task in common: to
reconcile the dual experiences of a faith in that which has already arrived
(the life, death and resurrection of the Messiah) and that which is still
to come (the biblical anticipation of his coming again and, relatedly, the
controversy of the prediction of a coming kingdom, or millennial reign).

In this chapter I consider the political implications of this distinction
between living in expectation and living 'as if' (that which is expected is
already present). I do this, first, by locating a key systematic eschatological
response to the 'problem' of the future in the form of 'radical eschatology'.
Sauter defines as 'radical' any eschatology that is rooted in a faith in the
future, which – as St Paul shows by the example of Abraham – is essentially
'hoping against hope' (Rom. 4.18). By exploring this notion of the radical
'otherness' of Christian hopes in the work of two influential theologians,
Karl Barth and Karl Rahner, I am subsequently more able to assess its relevance to contemporary practices of Utopian imagination. Next, I try to
draw further conclusions about the scope of eschatology by understanding
it more generally as a qualitative transformation of the 'time' of political
hope. This involves looking briefly at a contemporary interpretation of

---

[7] See Anthony Tyrrell Hanson, 'Parousia' in *A New Dictionary of Theology*, ed.
Alan Richardson and John Bowden (London: SCM Press, 1983), pp. 427–428
(p. 428).

[8] Harvey Cox, 'The Problem of Continuity' in *The Future of Hope: Theology as
Eschatology*, ed. Frederick Herzog (New York: Herder and Herder, 1970), p. 74.

St Paul's eschatological politics, in the work of the Italian political philosopher Giorgio Agamben.

What is radical eschatology?

The Swiss theologian Karl Barth crystallized the paradoxical nature of eschatology when he wrote:

> to wait is the most profound truth of our normal, everyday life and work [. . .]. In our journey through time, we are still men who wait, *as though we saw what we do not see*, as though we were gazing upon the unseen. Hope is the solution of the riddle of our 'As though'.[9]

These words reflect the problem of projecting the Utopian imagination of 'what is to come' within the everyday, mundane assumptions about what *is*. It articulates a 'disjunction' between the act of hope and the thing hoped for. It is therefore most appropriate to ground this chapter's study in the 'radical' formulations of eschatology. But what does the word radical mean here? The protestant theologian Jürgen Moltmann, famous for renewing an interest among theologians of the political significance of eschatological doctrine, recently commented, that:

> when the dreams about the end of history come to nothing – whether that dreamed-of end be Christ's Thousand Years' Empire or 'the global marketing of everything' – the lesson we learn is a simple one: it is impossible to complete history within history.[10]

In a similar way, radical eschatology can be seen as the expression of the insufficiency of human practices of hope to the object of their desire. However, Moltmann's celebrated 'theology of hope' is precisely a focus of criticism for Sauter's own interpretation of radical eschatology. This is because Moltmann's theology continually seeks the function of liberation within eschatology. It reconciles a vision of the continuation of the goodness experienced in the present with the ushering in of an entirely *other* order of creation. Sauter, however, sees in this historicist approach a dangerous conflation of eschatology with 'adjacent concepts such as utopia (or

---

[9] Karl Barth, *The Epistle to the Romans*, trans. Edwyn C. Hoskins (Oxford: Oxford University Press, 1933), p. 314, my italics.

[10] Moltmann, 'Is the World', p. 135.

utopian thinking), Apocalyptic, Messianism, Chiliasm and Futurology'.[11] According to Sauter, the new definition of eschatology, he writes, should be '*talk of God which is determined by God's coming. God's coming means adventus and futurum,* God's coming to be present both today and in what still lies ahead.'[12] But what then can practically be spoken with regard to the future? Sauter assumes, incorrectly in my view, that if our hopes lies in the coming of 'another world' – or God's world – then parallel secular hopes for social justice should be considered inappropriate or incongruous. Thus, he adds, 'eschatology would then be extricated from the almost explosive profusion of reflections on the nature of time, conceptions of history, ethical problems and their illustration, hermeneutical questions of the interpretation of biblical expectations and linguistic aporia'.[13] But if eschatology does *not* entangle itself in 'reflections on the nature of time, conceptions of history, ethical problems and their illustration' then it appears to contradict a claim Sauter makes elsewhere about its function and task:

> eschatology deals with everything that is in store for humanity. Thereby, it determines our direction and thus our behaviour and actions. Eschatology can become an almost perfect example of a theology that deals with the intellectual and political situation of its time.[14]

Sauter's watering down of a potential liberationist function of eschatology, on the grounds that 'for the sake of the promise of justice, God's free gift of salvation must be kept distinct from all human yearnings after what is just',[15] seems to imply a disconnection of theology from popular social struggles.

Sauter insists that 'what Christians may hope cannot be drawn from what they know to be their needs'.[16] What, then, can his analysis bring to a general theological appraisal of political practices? For one thing, Sauter *is* able to highlight a danger inherent to any formulation of 'historical eschatology' such as Moltmann's. That is the temptation to simply translate into divine language already existing projections of the future. This option lies in distinction from opening up social hopes as the projections of an

---

[11] Gerhard Sauter, *Eschatological Rationality* (Michigan: Baker Books, 1996), p. 145.

[12] Sauter, *Eschatological Rationality*, pp. 145–146, italics in the original.

[13] *Ibid.* p. 146.

[14] Sauter, *What Dare We Hope?*, p. 123.

[15] Sauter, quoted by Ted Peters, 'Eschatological Rationality: Theological Issues in Focus', *Theology Today* (October 1998) reproduced in *Findarticles.com*, www.findarticles.com/p/articles/mi_qa3664/is_199810/ai_n8827206 [accessed 17 March 2006].

[16] Sauter, *What Dare We Hope?*, p. 145.

incomprehensibly newer situation – a Utopian vision. The purpose of eschatology, if it is to be 'radical' (i.e. if it '[goes] to the roots'[17]), is to understand the process by which our Utopian desires are related to the promise of a definitively *new* reality. It is, Sauter makes clear, the content of that 'newness' that is in question. It is therefore possible to depart from the narrow remit ascribed by Sauter for applying 'eschato-logic' to extra-human concerns. At the same time we can affirm the importance that he gives to the imperatives of radical eschatology. The real purpose of this chapter's engagement with radical eschatology is to consider the 'new' questions it generates about political hope in contrast to the parameters of expectation defined by the narrow remit of a politics of fear.

The political currency of eschatology, as I have understood it, centres on the 'dialectical' relationship between historical context and eschatological formulation. It should therefore come as no surprise that the two most appropriate candidates for assessing the scope of radical eschatology are the Swiss protestant Karl Barth and the German Catholic Karl Rahner. Both theologians wrote within periods (both writing before and after the Second World War) of not only theological but also historical and political upheaval. And both men are influenced by a pandemic insecurity with regard to the future generated by that upheaval. I first consider Karl Barth's take on eschatology as marking out a distinction between God's time and human, 'given', time.

Karl Barth and given time

Dialectical theology, with which Barth is associated, has been described as a concern with 'the crisis through which the eternal threatens every stability in time'.[18] This means that theology interprets the reality of this world 'in time' in the light of faith in a reality – that of God's or 'the eternal' – that is radically different. The historical context of dialetical theology follows the shattering of linear progressivist interpretations of history in 1920s Europe. Barth's theology therefore represents a clear response to the more general crisis of hope as a 'serious philosophical category'. For Barth, the whole experience of human life should be oriented within the 'problem' of temporal living, the 'riddle' of our experience. As humans we are bounded by a past, a seemingly perishing present, and a radically uncertain future. 'Humanity', he writes, 'is temporality [. . .]. Humanity means to have been,

---

[17] *Ibid.* p. xiii.
[18] Schwöbel, 'Last Things First?', p. 222.

to be, and to be about to be.'[19] What does it means to reflect theologically upon this situation, to construct a 'theological anthropology'?[20] It means taking seriously the existential givenness of temporal living as a problem to human aspirations and the fact that people do, in fact, continue to strive and hope. Typically, for Barth, this problem is one and the same as the need to reorient theological reasoning Christologically. It means, in other words, orienting our philosophical questions towards the belief in Jesus as the incarnate God. To claim that Jesus is 'Lord of Time'[21] implies that time is first and foremost *God's*, and subsequently *given* to the world. A political imperative immediately arises from this belief; Barth thought it was a common failure to see the personal and social struggle of facticity and finitude as expressly *theological* problems. This failure leads to the 'Utopian' fabrications[22] of social projects. They were insufficient, thought Barth, insofar as they did not rely on a faith in the God who is *to come*: 'the New Testament looks forward, not merely to a better future, but to a future which sets a term to the whole time process, and in its perfection surpasses absolutely all the contents of time.'[23]

'Given time' is therefore infused with the paradox that the creator God is, on the one hand, equally past, present and future, and yet in the sense that it is given by *God*, it is 'real' time and not simply relative. Barth is quick to distance his own existentialist interpretation of time from philosophical abstractions that confine its 'reality' to the realm of perception and subjectivity. He does, nevertheless, pick up on Aristotle's problematizing of the experience of time as a series of indivisible 'nows'[24] by attaching much importance to the feeling of being 'trapped' in time:

> but what is now? What is this present? It is the time between the times. And this, strictly speaking and as we actually experience it, is no time at all, no duration, no series of moments, but only the boundary between past and future.[25]

The fact that we do not 'have' time, neither the past, nor the continually vanishing present, nor the unreachable future, forms the basis for Barth's

---

[19] Karl Barth, *Church Dogmatics*, vol. 3, part 2, ed. G. W. Bromiley and T. F. Torrance, trans. Harold Knight and others (Edinburgh: T&T Clark, 1990), p. 522.

[20] *Ibid.* p. 438.

[21] *Ibid.* p. 437.

[22] *Ibid.* p. 486.

[23] *Ibid.* p. 486.

[24] See *Aristotle's Physics*, Book 4, trans. Edward Hussey (Oxford: Oxford University Press, 1983), pp. 49–51.

[25] Barth, *Church Dogmatics*, vol. 3, part 2, p. 514.

dialectical contrast between the human condition and its need for the intervention of the eternal. Our lives are characterized by a 'continual loss of time',[26] as if the original human impulse was to be one's *own* lord of time. I shall have reason to reject this assumption in due course. For now, the important point for my argument is that Barthian eschatology looks for the transformation of modes of temporality, the ability to be 'in' a certain time. This comes about through the revelation of Christ *not* as the supreme example of living in time and outside of it, but as the *sole means* by which living in time may be truly hopeful at all. Barth provides a rationale for human hope based on an ineradicable and uncompromising need for the God-man-event that provides human time with its outside *in* given time. Before any assumptions about the character of this transformation and what events it alludes to (i.e. without alluding to any mention of the character of the promise of *parousia*), time established by the Christian message is simply time 'pregnant' with promise.

For all his emphasis on Christ being equally past, present and future, how does Barth account for this paradox of transtemporality, in which time is both fulfilled and awaiting fulfilment, and what are the consequences for political hope? Barth describes the concept given by St Paul of 'the fullness of time' (Gal. 4.4) as paradox. It is both an 'empty vessel' waiting to be filled,[27] and also that which *is* already filled. In *The Epistle to the Romans*, Barth reflects on St Paul's treatment of hope. Hope is a condition that requires that we think of 'special' time; time transformed *eternally* by God's presence, but contained within the agonistic state of waiting, of being 'in-between' times. As soon as the believer has accepted that hope can only be in a Christ who is past, present and future, the state of 'waiting' itself becomes relative to a sense of transtemporality. The notion of future fulfilment is already contained in the resurrection, whose reality was present (to God) before *any* lived, human time. The essential phrase that Barth gives us, in order to understand how he 'solves' the paradox, is that given time is infused with 'His future, for us'.[28] Barth's view of the new concept of time established in Pauline theology is therefore that the very notion of a delay of the *parousia* is fundamentally mistaken. It ignores the fact that it is only to us conditioned humans that the notion of 'delay' constitutes crisis. This obsession, which defined the spirit of 'consistent eschatology',[29] is shattered by Barth. He identifies it with a failure to see the 'consolation of

---

[26] *Ibid.* p. 516.
[27] *Ibid.* p. 461.
[28] Barth, *Church Dogmatics*, vol. 3, part 2, p. 490.
[29] See Sauter, *What Dare We Hope?*, p. 32.

the Holy Spirit' as the continued presence of Jesus in the community.
Essentially, that presence is to be seen as permanent *expectation*.[30] That time
has 'become short' (1 Cor. 7.29) signifies for Barth the character of a hope
that is both confident and that yet relinquishes control over the content
of the thing hoped for. It is time 'vaulted over the interim time of the
community'.[31]

What implications to my overall exploration of hope arise from Barth's
eschatology? On the one hand, the political limits of Barth's eschatology
certainly do not come from a failure to acknowledge the revolutionary
nature of human hopes and longings.[32] On the other hand, two specific
points of critique can be raised in relation to his concept of given time. The
first concerns his approach to time as the relinquishing of control over
the *content* of hope. For in this Barth could be seen to depreciate any
attempts to *re*politicize the anticipation of the future: the subject of this
book. Barth appears at times to insinuate that the 'final catastrophe' embedded into the condition of given time takes on the form of a kind of temporal
fatalism. It can therefore be argued that Barth's eschatology resembles that
rhetoric of fear and a paralysed 'waiting' for crisis contained in the secular
eschatology of a politics of fear. The experience of being trapped in time
would appear to focus political practice on a distant point that disturbs,
haunts and infects the very experience of a politics of time. Barth writes, for
instance, that 'the terrible end can come only once, and it may still be a
long way off. But come it will, and therefore the future that precedes it
cannot be other than unending terror'.[33] Elsewhere, he says, 'we are no
match for the future, which really comes and is so terribly menacing [. . .],
we do not seize the future; it seizes us and overpowers us.'[34] What is to be
made of this apocalyptic style, this fearful relationship with the future? To
respond fairly, it should be remembered that a focal target of attack for
Barth was the temptation succumbed to simultaneously by liberal theologians, existentialists and 'social gospel' advocates. These groups imagined
the eschatological impulse to project a 'beyond' that is in essence a projected continuation of our 'now'. Perhaps, therefore, Barth saw *this* trend as

---

[30] *Ibid.* p. 509.
[31] *Ibid.* p. 489.
[32] For an appreciation of the influence of socialist ideas on Barth's own theology, see,
    for instance *Karl Barth and Radical Politics*, ed. George Hunsinger (Philadelphia:
    Westminster Press, 1976); Timothy J. Gorringe, *Karl Barth: Against Hegemony*
    (Oxford: Clarendon Press, 1999).
[33] Sauter, *What Dare We Hope?*, p. 542.
[34] *Ibid.* p. 543.

the truly crippling form of fatalism, both theologically and politically. We can, for example, understand Barth's warning to those tempted to divinize and, in the manner of liberal theology, internalize projects of human aspiration. In reality these aspirations may amount to little more than the continuation of an ideology of 'endless progress'[35] or the pseudo-radicalism of political and social reforms. He is thus particularly averse to the word 'beyond' as a substitute in any way for actually speaking about 'the eternal God' for precisely this reason: he suspects that our natural attraction to the projection of a beyond is nothing more than an inability to see past a linear temporal trajectory. It is important to see this judgement of Barth's in the light of my previous description of war without end as a secular eschatology. It is clear that such a target leads Barth to place all eschatological importance on the political and ethical imperative to transform one's own temporal appreciation of the present moment, of 'now time'. It is not about politicizing in any way the imagination of the future.

The second point of critique comes from Barth's emphasis on the human condition of striving for an *ownership* of time. A condition for the disjunctive paradox of divine/human time is that it should point towards some kind of recognition of the incursion of eternal time in our lives. This implies a recognition that 'the man Jesus' is both wholly other and yet 'like us', in that he too lived in time. The consequence of this man is, for Barth, the crucial difference between a fatalism based on the failure to ever be able to step outside of time, and the hope based on one who has already achieved it. Barth tellingly writes that:

> to compare our lot with that of 'blessed spirits', with very different and purely eternal beings, may produce a gloomy Hymn of Fate, but it gives us the easy evasion that we men in time are so totally different. Our comparison, however, is with the man Jesus. And although as the Son of God He is so utterly different from us, yet as the son of Man He is wholly like us. Hence we cannot escape the contrast by pleading His absolute dissimilarity.[36]

This Christocentric anthropology (a comparison of the human condition with that of Jesus) is not simply a conceptual tool within Barth's eschatological teaching. It constitutes the 'presupposition of our [*sic*] whole enquiry'.[37] The suggestion is that if it wasn't for our palpable likeness to God (the

---

[35] *Ibid.* p. 516.
[36] *Ibid.*
[37] *Ibid.* p. 517.

historical fact of Jesus as God-man) then we would have good reason to despair. In that case time would be seen to 'take over' the creation of our hopes. Barthian eschatology, in other words, defines human hope as the affirmation of an interminable paradox of human striving: the fact that inhabiting time is *both* the foundation of political hope *and* cause for despair.

These two points of critique highlight the emphasis in Barth's Christian anthropology as a state of being both 'inside' and 'outside' of an existential experience of time. The principal Christian 'realities' of death, resurrection and final apocalypse therefore constitute for Barth a kind of simultaneous presence. This attitude requires a mode of waiting that relativizes the 'time of the community' as an 'interim'. To be able to act 'as though' we see this alternative time of justice, peace and love therefore requires, in Barth's view, a kind of suspicion and repulsion of lived time. In relation to this chapter's enquiry, this position can be seen to have negative political and ethical consequences. It could be seen to generate dissatisfaction with given time and an *envy* of its eternal counterpart. In the light of my study of Utopian imagination, for instance, it is difficult to imagine how such expressions of genuine human anticipation should be coloured by a disenfranchisement from time, an insatiable desire to 'have' time.

Despite these criticisms, it should soon become evident that Barth's radical eschatology continues to have an enduring influence on the theological understanding of hope and Utopian expectation. Towards the end of this chapter, for instance, I shall have reason to return to Barth's riddle of living 'as though we see what we do not see' when I explore the contemporary implications of Pauline *kairòs* time, time that shatters temporality itself. Before then, however, I must look to Karl Rahner for further possibilities generated by radical eschatology.

Karl Rahner and Utopian time

As I have suggested in the above analysis of Barth, there is a fundamental discrepancy among 'competing' eschatologies: namely, their position on the 'end' as either a reachable, transformative experience in time, or as a state that, but for the grace of God, is first and foremost entirely unreachable and also unimaginable. Barth's emphasis was clearly with the latter. But his position was expressed within categories of human error, guilt and the 'illusions' of humanist, liberal and existentialist attempts to explain the condition of alienation. The Catholic theologian Karl Rahner emphasized instead a strong *metaphysical* and philosophical imperative to maintain the unknowability and indescribability of the end. Rahner emphasized the importance of what we cannot know about the future. He declared that the role of the theologian is

> the guardian of this *docta ignorantia futuri*. [. . .] Only the *docta ignorantia futuri* provides a basic position for exercising a sustained critique of a present which is at all times only too ready to assert itself as the only right state of affairs.[38]

He thus defines eschatology as a state of the radical openness to the unknown. This state of being is described as a condition for the input of the Holy Spirit in the creative Utopian imagination. Only an attitude of expectation that incorporates a cosmic and collective Utopian tendency in human seeking can make sense of the *function* of eschatology in the modern world. Eschatology describes a future that transcends the scope of human knowledge and prediction. Rahner calls it the 'absolute future' (equivalent to 'God's time' in Barth): 'Christianity is the attitude of abiding openness to the question of the absolute future which seeks to bestow itself, which has definitively promised itself as coming in Jesus Christ and which is called God'.[39]

It is also clear, however, that Rahner, at least in his systematic writings, makes more explicit the balance that must be struck in everyday understandings of eschatology as a mode of 'waiting'. This balance is between hope in an 'absolute future' on the one hand and in the human 'this worldly future' on the other. He is quick to condemn, for instance, the temptation to assume on behalf of a radical eschatology that Christian teaching basically coheres with a conservative, quietist politics 'which favours the present rather than the future'.[40] Armed with this awareness, Rahner is able to orient eschatological rationality towards the possibilities of human creativity. More importantly still, he gives prominence to the function of the imagination (and, relating more specifically to Rahner's terminology, the realm of human freedom and conscience). The disjunction between God's time and human time should not be in opposition. They should instead be seen as a mutually 'conditioning relationship' between the transcendent future and a concrete human plan for that future.

---

[38] Karl Rahner, *Theological Investigations*, vol. 12, trans. David Bourke (London: Darton, Longman and Todd, 1974), pp. 198–200, italics in the original.

[39] *Ibid.* p. 190.

[40] *Ibid.* p. 201.

In comparison to Barth, Rahner is able to assert with greater conviction this notion of a confluence of temporal and eternal hopes by referring continually to the practical function of Utopian imagination. His context for doing so was a society that had unleashed some of the more extreme military and scientific consequences of a new-found ability to manipulate their surroundings and apparently direct their own future. Any creative Utopian drive derived from God represented an alternative to the 'modern militant political world-heresies of secular utopianism'.[41] Rahner may have been referring principally to totalitarian Marxism, but his comments fit within a more general position on eschatology as referring to very real *future* events. They do not express an extension of the desires of the present based on scientific extrapolation. His ideas thus remain firmly within the definitions of 'radical eschatology' set out by Sauter. In other words, he warns both theological and political thought of the dangers of extrapolating a vision of the future from the basis of human endeavour alone. Rahner calls on the church to renew its prophetic role concerning the historic future without defining its blueprint. Like Barth, this 're-eschatologizing' of theology itself is seen as a unique gift of the Christian message as a mode of waiting: eschatological assertions must not be 'pre-views of future events'.[42] They are not *only* concerned with the 'presentness' of future assertions but also with a prophetic confidence in that which can never be of scientific certainty. Thus, Rahner takes very sincerely the notion of 'hiddenness' in a far subtler way than Barth does when relating to the distance between humanity and that to which its prophetic role points:

> the end has for us a character of hiddenness which is essential and proper to it and affects all its elements. [. . .] Revelation is not the bringing of what was unknown into the region of what is known, perspicuous and manageable: it is the dawn and the approach of the mystery as such.[43]

It isn't immediately clear what form this 'hiddenness' should take, but a closer look at Rahner's views on salvation history clarify this concept. It operates as a form of *dialectical* history rather than, as was more the case for Barth, an irreconcilable antagonism between human time and God's time.

---

[41] Karl Rahner, 'Eschatology' in *Encyclopedia of Theology: A Concise Sacramentum Mundi*, ed. Karl Rahner, trans. John Griffiths, Francis McDonagh and David Smith (London: Burns and Oates, 1975), p. 436.

[42] Rahner, *Theological Investigations*, vol. 4, trans. Kevin Smyth (London: Darton, Longman and Todd, 1966), p. 329

[43] *Ibid.* p. 330.

A sharp distinction is made between 'profane history' (secular, purely human time) and 'salvation history' (the encounter of humanity with God). In doing so Rahner confirms the paradox of the incarnation as something that draws humanity *beyond* its own horizons rather than deifying them. Though this distinction sets out to relativize and 'put in their place' the great aspirations and hope of profane history, it can also be seen as an attempt to make sense of Utopian schemes as participating in a higher, divine scheme. As Morwenna Ludlow puts it, for Rahner profane history and salvation history are 'co-extensive and mutually dependent'.[44] It expresses, in other words, God's decision to make profane history an essential 'moment' in the consummation of salvation history. Rahner's answer to Barth's riddle of the 'as though' is therefore to refine our view of salvation as 'consummation' of profane history (i.e. a fulfilment or comple-tion of human history). True consummation of history can only be achieved through a power external to itself. This power Rahner describes as the attraction of the transcendent, or perhaps to put it another way, the fact that profane history has *need* of salvation history.

Rahner refines our understanding of 'end', then, by stating that consum-mation should be understood as 'the opposite of a mere end'. Its horizons are limited by its predetermined life span. Consummation therefore 'cannot have any meaningful application to a mere material event as such. The material event "runs out". It remains radically and constantly open to a further future so long as it is not thought of simply as having been termi-nated.'[45] When Rahner applies this distinction to the notion of the consummation of the cosmos, or the historical 'world' in its widest, collec-tive and ecological sense, this draws out the important consequences in respect of eschatology. It relies heavily on Rahner's belief that 'the world is a unity of spirit and matter'.[46] His key to understanding the fusion of matter and spirit in the incarnation of Jesus, in which the divine and the profane fuse, is to understand it as 'mutual interrelationship'.[47] Rahner thus defines the proper 'Utopian' desires of profane history as tending naturally (Rahner calls it a 'creative impetus'[48]) towards their transcendent consummation, to salvation history.

---

[44] Morwenna Ludlow, *Universal Salvation* (Oxford: Oxford University Press, 2005), p. 166.

[45] Rahner, *Theological Investigations*, vol. 10, trans. David Bourke (London: Darton, Longmann and Todd, 1973), p. 275.

[46] *Ibid.* p. 284.

[47] *Ibid.* p. 286.

[48] *Ibid.* p. 288.

What uses for my argument are contained in Rahner's eschatology? By emphasizing the incursion of God's will into human Utopian imagination through a 'creative impulse', Rahner contributes significantly to an affirmation of political aspirations. In much clearer terms than Barth, Rahner provides theological grounds for distinguishing a discourse of 'fantasy' of the end from the imagination of radical alternatives. In his attempt to go beyond a dichotomization of immanent and transcendent concepts of consummation, Rahner therefore opens up a new appreciation of the *visionary* function of radical eschatology. But what, in this case, does Rahner really believe of the reality of time? What are the consequences of articulating the problem of living in a time that is somewhere in between fulfilment and the 'not yet' of living creation? It is ironic that Rahner, who is thought of as having been significantly influenced by Heidegger much more so than Barth, has less to say explicitly on the existential question of time. Nevertheless, the way that he *does* bring time into his discussion with eschatology is instructive. Being wary of eschatological formulations that reinforce the conservative tendency of the church in the world, Rahner seems eager to describe the creative aspect of temporality as 'becoming'. But this becoming is defined as the unavoidably transcendent aspirations of spiritual humanity. Transcendence imparts an orientation to the *beginning*, which is not simply left behind as that which has never been achieved and never been conceived of. It imparts an orientation towards the 'absolute future'. Time is therefore a necessary component of the immanent self-transcendence of human destiny. But it requires a detachment from lived temporality with the general notion that God enters into time and provides a way of seeing *beyond* it. For Rahner 'consummation' implies a 'temporal event' that isn't bound to the contingencies of *human* temporality:

> this event not only has an end, not only 'ceases', but in time produces a result, something which is definitive from the event itself, independently of how this abiding result in its validity and 'lastingness' is to be conceived of more precisely as compared with 'time'.[49]

`The 'end of history' is something that can never be simply conceptualized, but must be a renewal and deepening of our understanding of the consummation of time itself. It is that which continually *opens*. However, none of this seems able to hide the fact that Rahner's radical disjunction between 'profane history' and 'salvation history' presents the political

---

[49] Rahner, *Theological Investigations*, vol. 10, p. 275.

potential of theological waiting as an essentially dead-end project. It is worth quoting Rahner at length to demonstrate this:

> Salvation history interprets the history of the world as something antago-nistic and veiled. Precisely because salvation is not simply the immanent fruit of profane history, Christianity is sceptical towards profane history. It lets man go out to his worldly task, because it is precisely in the obscurity and ambiguity of this earthly task that man must work out his salvation which is by faith. Yet for Christianity this very task in the world is some-thing which will ultimately always again end in failure. For as far as the individual is concerned, this task always finds an absolute limit in death. In the same way Christianity also shows that death is to be found even in the midst of universal history. This implies a futility arising from the fact that what can always be planned only partially will always remain incalcu-lable – a futility which always springs afresh out of man's evil heart.[50]

Implied in these words is the view that human concern for the future is a mode of waiting for a consummate end to those futural conditions. The *ethical* implication is therefore that a 'new earth' is impossible within human time:

> Christianity denies that the history of the world is progressing towards eternal peace – although this does not mean that war, which will always be with us, must necessarily be fought with halberds or atomic bombs. Christianity knows that all progress in profane history is also another step towards greater dangers and ultimate ruin. History will never be the place for eternal peace and shadowless light – rather if this life is measured by the absolute demands which God has empowered man to make or, indeed, which man has a God-given duty to make, it will always be the land of death and darkness.[51]

In the end, therefore, Rahner echoes Barth's lamentation of given time, the futility of time-bound projects. With a nod towards to Heidegger, Rahner writes that, 'man has been thrown out into this undeified world'.[52] When Rahner writes that 'Salvation-history interprets the history of the world as something antagonistic and veiled',[53] he is of course trying to colour the reality of an eschatological faith in terms of what it can *uncover*

---

[50] *Ibid.*, p. 111.
[51] *Ibid.* p. 112.
[52] *Ibid.* p. 110.
[53] *Ibid.* p. 111.

to the realm of human history. Ultimately, however, no credence is given by Rahner to the imaginative capacity for transcending – *within time* – the time of continual war to which he apparently condemns human fate. From this point of view Rahner's eschatology seems little more equipped to discern a 'purified' form of attention to the future as a political act than Barth's. With regard to these two systematic representations of radical eschatology, therefore, I must question whether their synopses of human desire, to 'have' time and be the lord of it, is consonant with the actual temporal expressions of Utopian protest. How, my enquiry demands, can a radical eschatological orientation be meaningful to the resistant and revolutionary subject grappling with the continually failing present?

St Paul and the politics of in-between time

It would be unfair to dismiss the contributions of Barth and Rahner as generating fatalistic conclusions about human aspiration without also appreciating their dedication to world history. Both were outspoken in the promotion of peace and the rejection of Christianity's accommodation with Fascism. Where their usefulness breaks down, however, is in negotiating the imaginative and discursive power of the prophetic role of living in a time that is Utopian or heaven-bound. What is sought is the quality of time that produces a political subjectivity through expressing the power of this 'to come'. Barth himself may have been able to account for the eschatological foundation for God's action in the world and the continued imperative to 'hope against hope'. But what about the individuals and communities charged with carrying that hope? What experience of time can be expected of them as collective political practices? And when Rahner cites as an example of the 'dialectical interplay' between the humanly foreseeable and that unconditioned future known only to the mind of God, he asserts that 'the absolute future of God appears as silent presence'.[54] But what room does he allow for articulating the shape and form of that silence? Could the future of God really be a silent one? Like the interpretations of the early Christian communities and their challenge of living in the shadow of the expected *parousia*, this question must be posed from the perspective of the performative function of discourse about time in the light of the experience of crisis. It is, for this reason, necessary to explore in greater depth one of Christian eschatology's primary sources for articulating the

---

[54] Rahner, *Theological Investigations*, vol. 10, p. 273.

qualitative transformation of life lived in expectation: the eschatological vision of St Paul.

St Paul's letters have enjoyed a recent revival of interest from both theological and philosophical circles. One work in particular, Giorgio Agamben's *The Time That Remains*,[55] provides a pivotal reflection of the political scope of eschatology. It supplements and makes broader the implications of theological-political dialogue than those offered by Barth or Rahner.[56] I am here in no place to defend Agamben as a *theologically* authoritative reading of St Paul's letters.[57] However, Agamben's ideas about St Paul are of particular relevance to a critique of a politics of fear, particularly in relation to his wider interest in the 'state of exception'. This theory states that liberal state sovereignty as much as dictatorship require a paradox of both being the law and suspension of the law if they are to monopolize violence. The sovereign is the one who must be able to suspend the rule of law in order to protect the law, as occurs in a contemporary state of emergency. Here it is known as the 'state of exception' where rights can no longer be guaranteed. A state of exception is: '. . . the point of indistinction between violence and the law, the threshold on which violence passes over into law and law passes over into violence.'[58] Today, such a logic is apparent in the context of the increasing erosion of civil liberties under the rubric of the war on terror. It is becoming clear that such an exercise of extrajudicial authority has become *un*exceptional. What does this have to do with Pauline eschatology? The state of exception represents a sort of *juridical* transcendence, the suspension of 'normal' political time. It therefore brings the wider political significance of eschatological thinking once more into focus. This draws principally on St Paul's opposition between the law and the *spirit*, or the law and *faith*. Essentially for St Paul, the promise of the Messiah replaces the concept of the norm, *nomos*, or law itself . The new 'law of faith', *nomos pisteos*, introduces an *excess* of temporal living. It is a notion that we are in

[55] Giorgio Agamben, *The Time That Remains*, trans. Patricia Dailey (Stanford: Stanford University Press, 2005).

[56] See also Alain Badiou, *Saint Paul: The Foundation of Universalism*, trans. Ray Brassier (Stanford: Stanford University Press, 2003); Slavoj Žižek, *The Puppet and the Dwarf: The Perverse Core of Christianity* (Massachusetts: MIT Press, 2003) and Jacob Taubes, *The Political Theology of Paul*, trans. Dana Hollander (Stanford: Stanford University Press, 2004).

[57] See, for instance, Bruno Blumenfeld, *The Political Paul* (London: Sheffield Academic Press, 2001).

[58] Giorgio Agamben, *Homo Sacer*, trans. Daniel Heller-Rozen (California: Stanford University Press, 1998) p. 38.

special time, that old norms may often be overturned. The march of time and with it the rhythm of power, law and force holds no purchase any longer.[59] The exhortation to live 'as though' the kingdom has come is, as argued by Paul Fletcher, one that liberates the believing community for an alternative understanding and practice of possessions, attachments and the concerns for this life:

> beyond the law (code) and between history and the future resides an opening that allows for another experience of politics and community in which the Christian lives as though they were not in a world that is all that is the case.[60]

This Pauline theology of a reinterpretation of law in the light of grace, in the hasty sense in which I have appropriated it, is instructive to any search for alternative manifestations of political eschatology to that of a state of exception. In today's political context there is much desire for a reinterpretation of legality and 'normal conduct' in the light of the crisis of sovereignty enacted by the state of exception. Any act of civil disobedience, for example, from the destruction of 'illegal' weapons of mass destruction on Western soil to the fox hunters breaching civil law, is expressed these days in the systematic suspension of traditional legal sovereignty.

Agamben makes much of the fact (in marked contrast to Barth) that for St Paul, the man Jesus and his historical life is of little importance in comparison to 'Jesus Messiah' – a figure imbued more with the future than the past. *Messiah* refers to a post-resurrection disclosure. It is the inauguration of a new post-Mosaic mode of awaiting: the 'Day of the Lord'. From this perspective it would seem that St Paul is to be read as an *essentially* eschatological thinker. However, ambiguity over whether St Paul's eschatological message is to generate a spirit of transformation or of quietism has led some to attribute to him an 'eschatological indifference'.[61] The new Christian community is told, on the one hand, that 'the appointed time has grown short' (1 Cor. 7.29) and that they are to await 'the end, when [Christ] hands over the kingdom to God the Father, after he has destroyed every ruler and every authority and power' (1 Cor. 15.24). On the other hand, the new challenge to imperial power from the authority of God is apparently not to alter their secular commitments. The transformation effected by the new

---

[59] Agamben, *The Time That Remains*, pp. 107, 120.

[60] Paul Fletcher, 'The Nature of Redemption: Post-Humanity, Post-Romanticism and the Messianic', *Ecotheology*, 9.3, (2004), 276–294 (292).

[61] Agamben, *The Time That Remains*, p. 22. Agamben is referring principally to Max Weber's critique of the passage.

message of Christ is principally a renewal of one's minds (Rom. 12.2) as opposed to one's political commitments. This hidden and yet hotly anticipated future signals, in Agamben's estimation, the birth of a new metaphysical and political outlook. And it is one that transforms our understanding of living in time.

St Paul's message to the churches under Roman rule is a complex development of a theme whose principal expression can be found in 1 Cor., ch. 7, v. 17: 'let each of you lead the life that the Lord has assigned, to which God called you'. The palpable anxiety of the new churches for how they should live in this time of waiting, anticipation and imminence of the messiah, seems to be further compounded by St Paul's 'negative' commands:

> from now on, let even those who have wives live as though they had none, and those who mourn as though they were not mourning, and those who rejoice as though they were not rejoicing, and those who buy as though they had no possessions, and those who deal with the world as though they had no dealings with it. For the present form of this world is passing away. (1 Cor. 7.29–31)

How can this ambiguous sense of temporal vocation have transformative political implications? Agamben is struck by St Paul's ability to turn a structurally and grammatically negative evocation of political commitments into a positive grounds for living. The new messianic imperative holds no positive content, but stands rather as an act of *refusal*. It takes the form of a complete relativization of secular vocations. Tension is created between a sense of being called to renounce and accept in the same movement. Agamben believes this was intended to generate an ethic of viewing the present as passage, transition or interim towards what is ultimately more real, and more universal. Agamben thus draws our attention to the messianic as the singular *event*. This event places all personality, identity and social role under a form of 'annulment' (the Greek word is *katargesis*). It involves the renunciation of attachments and possessions. It is an act that liberates new life under the messianic. The 'new' that is anticipated does not have a practical blueprint or universal political applicability. It is, rather, the power and capacity to invert and subordinate the logic with which previous attachments held us.

How does Agamben's reading of St Paul describe a 'radical' eschatology which I identified in the theologies of Barth and Rahner? How, for instance, might he avoid the emphasis of being 'captive' or bound to striving for 'ownership' of time? For one thing, St Paul's notion of living in the 'time that remains' can be seen to avoid the feeling of being 'defeated' by, or trapped 'in' time. This is because it does not dwell on the *end* of time. To do so would refer, Agamben believes, to an apocalyptic hastening of the end-times within the imagination of the present. St Paul refers instead to a time of the present that transports the values of the end and infuses it with a radical 'nowness'. St Paul's key term is the notion of time that 'contracts', or as the Revised Standard Version translation puts it, that has 'grown short' (1 Cor. 7.29). He therefore plays on the general state of anticipation among his audience without ever intending to temper that passion and anxiety. He gives it the flavour of the permanent 'not yet', or as Agamben puts it 'the time that remains between time and its end'.[62] St Paul does not therefore revel in the ambiguity of its temporal commitments (as Barth and Rahner tended to do). He can be seen instead to take a political risk. For Paul defines messianic time as that which transforms through its commitment to being neither 'here' (bound to the conditions of the present) nor 'there' (whisked away to a certain future), but totally transformed by the promise of the coming of the messiah. The messianic promise transforms distinctions of 'now' and 'the future' because once accepted, this message totally transforms the quality of living 'in the now'. There is little distinction, with St Paul, between the messianic message and its content. Agamben therefore concludes that the very meaning of the gospel is the character of *message* itself. It is a transmitted promise of things *to come* that unites a believing community. Philip Goodchild has developed this insight even further. He suggests that what Paul institutes is the revolutionary concept of universal *truth* itself. But this truth, revealed through the new medium of messianic time, is one which is purposefully put on hold, not totally revealed, one that people strain *towards*:

> Paul inhabits the interval between law and final judgment, between the vindication of the messiah and his return to power, between temporal worship and ultimate glory. As such, universality is not yet possible. Truth is conceived rigorously as that which is to come.[63]

Agamben's reading of St Paul is particularly important in the light of the concept of the state of exception. How can St Paul's own version of the

---

[62] Agamben, *The Time That Remains*, p. 62.
[63] Philip Goodchild, *The Exceptional Political Theology of Saint Paul*, The Centre of Theology and Philosophy, Nottingham University, www.theologyphilosophycentre. co.uk/papers/Goodchild_Exceptional.doc [accessed 6 June 2005].

'remnant' or 'exception' to the law become a style of political action? How might that style be any different than, say, the indefinite suspension of civil liberties by the state over the individual? And how might such a political style be consonant with the belief that that which is to come neither affirms nor denies the value of political activities or commitments? Does St Paul not simply describe a state of perpetual indecision? A form of messianic limbo? An eschatology of permanent anxiety? In his defence, Agamben does demonstrate that St Paul is committed to an understanding of *katargeo*, the 'remnant' or exception as a function within 'operational time'.[64] In doing so Agamben allows the concept of messianic time the role of suspension as a *disempowerment*, rather than simply a momentary annulment, of the power of secular political time. This can only make sense within St Paul's radical notion of strength in weakness, or the triumph of the crucified over the logic of (Roman) imperial domination.

A further benefit of introducing the notion of 'in-between time' or 'time that remains' through the interpretation of a thinker like Agamben comes from the radical potential of the concept of the time of 'rupture'. The notion of *kairòs* describes transformation of lived time into a time of action. The translation from the Greek is generally given as 'the right moment' or 'the opportune'. However, it is its appropriation by a few key historic thinkers to construct a critique and philosophy of time that is of most interest. Eric White notes, for instance, that the first to make such a use of the word was the rhetorician Gorgias, for whom 'kairotic' was the key to *invention* in discourse: 'cultural practice remains innovative, he suggests, only so long as the inventor is willing to modify the existing repertoire of things to say in response to the unique opportunity offered by the situation at hand.'[65] *Kairòs* is important, then, because it interprets the very character of a God-given *now*. Now is a special, chosen, timely time. It continually renews its own sense of vocation and engagement. When St Paul insists on the imperative for his listeners to remain 'in the condition in which you were called', therefore, the principal breakthrough is clearly not a manifesto for social revolution. It is in providing theological and political grounds for finding that source of temporal life that, without qualification, cripples the 'ideological closure' of secular powers. It destabilizes the conviction that this world is 'all there is' without *simply* positing the existence of another world somewhere in the manner of a Utopian fairyland.

---

[64] Agamben, *The Time That Remains*, p. 65.

[65] Eric White, 'Kairos' in *Encyclopedia of Time*, ed. Samuel L. Macey (New York: Garland Publishing, 1994), pp. 332–333 (p. 332).

To declare that 'the present form of this world is passing away' (1 Cor. 7.31) can, from this perspective, be seen to constitute a radical hope in the future without generating animosity towards existence of the present moment. St Paul defines the new grounds for social engagement based on election, adoption or vocation in a source that entirely transcends the glare of power of the secular. In so doing he is arguably liberating practices of hope as practices of now time. These practices might themselves also be the search for new places to 'be political'. They lie underneath, in spite of, against, but perhaps equally *within*, the determination of our given conditions, vocations and identities. The important thing for St Paul is that the hoper acknowledges allegiance (which for his Roman audience is expressed as being 'owned' by a new master) only to the one who promises the abolition of all authority and power. Such a master imbues time paradoxically with the quality of masterlessness: 'you were bought with a price; do not become slaves of human masters. In whatever condition you were called, brothers and sisters, there remain with God' (1 Cor. 7.23–24).

Conclusion

Eschatology may be a discourse normally explored through systematic theologians like Barth and Rahner, but its importance goes far beyond systematic concerns. It addresses, that is, a profound appreciation of the manner in which people can adhere to, or believe in, a vision of the future. This chapter has therefore posed more of an anthropological question than an explicitly theological one, though it has done so in the light of legacy of the Christian theological tradition. That question is: 'what kind of time do we inhabit?' Radical eschatology's response, in the shape of Barth and Rahner's respective theologies, was to emphasize a radical disjunction between human desire and the divinely inspired Utopian impulse. Many aspects of their ideas seemed unable to respond convincingly to a culture of futility and depoliticization. Nevertheless, both theologians provided conceptual resources for elucidating the paradoxical act of hoping for 'another world'. Barth's contribution has been a description of human hope as an anthropological phenomenon that is remarkable for its *embrace* of this paradox. Humans must embrace the puzzle of being oriented towards the future and yet bounded by the present. Rahner's contribution can be expressed as the theological appraisal, once again, of a fundamentally human trait. This time it is of the Utopian impulse at the heart of historically based human hope. He therefore provides a theological lens with which to interpret the ideas of Bloch and other Utopian theorists. He does this by specifying that such a Utopian function represents a conscious 'opening' up of time to its consummation.

What these systematic approaches have demonstrated, in other words, is the enduring influence of eschatology as a radically political mode of 'waiting'. Agamben's reading of St Paul, however, has suggested that to be disenfranchised and dispossessed of the absolute future is not enough. What is required instead is a willingness to give material, political meaning to this excess, this remainder, this 'extra' time. It is this extra time that, perhaps in the manner of St Paul's welcome ambiguity with regard to attachments/detachments of the secular, relativizes the very direction of time. It makes way for the visionary and transformative power of the imagination.

We are thus in a better position to recognize a kind of eschatology that replaces a fatalist obsession with the end as 'timelessness' with one of 'timeliness'.[66] For St Paul, the first eschatological 'crisis' of the Christian community can be seen as a creative and progressive process because the 'fullness of time' is a temporal category capable of mixing up all singular conceptions of future and past, forwards and backwards, now and then. This is because it announces a spirit of hope, paradoxically based on a past event that is both established and yet to come. If there is a 'radical' aspect of eschatology at all, it is in its ability to navigate between a commitment to a politics of the event *in the future* and an uncompromising rejection of the state of 'waiting' as endlessness.

I should at this point give stronger justification for introducing St Paul through the eyes of Giorgio Agamben, neither a theologian nor authority on Christian eschatology. My motivation, however, was in preparation for my analysis of 'apocalyptic time' in the following chapter. Apocalypse is a concept that both Rahner and Agamben dismiss as a politically disempowering temporal category. By way of contrast, my own evaluation is that to push eschatological rationality to its fullest consequences is precisely to end up with an ontology of time that reintroduces the importance of myth, narrative imagination and the imagination of destruction and rebirth in one. There is therefore still much work to do with respect to evaluating the potential of theological imagination. In particular I want to emphasize the rich and politically fertile ground of endist discourse more generally to confront the 'endlessness' of a politics of fear.

---

[66] This distinction is taken from Catherine Keller's essay, 'Why Apocalypse, Now?', *Theology Today*, vol. 49, no. 2 (July 1992), 183–195.

Chapter 6

Apocalypse: Radical Seeing

Introduction

Why have both Rahner and Agamben insisted in their own ways on the separation of eschatological and apocalyptic discourses? Rahner believed that to confuse eschatology with apocalypse was to dangerously misunderstand the task of Utopian desire. Apocalypse meant bringing into the present a received vision of the future, and thus guarantee a political blueprint to manipulate all desires. Agamben, meanwhile, suggests that the message of St Paul, an 'apostle' and not a 'prophet', should also be sharply distinguished from an apocalyptic obsession with the last days. Accordingly, what concerned St Paul was not the last day itself, but the quality of a present that is *presaging* that day and imbuing in it a new quality:

> the most insidious misunderstanding of the messianic announcement does not consist in mistaking it for prophecy, which is turned toward the future, but for apocalypse, which contemplates the end of time. The apocalyptic is situated on the last day, the Day of Wrath. It sees the end fulfilled and describes what it sees.[1]

These thinkers also had contextual motivations for distancing themselves from an apocalyptic theology. Both Rahner and Agamben are aware of the totalitarian connotations of prophecy as *authoritative* vision. This could refer equally to the apocalyptic blueprints of world war, as to the logic of terror closer to my own description of a politics of fear. From this point of view apocalypse stands in the way of hope. It also inevitably recalls some of the conclusions made in Chapter 1 about the political strategies justifying the war on terror as a battle of good against evil of almost cosmic proportions. The 'visionary' figure of America as the virtually sole arbitrator in the war on terror is powerfully symbolic in this respect.

---

[1] Agamben, *The Time That Remains*, p. 62.

What grounds, then, are there for investigating such a destructive discourse, and what light could it possibly shed on practices of hope? Do not the criticisms above define apocalypse as eschatology taken 'too far', as prophecy breaching its contract with the unknown? For one thing, a clearer distinction must be made than is normally between variations of the word. Literary apocalypse; apocalyptic rhetoric; apocalyptic prophecy; postmodern apocalyptic: all of these terms take on different explanatory roles. It should be noted, for instance, that there are no shortage of studies made of the progressive function of apocalyptic *texts*. The classic source of Christian apocalyptic belief, St John's book of Revelation, for example, has been described as a tool for local resistance against imperial oppression.[2] The visions of St John, *performed*, first and foremost, to a minority religious community who had been promised a kingdom of justice in their lifetimes, transformed political despair under Roman occupation into a cosmic battle of good against evil.

The very least that this chapter presumes in advance is therefore that a fearful, paralysing apocalypse is not *necessarily* the dominant mode of apocalyptic discourse in political culture. The need to explore alternatives is, moreover, an urgent one. To entertain the fulfilment that 'your sons and your daughters will prophesy, your old men will dream dreams, and your young men will see visions' (Joel 2.28) is to take a risk that perhaps eschatological rationality alone could not. It invites a challenge to Rahner's insistence that it is only the *church* that is principally endowed with the 'prophetic role'.[3] And this widening of the meaning of apocalyptic is possible *not* by sharply distinguishing apocalypse as event from apocalypse as more cultural sensibility. It is possible, on the contrary, by recognizing the ubiquity and vast diffusion of apocalyptic dreaming among political individuals and cultures. It means asking whether the rhetorical-dramatic function of apocalyptic discourse is integrally bound up with acts of political

---

[2] This chapter focuses in particular on the analysis of Adela Yobra Collins, *Crisis and Catharsis: The Power of the Apocalypse* (Philadelphia: Westminster Press, 1984). Other examples of the radical function of the book of Revelation can be found in Tina Pippin, *Death and Desire: Rhetoric of Gender in the Apocalypse of John* (Louisville: Westminster/John Knox Press, 1992); Alan A. Boesak, *Comfort and Protest: Reflections on the Apocalypse of John of Patmos* (Philadelphia: The Westminster Press, 1987); Elisabeth Schüssler Fiorenza, *Revelation: Vision of a Just World* (Edinburgh: T&T Clark, 1993); Richard Bauckham, *The Climax of Prophecy: Studies on the Book of Revelation* (Edinburgh: T&T Clark, 1993); Christopher Rowland, *The Open Heaven: A Study of Apocalyptic in Judaism and Early Christianity* (London: SPCK, 1982).

[3] Rahner, *Theological Investigations*, vol. 4 (1966), p. 326.

hope *as well as* the rhetoric of political fatalism and the incitement of violence on a global scale. Perhaps even Rahner wanted to concede the power of this interplay when he wrote, 'on the whole, nothing is more artificial than the apocalyptic style when it is employed without due measure, but its intriguing symbols lend it an undeniable poetic force.'[4]

Eschatology emphasizes a faith in the transhistorical 'beyond' of the end-times. Apocalypse, on the other hand, concerns itself with the bringing down to earth, in dramatic narrative form, of that visionary future. Apocalypse is a spatializing of eschatological hope. It is the license to take the form of a new *place* in our political and social reality. It gives eschatological narrative a shape, a message and mode of dispatch in the form (sometimes) of prediction, warning, vision or description of present reality. The previous chapter was able to contrast a secularized eschatology of permanent crisis with the 'radical eschatology' of Utopian imagination. Similarly, this chapter will provide an alternative mode of vision to a fearful and fantastic form of apocalyptic discourse. As a consequence, we will gain a deeper appreciation of those expressions, through acts of resistance, of imaginative and temporal rupture with a dominant political culture. How do I proceed with this task? First, by exploring the rhetorical function of the book of Revelation. In particular I assess the potential for a liberating or political 'cathartic' reading of its sense of crisis discourse. This cursory glance at diverse biblical hermeneutics then leads to a need to analyse wider cultural appropriations of apocalypse. Among these cultural productions the need soon becomes evident to distinguish which approaches specifically enable a critique of the apocalyptic terror within a politics of fear. In order to make this distinction I ask again which temporal constitutions are able to generate alternative political practices to a 'time of fear'. I thus return to the theme of *kairòs* time. Kairòs is the most obvious confluence between the theological 'vision' of radical expectation and the Utopian imagination. Through a journey of various political and philosophical readings of this category I arrive finally at a contemporary formulation. This is a politicized notion of future anticipation: namely, the practical implications of a politics of the 'impossible'. It is articulated most powerfully in Derrida's apocalyptic notion of a justice *to come*.

I wish from the outset to avoid a few linguistic pitfalls. By referring interchangeably to apocalypse and apocalyptic, I permit myself to play, at times, with the blurring of the adjective/noun distinction. The intention is to bring out both the descriptive quality of 'apocalyptic' literature, discourse, imagination, etc., at the same time as recognizing 'apocalyptic' as *a* genre,

---

[4] Karl Rahner, 'Apocalyptic' in *Encyclopedia*, ed. Rahner, p. 19.

existential state or cultural product. Thus my starting presumption is that apocalypse, apocalyptic and apocalyptic discourse all have this fundamental rhetorical function: they point towards the disclosure (*apokalyptein*) of that which is hidden within the social interpretation of a politically given reality.

The function of apocalyptic rhetoric

The persistent and almost cyclical resurfacing of apocalyptic movements and activists throughout human history can seem like the ultimate human paradox, given that the essence of apocalypse is rupture, discontinuity. As Stephen D. O'Leary puts it,

> the study of apocalypse, a tragic discourse that announces radical discontinuity, paradoxically leads to a comic reaffirmation of continuity: for critics may discover in this tradition a continuous history, always recapitulating itself, of human attempts to break the continuity of history.[5]

What this paradox means is that any analysis of the rhetorical function of apocalyptic discourse should be a search for the way in which the idea of a 'time of rupture' is a pervasive and constitutive element of human society. It is not, of course, universal and certainly not timeless, even within the history of Judaism. As Norman Cohn's authoritative account tells us, belief in the end of the present world and the inauguration of a new one (its 'consummation') in any definitive sense (as opposed to the cyclical revolution of cosmic death and rebirth of, for instance, ancient Babylonian traditions[6]) probably emerged some time after 1500 BCE with the teachings of Zoroaster.[7] It should not be seen simply as the privileging of certain historical contexts or identities. O'Leary, who has explored the function of apocalyptic as *performative* rhetoric, suggests that the power of apocalyptic messages and messengers has been in their ability to dramatize wider cultural topoi by which human communities may explain their place in the cosmos. Apocalypse, in other words, gives human cultures a beginning and

---

[5] Stephen D. O'Leary, *Arguing the Apocalypse: A Theory of Millennial Rhetoric* (Oxford: Oxford University Press, 1994), p. 90.

[6] See Mercia Eliade, *The Myth of the Eternal Return: Or, Cosmos and History* trans. Willard R. Trask (New York: Princeton University Press, 1954).

[7] Norman Cohn, *Cosmos, Chaos and the World to Come: The Ancient Roots of Apocalyptic Faith.*

an end. The move from eschatology to apocalypse has represented, for O'Leary, quite definable moments in the progress of such topoi of human discourse and social identity. The form that transition has taken usually corresponds to external historic events, the rise of charismatic leaders, the climate of 'feverish expectation' and, therefore, a politics of fear in many different guises.

An examination of the rhetorical function of apocalyptic 'argument' must therefore shift from asking how 'closed' or abstracted from human concern the vision of the future is, to the manner of its performance in a wider (social) field of narrative meaning. O'Leary notes that the book of Revelation shared enough characteristics with the devices of Greek cultic drama to be able to specify both its tragic and comic elements.[8] The tragic elements have often been rehearsed by social critics as prototypes for the religious motivation of political resistance. Adela Yarbro Collins is representative of this approach. Collins compares the techniques of cathartic expression of the Christian community's woes with those defined by Aristotle on tragedy generally. Like Aristotle's teaching on the cathartic function of tragic representation, Collins summarizes the political function of Revelation thus: 'to overcome the unbearable tension perceived by the author between what was and what ought to have been'.[9] According to this reading, therefore, the imaginative function of apocalyptic in first-century Asia Minor was to *deepen* the sense of social crisis, the reality of their persecution by both Romans and Jews. As Rahner was all too aware, apocalyptic literature gave the symbolism and imagination of cosmic destiny an extremely preordained order and an abstraction from the controllable events of human history. It did this through its tragic symbolism, its reaffirmation of Old Testament prophecy, and its narrative of God's complete control and direction of the events of cosmic destiny. Against a common prejudice that such tragedy invokes powerlessness and quietism in the face of social upheaval, however, Collins sees Revelation's ability to provoke a cathartic release of the hearers' fear and anger. Tragedy is not evaded, but rather intensified and continually repeated, presumably to be better able to polarize symbolically the dual realities of what is (suffering and marginalization), and what is hoped for (the triumph of the lamb of God). The cathartic process is therefore both a means of letting fear and resentment take its course and a heightening of the stakes in holding fast to faith in God; the production of 'cognitive dissonance'. That the book of Revelation is also *comic* lies in the fact that, at least

---

[8] O'Leary, *Arguing the Apocalypse*, p. 66.
[9] Collins, *Crisis and Catharsis*, p. 141.

for a certain proportion of the participants in the eschatological narrative, conflicts are resolved and goodness restored. The 'heroes' of the apocalypse are brought from despair to hope.

What does this dual narrativity signify to its audience, and what are the wider implications to a politics of apocalyptic discourse? O'Leary argues that because commentators on Revelation have tended to side with one or other emphasis, the tragic and comic devices become powerful tactical means of stressing either the cathartic tragic potential or a faith in its resolution for the just. The classic example of this is, he writes, the use of Revelation by early church fathers, such as Augustine and Origen, in its comic frame. Because the conversion of the empire to Christianity under Constantine made it difficult to continue Revelation's identification of empire with the Antichrist, these commentators stressed its predictive role in identifying the general presence of heresy and Antichrist within the Church communities themselves. Augustine's *City of God*, O'Leary argues, is a paradigm example of this 'anti-apocalyptic eschatology' because it 'cautions against ignoring the beast in ourselves and projecting absolute evil onto the tragic scapegoat'.[10] Instead, the comic 'substructure' reveals the unknowability of God's plan since calamities do not represent the 'end', but only 'periodic setbacks to the progress of the church'.[11]

Whether or not one agrees with O'Leary's conclusions about Augustine, the important point is that he identifies one of the key areas of contestation for the dramatic practice of apocalyptic imagination, and shows how such a distinction is inseparable from its political and rhetorical expression of hope. Perhaps Rahner, for instance, would side with a comic interpretation of apocalyptic revelation. As for Augustine (in O'Leary's interpretation), the function of its performance would thus seem to stress the ability for humans to avoid catastrophe by exercising their freedom. But O'Leary is correct to insist that neither comic nor tragic interpretations of Revelation *necessarily* lead to more or less preoccupation with catastrophe. The temptation, for instance, is normally to see the tragic view of apocalypse as a formalization of global catastrophe, the materialization of a wider, explicable cosmic battle between good and evil and therefore as a tacit justification or even legitimation of the catastrophe. However, it has also been the legacy of a *comic* view of the catastrophe's ultimate resolution to side with the violent dénouement of global events. We need only think of radical millennial movements whose predictions periodically reach a frenzy

---

[10] O'Leary, *Arguing the Apocalypse*, p. 74.
[11] *Ibid.* p. 75.

of numerical calculations of the end-times or the anticipation of the (often violent) Christianization of the world. Post-millennial interpretations of the cosmic battle as striving *towards* perfection have also often coincided historically with the evolutionary views of progress associated with enlightenment thinking. They show that an obsession with perfecting society moves followers into the style of pre-emptive cleansing and 'quickening' action against what they perceive as evil.[12]

These observations serve as evidence that the translation of apocalyptic text does not guarantee a certain political orientation. Rather, it reaffirms the nature of apocalyptic desire as a 'double-edged sword', blurring certain boundaries between the discourse of hope and fear, destruction and creation, fatalism and optimism. This opens up some important questions for the contemporary appropriation of apocalyptic discourse. Hope and faith do not have such clear distinctions between knowledge of the future and faith in the unknown as a dogmatist like Rahner might wish, or as an analyst of the audience of Revelation might attempt to infer. A reading of apocalyptic texts within a specific political context need not view it as a categorical source of either quietism or revolution in times of social crisis, but rather as the inevitable release of imaginative energies within a political context.

There are undoubtedly problems with this approach. What, for example, should be made of Collins' observation that '[Revelation] is a text that enables hearers or readers to cope in extreme circumstances. In a situation where direct political action is not feasible, it is a text that keeps alive the expectation of a better world'?[13] Does apocalyptic rhetoric offer *only* catharsis and, if so, how was it responsible for such religiously inspired popular uprisings as Thomas Müntzer's peasant revolts? Müntzer, leader of several violent and failed peasant uprisings of the 1520s in Germany, protested against political and spiritual oppression from the Church of Rome. Müntzer eventually turned solely to those biblical texts, like Revelation and the book of Daniel, which presaged a blood-bath of vengeance upon the Antichrist before establishing a reign of justice and peace.[14] In the following analyses I shall give my own grounds for distinguishing a particular 'style' of apocalyptic desire that can be affirmed as a resource for political resistance. For now, however, it should be recognized that what an engagement with the visionary 'excess' of apocalypse offers (that was not possible within a systematic reading of eschatology), is a very contextual

---

[12] *Ibid.* p. 85.
[13] Collins, *Crisis and Catharsis*, p. 156.
[14] See Andrew Bradstock, *Faith in the Revolution: The Political Theologies of Müntzer and Winstanley* (London: SPCK, 1997).

and grounded basis for exploring the dichotomy of engagement/ disengagement that was opened up by Agamben on St Paul. Leaving aside what the author of Revelation's political intentions were (the question of the authorship of this text is certainly beyond the task of this book), what unites many of its secondary political commentaries is a fascination with the way in which *disengagement* from a certain political order is seen as the political act *par excellence*. This recognition, in turn, will provide an important basis for analysing modes of contemporary political resistance as 'exit' and Utopian disengagement. Collins, for instance, compares the psychological function of apocalypse to the situation in which schizophrenics (crudely generalized), project a fantasy in which an unbearable existential reality is given 'sense'. Apocalypse is a form of imagination capable of reimagining the space of the political by denying the *legitimacy* of (sanctioned, official) political engagement. Perhaps, goes the argument, it is therefore capable of providing the space for an alternative politics. In its earliest (Christian) manifestations it was from the outset a representation of an order of political truth completely superseding that provided for by secular powers. And it is in this sense that we should read Collins' comment (even if it is not her original intention) that 'the solution of the Apocalypse is an act of creative imagination which, like that of the schizophrenic, withdraws from empirical reality, from real experience in the everyday world'.[15]

To pose this problematic of engagement/disengagement is parallel to pursuing the possibilities of another fascinating paradox of apocalyptic discourse, the conviction 'instilled in the hearers that what ought to be *is*'.[16] What might be the experience of an audience gripped simultaneously by the mesmeric hope in the victory of their God against the powers that crush them and the message that this victory has been *already won*? In what sense is *Revelation* the rending of a veil on reality as things already are? And in what sense can a people called to political engagement make sense of a vision that makes all given political reality melt away? This ritualized narrative form of the tragic events of apocalypse, has, as O'Leary argues, the task of eliciting a reaction more subtle than simply acceptance of a divinely ordered cosmic balance. It is to provide more than the 'assurance' of divinely guaranteed victory. Its function, he suggests, is

> not to convince, but to retrace the pattern of the divine revelation. Argumentation becomes only secondarily an instrument for achieving

---

[15] Collins, *Crisis and Catharsis*, p. 155.
[16] *Ibid.* p. 154.

conviction and belief; it is primarily ritual, a fulfilment of prophecy, a symbolic enactment that contains its own proof even (and perhaps especially) when it fails to convince.[17]

O'Leary is referring to Jacques Derrida's ideas about apocalypse, to which I will turn towards the end of this chapter. For it is Derrida's fascination with the concept of the mode of its *telling* as performative gesture in itself, the idea that in some way St John's imperative of 'come' that reveals, unveils, more than a mere prediction, but also a *mode* and *style* of political hope itself.

Is apocalypse everywhere?

This brief overview of apocalyptic text and rhetoric reveals at least three possible modes of analysis, which I must clarify in order to show which modes raise the most pertinent questions for my argument. There are, first, those reflecting the renewed attention given to biblical apocalyptic literature, and particularly Revelation. The exegete's task seems to have been either to lead its readers to a greater understanding of the social and political context, within which the apocalypse functioned, or to define the rules by which Revelation might be 'legitimately' read today.[18] Second, apocalyptic discourse has been identified as an enduring rhetorical tool, both in giving meaning and shape to such discourse-framing topoi as time (the notion of the beginning or end to the world) and the problem of evil, or to give force to political movements and thus to influence the consent of a populace.[19] Thirdly, that which informs most usefully my argument, apocalyptic has been interpreted as a style of cultural discourse itself. Apocalyptic discourses reach beyond the confines of biblical theology to inform the very mode of political language in which the imagination of the future, the meaning of political hope, 'messianism' and Utopia, make sense.

I have used the word 'style' increasingly to approach this topic. I should now clarify that its use bears some resemblance to Derrida's use of the word 'tone' in his critically acclaimed essay, 'Of an Apocalyptic Tone Recently

---

[17] O'Leary, *Arguing the Apocalypse*, p. 88.

[18] See, for example, Christopher Rowland, 'Upon Whom the Ends of the Ages Have Come: Apocalyptic and the Interpretation of the New Testament' in *Apocalypse Theory and the Ends of the World*, ed. Malcolm Bull (Oxford: Blackwell, 1995), pp. 38–57.

[19] O'Leary, *Arguing the Apocalypse*, pp. 20–60.

Adopted in Philosophy'.[20] Both 'tone' and 'style' suggest an ability to apply a sense or world-view, a cultural inscription to colour the mundane and everyday within a new perspective. 'Apocalyptic style' is, for instance, a term used by John Howard Yoder to get around the oddities and eccentricities of apocalyptic texts by framing their significance within a broad appraisal of biblical texts as the world 'made strange'. As David Toole argues, reflecting on Yoder's term, there is a style or vision by which history may be understood in a manner that echoes Foucault's search for discontinuous ruptures in history. Discontinuity functions in opposition to the linear progression of historical events described by 'normal' history. For Foucault, history and political possibility are constituted by everyday transgressions. To see apocalyptically is similarly to affirm the strangeness and *otherness* of the world. It is to affirm that

> history continues not because of what kings and presidents might do but because ravens keep prophets alive in the desert (1 Kings 17) and because even as kings and presidents count their people and take their polls and plan the future, the word of God comes into the wilderness.[21]

An apocalyptic style in this sense is a commentary about the power of the weak. It can therefore be justifiably interpreted as a narrative of justice and resistance.

This last feature is problematic, however. For it suggests adopting apocalyptic analysis as a purely descriptive literary or cultural appreciation of otherwise explicable events – in the case of the early Christian community, resistance of imperial repression by a minority group. How, in this case, does one account for the relationship between an apocalyptic mode of *seeing* the world anew? How should we view the proliferation of apocalyptic fantasies guiding a very destructive mode of apocalyptic anticipation, whether from tragic or comic motivations? An example of the former mode is explored in David Dark's recent book, *Everyday Apocalypse*. Dark comments on a vast spectrum of current cultural products, from the music of Radiohead to the cartoon series 'The Simpsons'. He attempts to generate a general conceptual framework from the symbolic complexities of texts like Revelation by arguing that its core function was, and is still, to liberate the social imagination from an authorized discourse of the same. Whether through the perspectives of music or film, this is possible only if people are

---

[20] Jacques Derrida, 'Of an Apocalyptic Tone Recently Adopted in Philosophy', trans. John P. Leavey, Jr, *Semeia*, no. 23 (1982), 63–98.

[21] Toole, *Waiting for Godot*, p. 210.

encouraged to think apocalyptically. Dark falls prey to the omnipresence of apocalyptic thought because *he* sees it 'everywhere':

> Apocalyptic testifies concerning a world both beyond *and* presently among the world of appearances, an unveiling of actions are fraught. [. . .] Like nothing else, apocalyptic undermines, driving us to doubt our nervously-defended selves. It pulls us out of the mental torpor of our already-made-up minds, and when we're looking closely, it is everywhere.[22]

As uplifting as this seems, we should question what exactly is achieved by the revelation of everyday practices and expressions in the light of the new understandings generated by apocalyptic. Is the imaginative practice of apocalypse simply an everyday artistic venture? Is it there to jolt us to attention, or is it a more strategic act of resistance that requires our participation, and hence a critique of its *absence* in popular enactments of political resistance? Dark, Yoder and Toole all seem distracted from the central question of the ambiguity of the ethics of apocalyptic rhetoric. They emphasize its plasticity, its being 'all things to all men'. They are thus able to concentrate on, in Toole's case for instance, the 'apocalyptic politics of Jesus and the Church'[23] as the defining rhetorical usefulness of the term. Indeed, the typical approach to apocalyptic studies is, if one wants to redeem the texts at all, to show how they may still contain some liberative 'elements'. However, just as a secularized and heretical eschatology was seen to describe the form of fantasy inscribed in the 'debt' and 'security' paradigms, equal and simultaneous attention should also be paid to the renaissance in apocalyptic rhetoric being currently witnessed within the war on terror. The similarities (or direct relations in some cases) between millennialist apocalyptic belief and the political rhetoric underpinning much White House policy making has been well documented[24] and continues to open new debates on the resurgence of fundamentalist religion at the heart of the Project for a New American Century (PNAC). As stated on its website, PNAC is an 'educational organization dedicated to a few fundamental propositions: that American leadership is good both for America and for the world; and that such leadership requires military strength, diplomatic energy and

---

[22] David Dark, *Everyday Apocalypse: The Sacred Revealed in Radiohead, the Simpsons, and Other Pop Culture Icons* (Grand Rapids: Brazos Press, 2002), pp. 139–140.

[23] Toole, *Waiting for Godot*, p. 227.

[24] See in particular Michael Northcott, *An Angel Directs the Storm: Apocalyptic Religion and American Empire* (London: I. B. Tauris and Co., 2004).

commitment to moral principle'.[25] The strategic goals it identifies for America's role in the world thus emphasize pre-emptive military intervention around the world where American interests are threatened. But what is significant is the *visionary* aspect of the neo-conservative agenda, a direct continuation of the nineteenth-century creed of Manifest Destiny. Madeleine Albright, then US Secretary of State, introduced an apocalyptic element to strategic policy thinking inimically in justifying air strikes against Iraq in 1998: 'if we have to use force it is because we are America. We are the indispensable nation. We stand tall. We see farther into the future.'[26]

But how does this visionary element identify with explicitly *millennialist* beliefs? Michael Northcott describes the transition in America since the classic 'post-millennial' movements that arose out of the Enlightenment's puritan projects of evangelization, to a more sombre 'premillennialist' emphasis on the *present* as the real end-times. The historicist tradition of building the promised kingdom through human choice has been consonant with the general victories of neo-liberalism and Fukuyama's end of history thesis. The current trend in American Christian-right politics, however, seems to be an impatience with any such vision of long-term progression. There is, instead, a fervent and often detailed interpretation of current catastrophic events as signs of the penultimate dispensation.[27]

In the light of this history, an interesting problem presents itself in Norman Cohn's argument that, historically, millennialism's principal trigger has been social dispossession. In the Middle Ages, found Cohn, 'these *prophetae* found their following [. . .], where there existed a surplus population [. . .]. Living on the margin of society [. . .], that amorphous mass of people who were not simply poor but who could find no assured and recognised place in society at all'.[28] Today, the attraction of so many in contemporary affluent societies such as the United States to apocalyptic narrative according to Cohn's thesis would require a significantly widened use of the notion of dispossession. It would mean suggesting that material dispossession has been replaced by the popular discomfort about the moral depravity of a nation or community, as the sign of the end-times. Premillennarianists such as William Miller in 1830s America, in this view, were able to capitalize on popular fears and anxieties, and identified apocalyptic 'threats'

---

[25] www.newamericancentury.org/index.html.

[26] Quoted in Northcott, *An Angel*, p. 77.

[27] Northcott, *An Angel*.

[28] Norman Cohn, *The Pursuit of the Millennium: Revolutionary Messianism in Medieval and Reformation Europe and Its Bearing on Modern Totalitarian Movements* (London: Mercury Books, 1962), p. 314.

with the secular state, world government, moral depravity and liberalism, and the prospect of post-cold war 'New World Order'.[29] And in our own times, George W. Bush, following in the footsteps of Reagan in his close association with the authors of such calculations such as Hal Lindsay, has shown the extent to which Augustine's original 'de-eschatologization' of apocalypse, its turning inwards, can be perverted. Such a transformation produces a kind of radicalism that, while being a tool of empire, does not pervert its own violent course. Thus, because the American population has struggled to identify itself as victims, the specific influence of far-right Christian groups has been to turn against those hindering the evangelizing mission of the United States itself, such as the UN, and radical Islam. The 'optimistic' comic frame guiding the moral community since Augustine's distinction has become transformed into a perverse celebration of apocalyptic opportunism of the moral majority. One consequence of this widened sense of 'marginalization' is an ambiguity towards the content of apocalyptic vision of what 'ought to be'. O'Leary has noted, for example, the attempt of American right-wing apocalypticists to identify with the social identity of the persecuted Christian community to whom the book of Revelation was first preached: 'there is an obvious difference between being torn apart by lions in front of cheering crowds and being forced to endure media onslaughts of sex, violence, and secular humanism.'[30]

The widening of apocalyptic desires to represent a wide spectrum of fundamentalist beliefs only affirms the rhetorical effectivity of an apocalyptic discourse. It opens up the possibility that apocalyptic desire need not be seen neither as 'everywhere' (and therefore hard to distinguish) nor the sole possession of religious fundamentalists. Rather, an apocalyptic historicism has found wider and greater means to be a *productive* discourse. It has also found myriad channels for its dissemination in globalized society. And while the means by which a political power has manipulated biblical tradition to justify its own crusade demands serious critique, this book is not the place for such an undertaking. The reason for highlighting it is rather to appreciate the metamorphosis that apocalyptic endist rhetoric has taken in order to 'harness' the effects of fear and terror ever more effectively and *deceptively*. Derrida, for instance, made much of this idea of a fantasy of the end that paralyses and mesmerizes, rather than provokes reaction, through

---

[29] See Michael Barkun, 'Politics and Apocalypticism' in *The Encyclopedia of Apocalypticism, vol. 3: Apocalypticism in the Modern Period and the Contemporary Age*, ed. Stephen J. Stein (New York: Continuum, 1999), pp. 442–460 (p. 452).

[30] O'Leary, *Arguing the Apocalypse*, p. 11.

his analysis of our own contemporary version of the imminent apocalypse: the nuclear threat. 'Nuclear criticism' acts as a penetrating critique of the popular anticipation of crisis: 'who can swear that our unconscious is not expecting this? Dreaming of it, desiring it?'[31] Through the proliferation of discourses in which nuclear destruction remains a permanent possibility, in which human extinction becomes a negotiable pawn in international relations, apocalypse becomes banalized and thus, as Derrida said, transformed into the supreme *non-event*. In nuclear criticism, then, 'there is no more room for a distinction between belief and science [. . .]. Not even for a truth in that sense. No truth, no apocalypse.'[32] With this insight we might add that the crisis in considering the tragic form of apocalypse in contemporary discourse and its (political) subversions acts as a kind of erasure of apocalypse's imaginative catharsis. Does a politics of fear also speak about an apocalypse without vision at all, a non-event, as Derrida says, a 'process of fearful domestication, the anticipatory assimilation of that unforeseeable entirely-other [. . .]. Some might call it a fable, then, a pure invention'[33]?

This brief overview of the contemporary proliferation of apocalyptic discourses has therefore cast in a new light the suspicion with which this book began: namely, the crisis of contemporary political life in imagining the future, of articulating hope as a serious philosophical concept. The apocalypses described above appear in the same mode of banality with which permanent anxiety was found to be 'low level' and background in my analysis of fear at the beginning of this book. *This* kind of apocalypse therefore represents a visionary mesmeric screen, promising no new future but only rapture. As Krishnan Kumar has put it, we have today

a millennial belief without a sense of the future. [. . .] It brings no pleasure, and promises no happiness. In this sense it seems not to make much difference whether we look with foreboding to a dismal future, or proclaim our good luck at the way things have turned out. Neither brings any comfort.[34]

---

[31] Jacques Derrida, 'No Apocalypse, Not Now (Full Speed Ahead, Seven Missiles, Seven Missives)', trans. John P. Levy, Jr, *Diacritics*, vol. 14, no. 2 (Summer 1984), 20–31 (23).

[32] *Ibid.* p. 24.

[33] *Ibid.* p. 23.

[34] Krishnan Kumar, 'Apocalypse, Millennium and Utopia Today' in *Apocalypse Theory and the Ends of the World*, ed. Malcolm Bull (Oxford: Blackwell, 1995), pp. 200–224 (p. 205).

Time has grown short:
The political nature of *Kairòs*

How has the preceding analysis helped with an identification of apocalyptic desire at the heart of practices of hope? An assumption behind my argument that apocalyptic discourse acts as a double-edged sword has been that, as a 'style' or 'tone', it cannot be monopolized by any one ideological motivation. The last comments about mesmeric, fearful and tragically associated apocalypses, therefore, need to be placed alongside a more detailed approach to the underside of this apocalyptic fear. This means returning to the themes outlined in the search for political eschatologies. I do so with this new perspective of visionary, prophetic desire at the heart of political life. The task will be in particular to pick up the thread of eschatology's temporal constitution and ask whether apocalyptic offers any further resources for transforming a time of fear into a time of hope.

Barth and Rahner both showed how Christian hope means a reorientation towards time, the relationship between what has been, what is and what is to come. Both theologians, however, left the disjunction between given time and God's time at the level of human tragedy, that which generates a need for divine intervention. It is appropriate, then, that the challenge of a more apocalyptically grounded appraisal of *kairòs* time has been taken up recently in the *materialist* political philosophy of Antonio Negri. The starting premise of Negri's *Time for Revolution* is that time represents not simply a metaphysics of being, but, as Marx made clear, is constitutive of power relations, such as defining the value or 'measure' of labour.[35] Whereas it is Negri's task to show how capitalist empire has taken the domination of time to unprecedented levels, his innovation is to define, on the other hand, '*kairòs* time' as even more fundamentally constitutive and irreducible. It is a political investment of the future at all times, a *permanent* quality as opposed to a moment of rupture. While it often seems that human aspirations are defined by a commitment to the past and the perishing quality of the present, he writes,

On the contrary, I cannot conceive of time other than as *kairòs*, and so never as corruption and death. In other words: the past is normally conceived of as the accumulation of the destruction of physical events. But to think that temporality could have 'destruction' as its name is

---

[35] Antonio Negri, *Time for Revolution*, trans. Matteo Mandarini (London: Continuum, 2003), p. 23.

meaningless, because the temporality that we experience and that we live through is that of *kairòs* and of the creative act that constitutes it – and only that. In being, 'all is created and nothing is destroyed within the immediacy of the present.'[36]

The transition made here from Barth to Negri could hardly be more acute. In particular, Negri seems to get away from the polarization of discourse about time and apocalypse into, on the one hand, existentialist concerns of personal transformation and, on the other, an interpretivist, religious prophetic narrative. Before returning to Negri in greater depth, however, it is worth pursuing the roots of this view of time (highlighted by Barth) to give a clearer idea of what *new* challenges are thrown up by the legacy of a certain philosophy of time.

Barth's view of the 'ethical demand' of hope as the unseen time is indebted to Heidegger's hugely influential existentialist study of ontology, *Being and Time*. There, time is examined as an ontological condition of lived experience or, more precisely, 'the primordial ontological basis for Dasein's existentiality is *temporality*'.[37] Integral to the condition of being 'thrown' into the world (a Heideggerian feature of both Barth's and Rahner's accounts of given, experienced time) and experiencing itself immediately in terms of its potentiality for being, is the being already temporally constituted and concerned for one's future. For my purposes, and in particular because of the effect it has had on Derrida, the most crucial aspect of what Heidegger says about temporality in the make-up of Dasein is its expression as a mode of 'being towards death'. For Heidegger, death has the character of a persistent presence, something that 'belongs' to Dasein in the negative, that is, the experience of 'no-longer-Dasein' which is 'not-yet'.[38] Death represents something of a blessing since it promises an *end* to the overall 'lack of totality'[39] at the heart of Dasein's angst. At one point Heidegger even likens it to the ripening of a fruit.[40] But inasmuch as this realization is itself an experience of Being, the 'not-yet' is not an event to be anticipated in the manner of a death-wish (which would thereby lead my research into an exploration of martyrdom and apocalyptic suicide, an area too vast

---

[36] *Ibid.* p. 164.
[37] Martin Heidegger, *Being and Time*, trans. John Macquarrie and Edward Robinson (Oxford: Blackwell, 1962), p. 277, italics in the original. I have used the pagination of the later German edition, marked 'H' in Macquarrie and Robinson's translation, throughout.
[38] *Ibid.* p. 286.
[39] *Ibid.*
[40] *Ibid.* p. 288.

to include here). It is rather a way of being, perhaps even a 'style'. As Heidegger puts it,

> just as Dasein *is* already its 'not-yet', and is its 'not-yet' constantly as long as it is, it *is* already its end too. The 'ending' which we have in view when we speak of death, does not signify Dasein's Being-at-an-end [Zu-Ende-sein], but a *Being-towards-the-end* [*Sein zum Ende*] of this entity. Death is a way to be, which Dasein takes over as soon as it is.[41]

From this perspective we can begin to see apocalyptic time as 'ever present' to Dasein. The purpose of history is to reveal the 'silent power of the possible'.[42] The effects of this can be described as a sanctification of the experience of 'abnormal time', or, in Heidegger's terms the *authenticity* of being towards nothingness, that is, towards death as Dasein's 'ownmost possibility'. If living in the world constitutes a constant tension of being towards one's end and being thrown into a world of temporalized facticity, then apocalyptic time, as Gabriel Motzkin says, is 'the sign of greatest tension between being and nothingness'.[43] This mode of anticipation does not conflate the *anxiety* of being trapped in time with *fearing* death. Instead, it seeks a way to 'be' one's own end here and now through a transformation and authentic appropriation of that experience of time.

This forms a crucial basis for interpreting St Paul's exhortation to live 'as though' the apocalypse was imminent as a re-evaluation of temporal living. If it is apocalyptic it is because it is between *chronos* and *kairòs*. Apocalyptic time is an experience that allows one to see differently, to unveil the possibilities/impossibilities of the present through the eyes of the future. The notion that Dasein *becomes* its own end, that it contains an eschato-logic in its very temporal 'thrownness' in the concerns of this life, dictates a creative mode of anticipation as opposed to one that restrictively delineates its possible options. And, problematic though it is, Heidegger's emphasis on distinguishing authentic from inauthentic approaches to the end can illuminate a parallel desire to distinguish paralysing effects of a fearful, conformist apocalypse from one that liberates time as opportunity, or the moment of *kairòs*. Heidegger contrasts inauthentic 'awaiting' with authentic 'anticipation', a mode of being-towards-death characterized by

---

[41] *Ibid.* p. 289, italics in the original.

[42] Heidegger, quoted in William Katerberg, 'History, Hope, and the Redemption of Time' in *The Future of Hope*, ed. Volf and Katerberg, pp. 49–73 (p. 62).

[43] Gabriel Motzkin, 'Abnormal and Normal Time: After the Apocalypse' in *Apocalyptic Time*, ed. Albert I. Baumgarten (Leiden: Brill, 2000), pp. 199–214, (p. 205).

'resoluteness'. He goes beyond the idea of *predicting* the future according to objects of one's most immediate concerns to holding the being of Dasein as potentiality. It is a state of 'ecstasis', a 'rapture' of resoluteness towards its future possibilities. Perhaps the most apocalyptic expression Heidegger uses is therefore of a 'moment of vision'.[44] With inauthentic 'fallenness' the future informs the present by a mode of everyday 'making present'. In the 'moment of vision' the 'authentic present' is informed by a realization of Dasein's potentiality as a being towards its end. It is therefore *not* a means of escapism but an embrace of the end and totality of one's being as that which unveils authentic being in the world.

It is interesting to note that the translation for this 'moment of vision', '*Augenblick*', or flick of the eye, is elsewhere in *Being and Time* simply translated as 'moment'.[45] If there appears to be something unavoidably theological in the importance given to *the moment*, a more than mundane, perhaps transcendent appreciation of the 'now', it is provided by subsequent reflections on messianism by writers such as Walter Benjamin. Though I do not have the space to explore his work further, it is worth mentioning that Benjamin was influential in this field for developing the concept of a 'messianic moment' as the substance of living in the creative potential of an apocalyptic 'now time'.[46] As Motzkin puts it, 'as a time of the special moment, apocalyptic time cannot then signify the unexperiencable end, but rather that moment of anticipation of the end which precedes through normal, mendacious time'.[47] In terms of an understanding of 'future-orientedness' of political practices, it is also significant that this approach to temporality releases certain motivations for acting 'as if' certain things were possible, where that distinction might normally come down on either side of despair or hope. Heidegger, for one, expresses the experience of hopelessness as yet revealing a fundamental orientation towards the future. Such an orientation is an equal function of the condition of 'care' at the heart of Dasein's existentiality, regardless of the motive for what makes one *move* in the first place: 'the primary item in care is the "ahead-of-itself". [. . .] Even when it still exists but has nothing more "before it" and has "settled [*abgeschlossen*] its account", its Being is still determined by the "ahead-of-itself".'[48] While Heidegger rarely mentions the phenomenon of hopelessness (and certainly not *political* hopelessness) in distinction to the

---

[44] Heidegger, *Being and Time*, p. 387.
[45] See footnote 2 to Heidegger, *Being and Time*, p. 376.
[46] See Katerberg, 'History, Hope, and the Redemption', p. 67.
[47] Motzkin, 'Abnormal and Normal Time', p. 204.
[48] Heidegger, *Being and Time*, p. 236, my italics.

individualist, existentialist concept of angst or despair, when he does, he insists that:

> hopelessness [. . .], does not tear Dasein away from its possibilities, but is only one of its own modes of *Being towards* these possibilities [. . .]. It is essential to the basic constitution of Dasein that there is *constantly something still to be settled* [*eine ständige Unabgeschlossenheit*]. Such a lack of totality signifies that there is something still outstanding in one's potentiality-for-Being'.[49]

Heidegger's approach to 'authentic time' presents two important problems to the direction of my argument. The first is the similarity of his comment on hopelessness to the one expressed by Noam Chomsky at the opening of this book: namely, the idea that neither qualities of hope nor despair are decisive in the motivations to *act*. If we act, then this shows simply that we are the kinds of beings that are *moved towards the future*. A central premise of my argument has been, throughout this book, to critique this approach by insisting that to be towards the future in hope is qualitatively different to being towards the future in despair. More importantly, these two phenomena release radically different potentialities for being. The second problem is Heidegger's individualizing reduction of the experience of time. For Heidegger, of course, the being of others, the experience of the 'they', is also a primordial constitution of the being of Dasein. However, it is so only in the sense that it represents an immediate threat to its authenticity, the tendency to get lost in the 'herd' and the life of everyday chatter. Heidegger's foundation for an apocalyptic opening of the experience of one's ultimate horizon, death, therefore ultimately leads one to an extrication from the concern for a collective notion of that horizon:

> *anticipation reveals to Dasein its lostness in the they-self, and brings it face to face with the possibility of being itself* [. . .], *in an* impassioned freedom towards death – *a freedom which has been released from the Illusions of the 'they', and which is factical, certain of itself, and anxious.*[50]

Ultimately, this kind of being towards death concerns itself with a disengagement from the inauthentic everydayness of the hopes and fears of others as they appear to us.

---

[49] *Ibid.* p. 236, italics in the original.
[50] *Ibid.* p. 267, italics in the original.

Both of these concerns reveal themselves quite brazenly when, caught in the rapture of his apocalyptic 'ecstasis' of authenticity, he claims that "in the moment of vision', nothing can occur'.[51] What, with respect to the notion of political hope, is to be read into the priority afforded now time if this includes a sanctification of pure existential introspection and disregard for a teleological *apprehension* of the future, or regard for the past? If, as Paul Fletcher has already noted, the suspension of historical, teleological *chronos* time also suspends the notion of time in relation to *law* and the guarantee of an ethics that points towards an ultimate end, then we are left with a 'now' without (ethical) content.[52] Even worse, it provides the basis for the perpetual suspension of juridical norms that characterizes the 'state of exception' by which Agamben has described contemporary sovereignty. We are already witnessing the incarnation of this apocalyptic 'now time' in the new modes of sovereignty characterized by the war on terror as war without end and without desired resolution. With this 'martial aspect of eschatology',[53] as Fletcher puts it, the answer to the question 'what kind of time do we inhabit' returns us back to the production of fear. The historicization of eschatology has, in the paradigm of exception he describes, become a 'metaphysics of crisis'. It is the suspension of normal time, by which 'political time is terminated'.[54]

With these criticisms in mind it is now possible to return to Negri's own take on the political philosophy of time. Despite what he has to say about the centrality of revolutionary *kairòs* time, it is his account of the transformation of Heideggerian '*jetzt-zeit*' into capitalized time that truly opens up the urgency of constructing an alternative apocalyptic function of time. Capitalized time is time of administration, simultaneity and a paralysing equilibrium by global capitalism. It has 'invested the whole of life'[55] with the linear notion of work-time. Recalling Paul Virilio's paradigm of modern warfare, 'war at the speed of light',[56] we can now equate the new dominance of political subjects through this transition from spatial dominance to oppressive 'commanded time' of rapid response. Capitalism has achieved a transition to a perfect, static equilibrium of working subjects. It is 'the transformation of Prometheus into Narcissus, the ideal of the

---

[51] *Ibid.* p. 388.
[52] Fletcher, 'The Nature of Redemption', p. 290.
[53] Fletcher, 'Political Theology' (p. 59).
[54] *Ibid.*
[55] Negri, *Time for Revolution*, p. 144.
[56] See Paul Virilio, *Desert Screen: War at the Speed of Light* (London: Continuum, 2002).

complete self-sufficiency of the schema of production and of automatic functioning. *Ecstasy*'.[57]

Even if Negri was not thinking of Heidegger at the time, this echo of his 'ecstasis' allows an interesting juxtaposition. For the rapture of authentic being towards one's end could be seen to be complicit in the ecstasy of global capital's command of every time of local, everyday life. This means that the allure of authentic awareness of one's own death does not necessarily imply a freedom to *shape* that end or to strive towards it. It might instead represent one more desire to be commodified, much in the manner that Massumi argued in Part I that capitalism represents a warding off of death through the fantasy of the never-ending moment. Instead of an attitude of openness to one's finitude, being 'in' time might, in today's capitalist society, constitute a mesmerizing fantasy, 'filling' the present with the illusions of permanence. Negri in this way increases the need to be vigilant in the way in which one would appropriate both St Paul and Heidegger, concerning the revolutionary potential of apocalyptic time, by warning us that it can also become 'time zero'.[58] For the desires that emerge out of living *in-between times* might also suggest the face of the innovation of the time of empire, its flexibility and command of the whole of life:

> political economy is entirely directed towards drawing the *innovative element* that history – in any case – produces into the time of administration [. . .]. *Now-time* (*Jetzt-Zeit*), innovative precision, utopia: capital considers them as its own. [. . .] Administration is illuminated by charisma. The city of the devil is illuminated by grace.[59]

Negri quotes the biblical passage from Revelation that formed the crux of Rahner's theology of the future, in the *Prolegomena* to his essay, *Kairòs*:[60] 'And I saw a new heaven and a new earth; for the first heaven and the first earth had passed away; and there was no more sea.' (Rev. 21.1). His own Marxist appropriation of the quasi-theological category of *kairòs* time, however, occurs within a strict *materialist* philosophy. Negri's commitment to materialism frames his appreciation of *kairòs* in ways that open up the analysis of this chapter to the materialist effectivity of apocalyptic desire. This is because for Negri the new task of political materialism has far superseded the old demands of Marxist critique and must reach into the 'ontological

---

[57] Negri, *Time for Revolution*, p. 48, italics in the original.

[58] *Ibid.* p. 68.

[59] *Ibid.* p. 108, italics in the original.

[60] *Ibid.* p. 147.

imagination'. That is, the production not only of social goods but of 'bodies', 'subjectivities' and the type of innovation he calls the bringing about of the 'new being'.[61] The 'materialist field' is for Negri the terrain of bodies, desires and social constitutions that are constantly productive,[62] and the kind of production that interests him is that of the creative and subversive play of human subjectivities.

How does temporal constitution become so important within this scheme? As we have already seen, paradigms of production, biopower, and societies of control are essentially framed by ontologies of time. But so, too, are the conditions of political possibility opened up by the conscious reorientation of time, through the category of *kairòs*. The emphasis is always, for Negri, on temporal constitution as praxis, but he orients this praxis also as the ultimate epistemological task. In other words, by interpreting time as opening up permanent ruptures or opportunities for the new, for innovation, one is not only directing political action but also the possibility for discourse, the ability to make 'be' that which was once condemned to fantasy. Negri calls this the 'event of knowing, of naming, or rather knowing as singularity, interweaving of logical innovation and ontological creation'.[63] Innovation, invention and imagination are therefore code-words for the practical sense that can be gained from this temporal reorientation. *Kairòs* used to be a classical image of 'the act of releasing the arrow', the favourable moment, the instant of rupture, but in the context of post-modernity its radical new use is perhaps even simpler. Negri frames it at the outset in terms of this basic question: in the context of biopolitical subsumption and 'zero-degree' dialectic, 'how is a decision to be made by the multitude?'[64] The ability to *decide* is all-important within a cultural context that has eroded dialectical possibility, the absence of choice underneath the market fantasy of *endless* choices.[65] And if *kairòs* refers to the permanent ability to create anew, its translation into praxis is the ability to make a *decision* on the common human project: the constitution of the political realm.

How, then, does Negri's thought affirm apocalypse as the most appropriate conceptual tool for countering a politics of fear? It engages with apocalyptic insofar as it takes the risk, as I put it earlier, of recognizing both the destructive and creative aspects of apocalyptic time, and seeks continually

---

[61] *Ibid.* p. 154.

[62] *Ibid.* p. 171.

[63] *Ibid.* p. 142.

[64] *Ibid.* p. 143.

[65] See my comments about the 'false choice' of the society of the spectacle, p. 30, above.

to develop that latter part that has freed itself from command time. His ideas are imbued with the theological sense of 'opportunity' and the license to constitute politics according to an order of reality that comes close to a desire for transcendence. Not only the idea of the 'new' then, but the figure of the 'new *being*' is central to Negri's politics, indicating perhaps that it is through human *action* that we should seek the (materially) *new*. '*Kairòs* is the Christ that empties itself so as to produce new being, it is temporality augmented by expression, it is *praxis* of the common name'.[66]

It would, nevertheless be unfair to start making theological assumptions about this apocalyptic orientation without also acknowledging the extent of Negri's materialist commitment and aversion to the concept of God as a transcendent, more than material reality. Liberated time, he argues, allows no place for 'transcendence' or 'mysticism' precisely because of its temporal constitution, its basis in the life, or the lifetime, of the multitude, the proletariat:

> the temporal machine of proletarian liberation invests the inside and the outside of life, the *soul* and the *body*, and makes them operate – together – collectively, *as collective power*. All transcendence, even logical, is removed. All mediation that is not from the start within the materiality of the temporal, collective, productive existence is pure and simple mystification.[67]

Suffice to say here that what Negri *does* achieve is a distinction that I have also attempted to articulate in the process of this book: namely, between a Utopian desire of future-orientation, and an apocalyptic desire as an 'experimentation' and creativity of what it means to 'see' the time that is to come. This distinction is consonant with my critique of the 'futurist' fantasy of contemporary capitalism and liberal notions of progress as a perverted desire for the endless repetition of the same, seen in the examples of limitless consumption and war without end. As Negri puts it:

> Many see in the name of the 'future' the identical repetition of what has already happened. From this point of view the future means that which persists. And even when others see the future as a progression that modifies the conditions of arrival in comparison to those of departure, it is still the case (with greater or lesser variations) that the future will be

---

[66] Negri, *Time for Revolution*, p. 158, italics in the original.
[67] *Ibid.* p. 125, italics in the original.

positive or negative – but continuous – reproduction of itself. [. . .] What is missing is the apperception of the creative moment that establishes that which is yet to arrive.[68]

Crucially, the exploration of an apocalyptic imagination has also revealed its proximity to Utopian imagination: namely through the importance attached to the concept of the 'impossible' in alternative political practices. It is precisely to this concept that I now turn by looking at Jacques Derrida's fascination with the 'apocalyptic' genre.

A politics of the impossible:
Derrida's apocalypse 'to come'

The expression that Negri prefers to *Utopia* and *futurism* is one that has unavoidably crept into my previous analysis and can now be explored a little deeper. It is the 'to come', a concept central also to Jacques Derrida's messianic and apocalyptic themes. Picking up Derrida at this critical point in my argument will concretize a highly influential and controversial theme in political philosophy; the influence of deconstruction has arguably reignited a passion for the messianic element of global political movements and new political practices generally. This was evident, for instance, through Derrida's interest and involvement in the 'BRussels Tribunal: People vs. Total War Incorporated' [*sic*], held in Belgium, April 2004. In an interview he states:

I would say that today, one of the incarnations, one of the implementa-
tions of this messianicity, of this messianism without religion, may be
found in the alter-globalization movements. Movements that are still
heterogeneous, still somewhat unformed, full of contradictions, but that
gather together the weak of the earth, all those who feel themselves
crushed by the economic hegemonies, by the liberal market, by sover-
eignism, etc. I believe it is these weak who will prove to be strongest in the
end and who represent the future [. . .]. It is these alter-globalization
movements that offer one of the best figures of what I would call messianicity without messianism, that is to say a messianicity that does not
belong to any determined religion. The conflict with Iraq involved
numerous religious elements, from all sides—from the Christian side as
well as from the Muslim side. What I call messianicity without messianism

---

[68] *Ibid.* pp. 162–163.

is a call, a promise of an independent future for what is to come, and which comes like every messiah in the shape of peace and justice, a promise independent of religion, that is to say universal. [. . .] My intent here is not anti-religious, it is not a matter of waging war on the religious messianisms properly speaking, that is to say Judaic, Christian, Islamic. But it is a matter of marking a place where these messianisms are exceeded by messianicity, that is to say by that waiting without waiting, without horizon for the event to come, the democracy to come with all its contradictions.[69]

What does the messianic actually mean here, and within the broader context of deconstruction? Derrida's writing had long explored the related themes of abnormal time; time off its hinges and the expectation of the unexpected.[70] They have their roots in a wider philosophical concern, moreover, to illuminate the illusions of a pure 'meaning' that Western metaphysical discourse has assumed since Plato. A principal feature of deconstruction is the rejection of the Platonic 'logocentrism' (which asserts the 'real' presence of the meaning of the thing spoken in speech or writing). Thus desconstruction affirms language and sense as in a constant state of flux. Challenging logocentrism means permanently *differing* and *deferring* meaning. It means affording no permanence to the meaning we give to things. Derrida's critique of Western metaphysics is a condemnation of nothing less than 'phenomenology and ontology' as tending towards 'philosophies of violence. Through them, the entire philosophical tradition, in its meaning and at bottom, would make common cause with oppression and with the totalitarianism of the same'.[71] What Derrida means is that by affirming the reign and 'totality' of the subject, we get a politics of possession. We rationalize and homogenize the 'other', the subject's outside.

Deconstruction also generates an implicitly ethical and political imperative to reject the illusion of ideological certitude in historical 'epochs'. It means, therefore, a radical questioning of the ability to define the shape of the future. History often appears as a kind of authoritarian writing of the hierarchy of events and truths that give it cohesion and direction. The purpose of deconstruction is to show that such judgements are contingent upon a dictatorship of the narrator. It must reject, fundamentally, the

---

[69] Lieven de Cauter, 'For a Justice to Come: Interview with Jacques Derrida', trans. Ortwin de Graef, *Ris Orangis*, 19 February 2004, www.brusselstribunal.org/pdf/Derrida_EN.pdf [accessed 18 January 2006].

[70] See, in particular, Derrida, *Specters of Marx*.

[71] *Ibid.* p. 91.

principle of closure. And this closure is the same as that by which I have already described endist discourse: the ideological rejection of alternative imagination. It is hardly surprising, therefore, that Derrida's major application of a deconstructionist method to the subject of apocalyptic comes primarily through direct confrontation, in *Specters of Marx*,[72] with the triumphalist and logocentric closure of historical epochs in Fukuyama's End of History thesis. Derrida makes an ethical judgement on the naïveté of attempting to banish an historic idea from the realm of political possibility. He wishes thus to affirm the permanent possibility of rupture in history. As such, his thought touches and illuminates two themes with which my study has engaged. First, the idea of politics as a practice of the impossible; second, St Paul's expression of time becoming 'short' and derailed from its predictable course.

Derrida does this, in *Specters of Marx*, in the context of a discussion of ghosts; he appears obsessed with the difficulty of conceiving moments or eras passing and superseding one another synchronically or in terms of progress. He therefore reveals something about approaching both the future (of revolution, for instance, or of striving for justice) and the past (the persistence of 'spirits'). But he does it in such a way that does not, as I believe Heidegger did, isolate the present as a state of introspective, existentialist angst. Instead, Derrida's counterpart to St Paul's 'the time has grown short' can be seen in the way he develops the theme of 'abnormal time'. It relates also to Hamlet's expression, 'the time is out of joint', '*hors de ses jonds*' (off its hinges). The aim is to show 'the impossibility of thinking or rather of conceiving of the contemporary, of synchrony'.[73] To think of time within the experience of the special moment is to accept disjunction, the rupture in normal synchronic logic of events and their meaning. This ultimately concerns a continual striving for *justice*. Derrida was convinced that the spirit of Marxism, particularly in its messianicity, that is, its promise of a decisive rupture in historical events towards greater liberation, could not be as easily superseded as the champions of liberalism might want to suggest. That time is 'out of joint' means that that which confronts people as possibility is the unforeseen, the unpredictable. It appears more in the shape of a dream than a programme of events. More precisely, it refers to the importance of 'the impossible'. The impossible signifies both a

---

[72] These observations of the link between deconstruction and spectrology are influenced largely by Stuart Sim. See Sim, *Derrida and the End of History*.

[73] Jacques Derrida, 'The Spirit of the Revolution' in *For What Tomorrow: A Dialogue*, ed. Jacques Derrida and Elisabeth Roudinesco, trans. Jeff Fort (Stanford: Stanford University Press, 2004), p. 80.

transgression of the limit of language and meaning, but also, in more overtly messianic terms, the dream of the impossible event – he who comes: the '*arrivant*'.[74]

Long before *Specters of Marx* Derrida had developed the theme of 'the impossible' as a central tenet of deconstruction, following a close and critical reading of his contemporary, the Jewish philosopher Emmanuel Levinas, in *Writing and Difference*. While there is not space here to do justice to this influence, it is worth noting Derrida's interest in developing the centrality of the 'other' for Levinas' basis for ethics and the ultimate limit of ontology. Following Levinas, Derrida situates the alterity and other-ness of others as an 'ethical transcendence' that leaves the solitude and 'totalitarianism of the same'[75] behind in pursuit of the other. From reject-ing a Platonic obsession with the ego that speaks, Derrida moves to an ethics of welcoming the other. This is fundamental to an affirmation of politics as an impossible movement. It upsets, in other words, the normal perception of political possibility; the other is not simply outside of the self, but points to the possibility of an *infinitely other*, that which 'cannot be bound by a concept, cannot be thought on the basis of a horizon'.[76] In the pursuit of *justice*, therefore, in place of the hegemony of a given political idea, one must expect 'eruptions and surprises'. We must expect that which is literally unreasonable because incongruous with the present, the same: 'It is *the* encounter, the only way out, the only adventuring outside oneself toward the unforseeably-other. *Without hope of return*'.[77]

How might Derrida's work shed further light on an apocalyptic appraisal of practices of hope? Derrida is concerned with a primal movement of anticipating an absolute other. He understands political practices according to their enunciation of the unforeseen. For the sake of my argument the importance of this concept is in generating credibility for political desires (such as absolute justice or absolute truth) as in some very practical sense impossible, unachievable, and for that reason *only*, worthy of striving. The revolutionary potential of desire introduced by Deleuze and Guattari therefore returns with both Derrida and Negri as the possibility of transforming lived time into time of endless potential. The impossible comes from a desire to deconstruct the 'heritage' of: 'such concepts as

---

[74] Derrida, *Specters of Marx*, p. 65, italics in the original.

[75] *Ibid.* p. 91.

[76] Derrida, *Writing and Difference*, trans. Alan Bass (London: Routledge, 1978), p. 95.

[77] *Ibid.*, italics in the original.

"possibility", "power", "impossibility" and so on'.[78] This approach does not shy away from Negri's challenge to contrast the time of collective power with that of command time. This movement towards the impossible is *not*, as Caputo notes, an affirmation of 'impossible things' and projects, but rather '*the* impossible *simpliciter*' which is inforseeable and 'tout autre'.[79] What should be sought treads a precarious line between ineffability and the very vocal and expressible desires that emanate from revolutionary desire of *every* attempt to act with justice.

The result of this tension, Derrida believed, was a refusal to translate revolutionary desire – as desire for the impossible – into a programme:

> There is no ethical responsibility, no decision worthy of the name, that is not, in its essence, revolutionary, that is not in a relation of rupture with a system of dominant norms, or even with the very idea of a norm, and therefore of a knowledge of the norm that would dictate or program the decision. All responsibility is revolutionary, since it seeks to do the impossible, to interrupt the order of things on the basis of nonprogrammable events. A revolution cannot be programmed.[80]

Derrida's thought thus contributes to the notion that acts of resistance display a visionary sense of that which is 'to come' – an apocalyptic impulse – without requiring a definition of what that future looks like, and certainly without tying it to religious tradition. His idea of disjunction and the 'special moment' also opens up the possibilities of thinking through a politics of uncertainty. It is this concept which allows a deeper exploration of an apocalyptic theology that, to go back to Barth's original riddle, *sees what it does not see*. Derrida is able to express the impossible dream as a transformation of living-time. This is because he expresses an agonistic notion of the future as being not a 'future-present' but as something perpetually out of reach. It produces, like death, the effect of interminable non-occurrence.[81]

The latter concern with death itself as a form of impossibility relates to a principal influence on Derrida, his contemporary Maurice Blanchot. Blanchot had written extensively on the paradoxical nature of writing

---

[78] Derrida in Giovanna Borradori, *Philosophy in a Time of Terror: Dialogues with Jürgen Habermas and Jacques Derrida* (London: University of Chicago Press, 2003), p. 120.

[79] Caputo, *Prayers and Tears*, p. 23.

[80] Jacques Derrida and Elizabeth Roudinesco, *For What Tomorrow: A Dialogue*, trans. Jeff Fort (Stanford: Stanford University Press, 2004), p. 83.

[81] Caputo, *Prayers and Tears*, pp. 77–78.

itself. More specifically it was writing's exteriority to, and passivity in the face of, the reality of experience. What fascinated Blanchot in particular was the proximity of this impossibility of writing to the notion of the disaster. In *The Writing of the Disaster* death is understood as the very thing that can never be experienced or overcome. It is never cheated (through murder, or suicide) or understood. But disaster also represents something not dissimilar to my analysis of crisis: namely, the unease caused by the unpredictability of the event, its appearance as untimely and uninvited. There is a sense in which, in response to disaster, fatalist political thought has continually sought to silence the unpredictable, and to install in its place a false fantasy of the end.

Derrida also inherits an aversion to the desire for completeness and metaphysical unity in history. In distinction to Heidegger's treatment of death and dying, both Derrida and Blanchot's attitudes towards the Disaster lends itself to my critique of the imagination of the future politically and socially. Blanchot identified the Disaster as that which never comes but which frames the world in which we live, which '*takes care of everything*'.[82] It renders the future of dreams meaningless because 'there is no future for the disaster, just as there is no time or space for its accomplishment.'[83] The darkness of this idea is only tempered when we connect it to Blanchot's – and Derrida's – wider concern with the messianic. The ethic that emerges out of *The Writing of the Disaster* is for never giving up, for never being allowed to say, 'it is accomplished'. It therefore becomes a credo for ceaseless striving, an apocalyptic refusal of death's finality.

What deconstruction offers to my argument is therefore a critique of the Western metaphysical reflex of privileging crises that are treatable, domesticated or else endlessly *deferred*. This stands in contrast to acknowledging that crisis is more akin to Blanchot's disaster, that is, which is abstract and all-consuming. In his essay 'Economies de la crises' Derrida identifies this abstract threat as threatening the very formation of desire, which, I believe, must include one's Utopian desires, or the desire for the new. Thus, when 'the crisis' is transformed into domesticated 'crises' the end is deferred and fragmented into myriad fantasies of crisis management:

> The 'representation' of crisis and the rhetoric it organizes always have at least this purpose: to determine, in order to limit it, a more serious and more formless threat but that holds some desire in suspense: a threat to

---

[82] Maurice Blanchot, *The Writing of the Disaster*, new edn, trans. Ann Smock (Lincoln: University of Nebraska Press, 1995), p. 3, italics in the original.

[83] *Ibid.* p. 17.

desire. By determining it as crisis, one tames it, domesticates it, neutralizes it – in short, one *economizes* it. One appropriates the Thing, the unthinkable becomes the unknown to be known, one begins to give it form, to inform, master, calculate, program.[84]

Rather than framing an ethical imperative, Derrida and Blanchot's expressions seem more like arguments for the absence of reasons to *cease* striving, or hoping, or seeing apocalyptically, through an apocalyptic lens. Only in this sense can we read the politics of uncertainty, or the writing of disaster, as a challenge to a politics of fatalism. When Blanchot talks of the hypothesis of a Messiah who has 'come again', it is to postulate that he would have to be asked, when recognized, 'when will you come?'[85] Derrida concurs that to answer 'now' would be unsatisfactory, for the power of the messianic comes not in the actual return but in the power of its anticipation. It is the promise of *I will come* that has gripped apocalyptic audiences since its first enunciation. This is precisely the manner in which, in *Specters of Marx*, Derrida turns the power of expectation into an ethical imperative not to transform political desire into law. Whether it emanates from Christian eschatology or Marxist teleology, what should haunt all those who still hold on to a dream of democracy and a future for justice is the notion that 'its formal structure of promise exceeds them or precedes them. [. . .] What remains as undeconstructible as the possibility itself of deconstruction is, perhaps, a certain experience of the emancipatory promise; it is perhaps even the formality of a structural messianism.'[86]

How far does this consideration take me from my original concern with the rhetoric of crisis and the cultural obsessions with endist discourses? Has anything been resolved? A consequence of inviting Derrida to be my guide has been to invite the controversy he produces by rejecting the very notion of 'horizons' of possibility in the formation of political desire. The question now must be, what will distinguish the apocalyptic styles, the modes of anticipation, so far critiqued as inauthentic, paralysing, individualist or enthralled by capital, from a 'true' messianic impulse. What sense is given to political hope if it is simply 'awaiting without horizon of the wait, awaiting what one does not expect yet or any longer'?[87] Can this waiting really resemble

---

[84] Derrida, 'Economies de la Crises' quoted in Mark Wigley, *The Architecture of Deconstruction: Derrida's Haunt* (Massachusetts: MIT Press, 1995), p. 182, italics in the original.

[85] Caputo, *Prayers and Tears*, p. 79.

[86] Derrida, *Specters of Marx*, p. 59.

[87] *Ibid.* p. 65.

a hope that, phenomenologically speaking, at least, seems to require an object or a ground, in other words some *thing* to hope *for*? As James K. A. Smith argues, Derrida's position would be roundly rebuffed by Husserl, to whom Derrida is indebted for precisely this assumption – that 'any mode of intentional consciousness, such as hope, cannot escape the conditions of horizonality'.[88] Deconstruction attacks not only the false fantasies of 'certain' historic *projection*, it is also able to confront the depoliticizing inertia of an obsession with the stasis of the *present*. It does this by refusing the present moment its isolation and totalization against the flux of history. As Graham Ward puts it,

> the concept of logocentrism is a magnification of modernity's obsession with the purity of the present, the isolation of the moment, the now, the instantaneous, the immediate. As such, the critique of logocentrism takes the form of attention to the mediated, the time lag of *re*presentation, that which is un*present*able. Logocentrism is implicated in a certain metaphysics, mathematics, and technology of time.[89]

Derrida's exploration of anachronous time, time out of joint, therefore represents more than just an 'empty' hope. It can even be seen to supplement a radical eschatological notion of hope. Derrida's use of the term 'spectrality' to denote the undecidability between body and spirit in the realm of ideas is intimately bound up with his notion of the pursuit of some absolute other, some transcendent goal, in very material practices. It asserts both the presence of an ideal, the invisible 'spectre', and its craving to take physical form:

> for there to be a ghost, there must be a return to the body, but to a body that is more abstract than ever. The spectrogenic process corresponds to a paradoxical *incorporation*. Once ideas or thoughts (*Gedanke*) are detached from the substratum, one engenders some ghost by *giving them a body*.[90]

There is not room to fully explore the complexity of this notion of incorporation. We can at least now appreciate how Derrida's messianism goes

---

[88] James K. A. Smith, 'Determined Hope: A Phenomenology of Christian Expectation' in *The Future of Hope*, ed. Volf and Katerberg, pp. 200–227 (p. 223).

[89] Graham Ward, 'Questioning God' in *Questioning God*, ed. John D. Caputo, Mark Dooley and Michael J. Scanlon (Bloomington: Indiana University Press, 2001), p. 284, italics in the original).

[90] Derrida, *Specters of Marx*, p. 126, italics in the original.

some way to affirming the refusal to *end* a state of tension and political struggle. The act of striving therefore bears a function similar to the imperative, in St Paul, to carry on living 'as though', but to *carry on living* nevertheless. What is essentially affirmed is the possibility of opening up the practice of political hope to the impulse to go beyond mere possibility, mere 'normal time', or the time of fear. Derrida's own version of apocalyptic time therefore fills, it seems, a conspicuous gap in most mainstream political commentaries on the apocalyptic function of apocalypse. That is, he questions the presumption that apocalypse *only* satisfies a vacuum in the imagination of an oppressed people. I have already demonstrated how identifying apocalyptic desire as the fruits of alienation or oppression is as open to interpretations by white supremacists as it is to an oppressed minority. What Derrida introduces is the apocalyptic emphasis on the ability to *go on* announcing in spite of this struggle. He affirms the possibility of further imaginations, of inviting myriad messages of a revealed reality just as John of Patmos invites. To take seriously the question of *announcement* means understanding a general problematic in language and logocentrism. As 'people of the word' humans inherit the enlightenment desire to clarify and illuminate, to reveal and invite illumination. Just as the original apocalyptic texts signified the revelation of divine mysteries, secular apocalyptic desire represents a seeing or *rending the veil.*

That same fascination is at the root of my enquiry, particularly in relation to what 'apocalypticists' are attempting to achieve, what the saying, or announcing, of it *does* to society:

> what effect do these noble, gentile [*gentils*] prophets or eloquent visionaries want to produce? With a view to what immediate or postponed [*ajourné*] benefit? What do they do, what do we do in saying this? For whom do we seduce or subjugate, intimidate or cause to enjoy, to come?[91]

For Derrida there is something primal to Western thought in John's act as the *messenger*, this role of being the favoured dispatcher of revelation and denouncing the 'false' ones, the 'impostor apostles'.[92] We can already see a shifting trend in world politics in the way apocalypticism contests acts of 'veiling' and 'unveiling', the true function of its *address* and its *announcement* to the world. Northcott's argument has to this effect already expressed the irony of premillennialism. For this version of 'living-in-the-end-times'

---

[91] Derrida, 'Apocalyptic Tone', pp. 82–83.
[92] *Ibid.* p. 89.

apocalyptic at the heart of the evangelizing, messianic tone of the Project for a New American Century is a fundamental *veiling*, not an *unveiling*, of the true nature of its imperial ambition.[93] But who, in this case, if anyone, holds the key to the function of eschatological promise? Who commands our apocalyptic attention? As Derrida's 'spectrology' recommends, we would do well to look for a multiplicity of voices, unlocking various doors and opening a number of discourses: 'this demystification . . . [unveiling] is interminable, because no one can exhaust the overdeterminations and the indeterminations of the apocalyptic stratagems'.[94]

Derrida's challenge to hear myriad voices of an experimental and imaginative political and 'apocalyptic' style has, I shall argue, been taken up through a variety of Utopian political practices. These are acts that point towards a world turned upside down, in which politics reveals rather than veils. They describe a multitude united in diversity, in which bodies transgress the boundaries of power; all point towards the apocalyptic, visionary enunciation of the new and the unforeseen. Gathering the evidence of contemporary formulations of the apocalyptic should, then, without attempting to monopolize the meaning of apocalyptic *per se*, point us to an alternative style of political engagement. This style is one that contests an accepted, domesticated vision of 'what is to come'. Derrida's interest in the role of *announcing* adds to this. For he affirms the possibility that an apocalyptic style favours the visionary predictions of a completely different global order. To announce 'the new' is to flood the production of cultural imagination. It takes full advantage of the post-modern fragmentation and diversifications of discourses and 'truths' against the homogenous voice of authority and tradition:

> by its very tone, the mixing of voices, genres, and the breakdown [*le détraquement*] of destinations, apocalyptic discourse can also dismantle the dominant contract or concordat. It is a challenge to the established admissibility of messages and to the enforcement or the maintenance of order [*la police*] of the destination, in short to the postal regulations [*la police postal*] or to the monopoly of the posts.[95]

Eschatology can thus rightly be seen as the dimension of theological imagination that contests (and is contested) an ideological monopoly over the imagination of the end. But it is the *apocalyptic* imagination that opens

---

[93] Northcott, *An Angel*, p. 75.
[94] Derrida, 'Apocalyptic Tone', p. 89.
[95] *Ibid.* p. 89, italics in the original.

up the anarchic, untameable world of prophecy and visions that ideology cannot contain. The very idea of the incarnation of this 'affirmative' formulation of St John's 'Come' is, as Derrida writes, an event whose power precedes all discussion of place (where it came from) and content (*exactly* what it announces, in what time-scale, etc.).

Conclusion

In this chapter I have tried to show that an exploration of much more than Rahner's appreciation of the 'undeniable poetic force' of apocalyptic discourse is needed in order to do justice to this complex theological concept. Indeed, Sauter asks (whether rhetorically or not) whether, in the light of Rahner's apocalypse/eschatology distinction, 'one might ask if it is true that Christianity has no need for visions'.[96] We can see at very least that there is a certain contemporaneity to this question, and an element of ambiguity on the position of Christian theology's contribution to a politics of Utopian imagination. Whether it is invited or not, apocalypse appears, in the narrative imagination, as a potent and unavoidable current of theological and political reflection on historical crises and the anticipation of the future. It consequently seeks creative responses on the part of the hopers themselves, that is, the *hearers* and not just the bearers of the apocalyptic promise.

How has deconstruction contributed to an understanding of practices hope? Derrida increases our creative understanding of apocalyptic time. He does this by illuminating what it means to critique a politics of fear through an affirmation and imagination of the new. Even more powerful than the image of the wandering prophet, the apocalyptic messenger, coming *unannounced*, represents the collapse of the legitimacy of the voice of authority. It therefore points towards practices that open the path towards the impossible. It articulates political resistance and protest as Utopian imagination. Apocalyptic time also overcomes the theological problem of false, secularized eschatology, that fantasy of an eternal ending. It does this by returning to an original paradox that was found to lie at the heart of St Paul's eschatology. That paradox is a form of transformation of social engagement itself that acts *as if* what is to come also *is*.

I have thus tried in this chapter to make clearer an important distinction between two understandings of apocalyptic belief. The distinction, that is, between a fantastic apocalyptic vision of inevitable catastrophe on the one

---

[96] Sauter, *What Dare We Hope?*, p. 104.

hand, typical of premillennial apocalyptic faith and the spirit of 'war with
no end' implicit to the war on terror. And on the other, the imaginative
apocalyptic desire that is witnessed as the transformation of myriad political
practices. The latter fulfils the contemporary meaning of the time of opportunity and rupture so favoured by political theorists like Negri, *kairòs* time.
And through Derrida's recommendation of welcoming many different
apocalyptic 'voices' that announce the new, we can fully appreciate how
apocalypse may signify, as its etymology suggests, an opening and unveiling
as opposed to a veiling and foreclosing. Rather than holding fast to the
idea that apocalypse represents the revelation of an unambiguous message
and destiny for the world, we can instead affirm an attitude of openness to
the future: an active faith that liberation is *yet to come*. By exploring the
theme of this 'to come', the emphasis has been on the need to define
a character of living both without controlling any hold on the future – a
temporal *renouncement* – yet with a visionary confidence in its conclusion –
a temporal *affirmation*. Blanchot put it well by suggesting that what we desire
in *the new* is a kind of retrospective nostalgia for what is beyond our wildest
imagination:

> The new, because it cannot take its place in history, is also that which is
> most ancient: an unhistorical occurrence to which we are called upon to
> answer as if it were the impossible, the invisible – that which has always
> long since disappeared beneath ruins. [. . .] How could we know that we
> are forerunners, if the message which ought to make us messengers is
> ahead of us by an eternity, condemning us to be eternally tardy?[97]

For Derrida, too, what compels about the expectation of a Messiah
whose essence is the promise itself of coming is that the waiting, and not the
arrival, transforms life: 'one does not make the other come, one lets it come
by preparing for its coming.'[98]

I have therefore gone beyond both Agamben and Rahner's obsession
with erasing the prophetic role of visions from the permissibility of eschatological assertions. In doing so I am suggesting that in visions, too, an amount
of blindness is necessary. As Caputo puts it,

> messianic time is through and through a time of hope and faith and
> blindness, of the passion of a blind faith. It does not engage, does not get

---

[97] Blanchot, *The Writing of the Disaster*, p. 37.
[98] Derrida, quoted in Caputo, *Prayers and Tears*, p. 76.

in gear, until one is lost, destinerrant, having been divested of the guiding light of a future present. The secret, *sans vision, sans vérité,* impassions.[99]

Resurrecting ghosts of a past future, tampering with the 'postal regulations'[100] and the authority of received messages, the received and sanctioned 'truth' about the future – these are tools that are needed to hear, fighting against the ticking of imperial, fearful and paralysing time, with the clamour of apocalyptic time(s) and the promise of that which is 'to come'. It is a practice of the future in its refusal of the 'time' of death and acquiescence. It is the sound of *imaginary* and not *fantastic* deferral, the living *as if* but *not quite yet.*

---

[99] *Ibid.* p. 92, italics in the original.
[100] Derrida, 'Apocalyptic Tone', p. 89. See also *The Post Card* (Chicago: University of Chicago Press, 1987), translator's glossary, p. xxvi.

Reflections on Part II

I have tried to outline some of the conceptual resources that offer alternative philosophies of the future to those assumed by a politics of fear explored in Part I. In place of a state of endlessness, paranoia and inertia towards the future, this section has sought to recover the *imaginative* engagement with the future through the rich conceptual resources of Utopian, eschatological and apocalyptic beliefs. By crossing the disciplines of politics and theology we can appreciate fully how human cultures have continuously experimented with the notion of hope in 'another world', a reality defined by its radical otherness to the present one. Hope, seen through the concepts here explored, appears as the refusal of an ideology of fear, closure and a philosophy of '*there is no alternative*'.

The way is open, then, to explore what evidence there is for contemporary practices that experiment precisely with this sense of openness towards the future, through acts of resistance and protest. For I do not wish to give the impression of restricting analysis to purely symbolic and imaginative acts. We are still essentially speaking of the *movement of people*. Utopian, eschatological and apocalyptic beliefs are not monopolized by any confessional faiths, and are frequently shared across many boundaries. If I have relied upon Christian and largely Western philosophical resources it is, as I have already stated, because it is often from those very traditions that the perverted desires of endless war, capitalism and depoliticization draw. I have thus sought to do justice at very least to the complexity of Utopian, eschatological and apocalyptic beliefs in order to liberate their more radical potential. This potential should reveal itself in our richer appreciation of experiments in hope.

Part III

Experiments in Hope

No weight could be heavier to bear than the possibility that everything we want is possible [. . .]. Nothing could be more tragic, and more ridiculous, than to live out a whole life in reach of heaven without ever stretching out your arms.

CrimethInc. Workers Collective[1]

The following chapters are, in essence, a search for active responses to those conditions outlined in Part I with the help of those theoretical tools unearthed in Part II. Actions that challenge an ideology of fear and fatalism may open out and give life to the concepts, beliefs and traditions about the future that I have outlined. The following analysis does not form an overview of the most popular or effective acts of protest today. Instead, acts of resistance have been specifically chosen for their ability to open up questions about the nature of political hope as a response to the depoliticizing trend of a politics of fear.

---

[1] CrimethInc. Workers Collective, *Days of Love, Nights of War: Crimethink For Beginners* (2001), pp. 15–16, my emphasis.

Chapter 7

The Performance of Dissent

Introduction

A commentator on the events of May 1968 in Paris once wrote that 'the first stage of an uprising [. . .], of any revolution, is always theatrical'.[1] Appraisals of political performance or art often look to those creative 'precedent' moments before popular uprisings: periods or events able to capture, quicken or mirror key shifts in the public domain. Public street performances are a historically powerful example of this. They have frequently been at the forefront of popular critique and practical resistance to the social effects of fear. Whether that fear be a product of the dominant discourses of state or of church, it is often the parodying of power that signals an emergent counter-discourse. The task of this chapter is not only to acknowledge this historic legacy, but to address the very concept of the imagination as a political tool of resistance. It is thus a search for acts of resistance as examples of the Utopian imagination's ability to repoliticize.

The policing of spatiality, location, participation and representation are all features of a politics of fear. They are also both represented and contested through political performance. The often austere historical legacy of this ranges from Agit-Prop revolutionary parades and artwork of communist states to the immaculately orchestrated mass rallies and parades of Hitler's Nazi Party in Nuremburg in 1934. In both instances ideology had required a command of performance techniques to become a truly public discourse. What they both show, nevertheless, is that to explore acts of creative resistance is to recognize the value of focusing on discourse as more than just speaking. It means asking: what resources emerge out of the *creative* and *performative* elements of protest that transcend a politics of fear? What performances promise the radically new, and in so doing bear seeds

---

[1] Jean-Jacques Lebel, 'Notes on Political Street Theatre, Paris: 1968, 1969' in *Radical Street Performance: An International Anthology*, ed. Jan Cohen-Cruz (London: Routledge, 1998), pp. 179–184 (p. 180).

of an apocalyptic desire, of a rejection of the present order through imagination of the *to come?*

I begin to answer these questions by explaining in a little more depth the implications of a discursive element to practices of hope. A theoretical foundation laid by James Scott and Michel Foucault is central. I am then able to refer to two broad approaches to political performance. The first is an exploration of the enactment of Utopian imagination through carnival protest. The second represents its reverse – the imaginative reflection of a *dystopian* present.

Discourse and protest

Key moments in the history of protest have demonstrated the need to blur often polarized distinctions between discursive and non-discursive resistance, or, to put it crudely, between *expression* and *action*. Roland Bleiker, for example, uses the example of the role of poetry in the popular revolution in East Germany. The communist regime had represented to many people a systematic attempt to suffocate discursive space, or the places of free expression – literature, the arts, media critique and so on. In such an environment 'discursive transgression' arguably became a precondition to more explicitly revolutionary demands. And in Bleiker's view it ultimately contributed to the collapse of the regime in 1989. Poets based in Prenzlauer Berg found expression, movement and popular identity through their work. Through a subversion of the propaganda of political dualism they effectively challenged a persistent mentality that one is 'either with us or against us' dominant in cold war propaganda.[2] The function of poetry here is an opportunity to widen our perception of what is meant by political resistance to include the background production of the imagination of alternatives. Poetry

> generates more questions, creates ambivalence and doubt, and in doing so it comes to terms with the death of God, makes room for a more tolerant politics, recognises that society is oppressive and closed if all major questions either have an answer or are considered irrational, absurd, taboo.[3]

---

[2] Roland Bleiker, *Popular Dissent, Human Agency and Global Politics* (Cambridge: Cambridge University Press, 2000), p. 252.
[3] *Ibid.* p. 45.

A more general question about practices of resistance thus presents itself to a culture imbued by a politics of fear. How do social and political acts, no longer guaranteed space in the depoliticized public sphere, subvert ideological closure? We can learn much by beginning with James C. Scott's concept of the hidden transcript. Scott's theory takes up Foucault's appreciation of discourses that, while ignored by the 'dominant discourses' of history, are pushed to the fringes of society. It is for this reason a powerfully descriptive tool, on behalf of the subordinated, of 'weapons of the weak'. Scott acknowledges an underside to relations of power that mimics the subtleties of dramatic form. There is a 'dramaturgy of power'[4] in which not all is spoken out loud, or takes centre stage. Within the nuances of this 'infrapolitics'[5] the weak contest their status through the performance of both 'backstage' and 'on-stage' discourse. Both dominant and subservient 'social actors' develop masks in their everyday speech and action. Official slavery affords only the most obvious illustrations (and forms the backbone of much of Scott's research). The exaggerated obedience of the slave to gain trust from his master plays the game of power relations as the dominant wish it to be played. But neither are fooled that what occurs on the surface is equal to what goes on behind the masks. The oppressed find sites where, either individually or collectively, the mask can be removed and a truer discourse can be fostered, whether it is servants' quarters, working-class environments or spaces of confinement such as prisons.

How might this relate to the subversion of a politics of fear? Scott is motivated by dissatisfaction with popular understandings of domination. To this effect he provides a critique of the notion that fear operates as a top-down control mechanism. He demands a more nuanced appreciation of the relationship between ideology and agency. Looking only at the 'public transcript' ignores processes of deception and disguise and the relation between hidden discourses and acts of open rebellion. Political dissent has, in other words, a long history of finding a lasting breathing space before it becomes crushed. In the creative command of public spaces for artistic and theatrical performance, the imagination can be captured in ways that avert sanctioned propaganda of the public transcript. This capture is likely to manifest itself first in discourse, such as conversations between oppressed parties naming their abuses and imagining retribution. The significance of the hidden transcript is not that it replaces physical resistance or retribution, but that it enables a challenge to the dominant ideology without requiring

---

4 *Ibid.* p. 50.
5 Scott, *Domination and the Arts of Resistance*, p. 19.

a structure. What both Bleiker and Scott's analyses reveal is that the potential for 'creative resistance' to shed light on practices that contest a politics of fear is closely related to an appreciation of protest that has as much to do with resistant speech and imaginary representation as it does with physical protest. The legacy of thinkers like Foucault through this idea of subversive 'backstage' transcript, and thus to political artistic expression in particular, introduces an important concept for practices of hope today: the 'lyricism' of resistance.[6] Foucault's ideas renewed an interest in the exclusionary structures of language. But he was also concerned to show the ability for language to subvert dominant discourses and to contain a hidden, unpredictable element, a resistant discourse. Turning more specifically to the phenomenon of the art of the insane, Foucault also tried to identify resistance as a kind of *reversal* of dominant discourse, something we can identify within the scheme of a politics of fear. In *Madness and Civilisation*, for example, Foucault describes the history of a discourse that becomes polarized into reason and unreason. It does not appear in the manner of victory for one over the death of another, but the *transformation* of unreason and madness, through confinement, into a voice on the fringes.[7] It is these voices that contest the 'scientific gaze' of reason, and declare the sovereignty of madness through lyric fantasies. Similarly we might say that not only 'political activists', however that term might be interpreted, engender popular resistance. We must look also to the poets, *broadly* conceived: those that speak with the 'untamed, imperious being of words'.[8] Those who can speak in detachment from their conformity to the 'order of things'. Like the visions of the madman, the artist and the poet represent the untying of 'historical knots'. They are, as David Toole has written in commenting upon Foucault's legacy to a 'counter history' of protest, the 'last line of defence'[9] in the hegemonic world of reason as ideological closure. Could the same importance be attached to contemporary artistic expressions that attempt to challenge an accepted order and style of living? On the one hand, Foucault's analysis of language as *excluder* reminds us that resistance is not the opposite of power, and neither is it ever free from power. A discourse of resistance will therefore never emerge as something spoken that is *wholly* new or detached from a discourse of domination. But he also re-emphasizes

---

[6] Toole, *Waiting for Godot*, pp. 129–165.

[7] See Michel Foucault, *Madness and Civilization: A History of Insanity in the Age of Reason*, trans. Richard Howard (London: Routledge, 1971).

[8] Michel Foucault, *The Order of Things: An Archaeology of the Human Sciences*, trans. from the French (London: Tavistock/Routledge, 1970), p. 300.

[9] Toole, *Waiting for Godot*, p. 165.

the anarchic nature of 'epistemic' change. Discourse is capable of taking sudden twists, catching us by surprise and, though caught in the interstices of power, is liable to undermine it. Could the sense of hope that is expressed in the desire for 'the new' in fact be an affirmation that these power relations lie permanently at risk of having the rug pulled from underneath them? Could their monopoly over cultural discourse be suspended, even momentarily?

Performing Utopia

The preceding analysis could be applied to many different sites of political creation. One that lends itself directly to a critique of a politics of fear, however, is the practice of the Utopian imagination through the legacy of the *carnivalesque*, to use a well-known Bakhtinian term. Traditionally the carnival is the site where dangerous discourse, as Scott puts it, attempts to make a 'foray into the public transcript'. It is 'the occasion for recrimination from subordinate groups, presumably because normal power relations operate to silence *them*'.[10] In the 1960s Mikhail Bakhtin had made popular the idea that spatial and public practices such as 'ritual laughter' or 'popular-festive forms' of folk and carnival culture were simply persistent examples of the tactics of the fearless, expressions of a boundless hope of dispossessed classes. Medieval celebrations linked with the Mardi Gras carnival, the Festival of Fools or harvest and spring festivals often became the opportunity for performing narratives in which social roles were reversed. Rules of etiquette were replaced with a glorification of crude bodily functions and the cycles of nature, where kings become slaves, blood turned into wine, women beat their husbands and acts of murder turned into merry banquets.[11] As 'Utopian critique' this carnivalesque system of fearless and festive images was, thinks Bakhtin, a way of affirming the 'immortal, indestructible character' of ordinary people by the relativization of the established order and established truth itself. The indestructibility of natural cycles were glorified, and values and rules of established ones were mocked. In the process, the cause of ordinary people was granted Utopian fervour by its association with inexorable time, 'time which kills and gives birth, which allows nothing old to be perpetuated and never cease to

---

[10] Scott, *Domination and the Arts of Resistance*, p. 174, italics in the original.

[11] Michael Bakhtin, *Rabelais and His World*, trans. Hélène Iswolsky (Bloomington: Indiana University Press, 1984), p. 211.

generate the new and the youthful'.[12] If these images genuinely 'absorbed the new hopes and thoughts of the people'[13] then carnivalesque practices confirm what Bloch had long argued about ritualistic Utopian activity. Practices that affirmed the intrinsically transcendent (in the sense of reaching *beyond*) human desire for the 'not yet' could already claim a victory for the function of hope: by overcoming the passivity of fear. In Bakhtin's words:[14]

> Popular-festive forms look into the future. They present the victory of this future, of the golden age, over the past. The victory of the future is ensured by the people's immortality. The birth of the new, of the greater and the better, is as indispensable and as inevitable as the death of the old. The one is transferred to the other, the better turns the worse into ridicule and kills it. In the whole of the world and of the people there is no room for fear.[15]

In the institution of popular creative forms, in other words, the carnivalesque represents strategically thinking 'the new'. It is a tactic of disempowering the fearfulness so often desired by the powerful. More often than not this has been achieved through the use of humour and frivolity, a concerted campaign against fatalism and despair. In both Rabelais' and Bakhtin's times (Renaissance France and Stalinist Russia, respectively), this occurred specifically in response to a 'cosmic terror' that was used to subdue the population. Folk laughter represented 'the defeat of fear presented in a droll and monstrous form, the symbols of power and violence turned inside out, [. . .]. All that was terrifying becomes grotesque [. . .]. The people play with terror and laugh at it; the awesome becomes a "comic monster".'[16] And because carnival has frequently given voice to visions and enactments of a world turned upside down, with equalities restored and injustices redressed, they have been widely described as performances of Utopia. Even if for a fleeting moment, the carnivalesque can be seen to open up the capacity for political subjects to imagine and act out their desires for a better world.

If this celebration of laughter is truly at the heart of carnival as Utopian discourse, if it makes Rabelais' novel (a subject of Bakhtin's study) 'the

---

[12] *Ibid.* p. 211.
[13] *Ibid.* p. 211.
[14] Bloch, *The Principle of Hope*, vol. 1 (1986), p. 3.
[15] Bakhtin, *Rabelais and His World*, p. 256.
[16] *Ibid.* p. 91.

most fearless book in world literature',[17] how is it present today as both discourse and practice of resistance? In attempting to categorize the many
different functions, intentions and methods of contemporary 'radical street
performance', writer Jan Cohen Cruz's definition of what links these practices together are in line with Bakhtin's. They are 'acts that question or
reinvision ingrained social arrangements of power. [. . .] Radical street performance draws people who comprise a contested reality into what its
creators hope will be a changing script.'[18] Carnival remains as a discursive
tactic of confrontation with a discourse of fear primarily through its ability
to metaphorize, as Ricoeur would say, established notions of authority
and order. We can see this in the different spaces in which carnivalesque
theatre has inserted itself into the concept of political activism itself. The
changing shape of the direct action movement embraces the *theatrical,*
broadly conceived, as a new terrain of contestation. Descriptions of the
paradigmatic – but certainly not isolated – sites of such struggles, from
the anti-WTO protests in Seattle, 1999 to the G8 summit protests in
Gleneagles – have become unavoidably connected to their carnival roots.
What does this incursion of carnivalesque signify to the function of discursive resistance? The implicit, perhaps naively bold claim seems to be
that the imagination of ordinary people remains to be the unconquered
terrain of social power. As a group of samba band activists exemplary of this
philosophy, Rhythms of Resistance, have put it, the aim is to 'reject any false
opposition between militancy and creative forms of resistance'.[19] Their
successes in mobilizing groups of people during protest, providing a festive
element to potentially dangerous, aggressive stand-offs, and to making such
confrontations *enjoyable,* has been not only infectious to other resistance
groups around the world, but made them the target of intense police
surveillance. As John Jordan and Jennifer Whitney have put it,

> when the FBI identify Carnival Against Capital as a terrorist group, they
> expose their greatest fear, and perhaps their greatest weakness. [. . .]
> As they attempt to isolate, influence and infiltrate groups in a great effort
> to break these varied and diverse movements, our spontaneity, unpredict-
> ability and irresistibility are blossoming, scattering seeds of inspiration
> across cultures and continents. We learn to work together, we become

---

[17] *Ibid.* p. 39.
[18] Jan Cohen-Cruz, 'General Introduction' in *Radical Street Performance*, ed. Jan
Cohen-Cruz, pp. 1–6 (p. 1).
[19] Rhythms of Resistance, www.rhythms-of-resistance.org/spip/article.php3?id_
article=6.

better at being human, and we are able to live prefiguratively, in the most radical of all carnivals – a world which will not wait for the future, a world which embraces paradox, a world which contains many worlds.[20]

Or again, in the words of a participant in Quebec City's 'Carnival Against Capital' during the Free Trade Area of the Americas summit in April 2001: 'freed from the clutches of entertainment, the anti-capitalist movements have thrown it back into the streets, where it is liberated from commerce for everyone to enjoy once again.'[21] What these testimonies add to our analysis is thus a powerful reason to suppose that imaginative, creative resistance might also be the one that threatens the fabric of the 'culture of cynicism'. Another illustrative example is the anti G8 resistance that took place at the G8 summit in Gleneagles, Scotland.[22] As on many similar mobilizations, the protests featured the theatrical political collective known as the Clandestine Insurgent Rebel Clown Army (CIRCA). The clowns use 'tactical frivolity', humour and fluid, carnivalesque bodies in acts of civil disobedience. They use public demonstration as a principle of ridiculing the assumed 'order' of the system against which they protest. But once more we might see in all such performative protests the principle of rejecting the legitimacy (or at least seriousness) of the present at the same time as affirming the possibility of a radically altered future. As it is written on the clowns' website, 'We are **circa** because we are approximate and ambivalent, neither here nor there, but in the most powerful of all places, the place in-between order and chaos.'[23]

Performing dystopia

The performance of Utopia through carnival practices is not the only example of this reinscription of political space with the lyrical or discursive acts of the imagination. Other forms of political artistic representation openly critiques of this infectious rhetoric of frivolity and of turning the

---

[20] John Jordan and Jennifer Whitney, 'Resistance is the Secret of Joy' in *The New Internationalist*, no. 338 (September 2001), www.newint.org/issue338/secret.htm [accessed 21 March 2006].

[21] Notes from Nowhere Collective, *We Are Everywhere: The Irresistible Rise of Global Anti-Capitalism* (London: Verso, 2003), p. 177.

[22] See Stefan Skrimshire, 'Anti-G8 Resistance and the State of Exception' in *Shut Them Down! The G8, Gleneagles 2005 and the Movement of Movements*, ed. David Harvie et al (New York: Autonomedia, 2005).

[23] www.clownarmy.org/about/about.html [accessed 4 January 2008].

world upside down through expressions of political desire. They are wary of its aesthetic becoming an *an*aesthetic, a flight *from*, not *towards*, the political realm. A recent art installation in Hulme, Manchester is of particular interest in this respect, as it shares many of the hopes and tactics of street theatre and the carnivalesque, at the same time as representing its flip side. *This Is Camp X-Ray* was a 9-day long, fully functioning replica of the internment camp in Guantanamo Bay. Local volunteers acted as guards and prisoners. Its very location and context alone draw it into the sphere of my analysis. By means of this installation, the by then infamous Camp X-Ray internment camp appeared in a wasteland backyard of the Hulme/Moss Side border, the neighbourhood of one of the real camp detainees, Jamal al Harith.[24] It was not the teasing of public reactions to join in a shared joke, to desecrate popular traditional hierarchies with an alternative language. Nor was it a performance of Utopia intended to disempower the popular effects of a politics of fear. Every morning the raised American flag and national anthem declared itself to Hulme from the guarded watch-tower. A razor-wire perimeter fence stared at Jamal's Mancunian neighbours every day only as that: an internment camp, visibly subjecting its inmates to inhumanity and deprivation.

This kind of art represents a form of *hypervisible* theatre in its attempt to make real, make present and as an almost banal feature of someone's walk to work or school each morning, the latest iron fist of the war on terror. It was important, says Jai, that

> the people who came to the viewing saw prisoners arrive, saw them being processed and experienced that powerful, that horror . . . there's perhaps a role for art that hurts people in some respect . . . since the renaissance its been art's role in the west to redeem the white man's soul . . . what I'm doing, it's like redemption through confrontation with those fears.[25]

The suggestion appears to be that to address a politics of fear is to stare it in the face as much as to transcend its effects. As a political statement, the installation attempted (among other things) to remove geographical boundaries that create distance between people and a given political reality. This act of the capture of the imagination therefore addresses the depoliticizing nature of the war on terror. It also questions what, in general

---

[24] Who was subsequently released without charge, explanation or apology, for his detention.

[25] Jai Redman interviewed 2004.

terms, creative expression is able to *do* in response to the climate of permanent anxiety produced by the war on terror. Does it represent the presence
of American hegemony in our midst? Does it also attempt to reinsert
cultural texts or paradigms that otherwise only appear in academic critique?
If these suggestions ring true, they go someway to applying the critique of
modern sovereignty by Giorgio Agamben explored in Chapter 5.[26] For
Agamben, 'the camp' is a materialization of the state of exception, that
zone of absolute exclusion because of its utter indifference to the norms
ascribed to by any other concept of prison. The camp, writes Agamben, is
materialized whenever people are reduced to 'bare life', stripped of any
rights or values. It is 'a space in which power confronts nothing other than
pure biological life without any mediation'.[27] That may justifiably include,
as Agamben suggests, detention centres and 'zones d'attentes' where European governments have frequently herded refugee populations before
sending them back. Agamben insists that our task is to recognize the camp
'in all its metamorphoses'.[28] That would involve, for instance, interpreting
and communicating every step taken by authorities to suspend and exclude
the rights of civilians in the name of a transcendent, but invisible, paradigm
of security. It increasingly also involves identifying places in which dissent is
also stripped of its rights of engagement. Those sites in which, like the
terror suspect, the act of protest itself is seen as a kind of underclass activity,
subject to exclusion zones and permanent surveillance.

Dystopian performances such as *This Is Camp X-Ray* suggest that there is a
political imperative to manifest the sites of fear within a context of everyday
life. Not only our personal fears, but of the political construction of fear as
incarceration that is continually justified in the name of the war on terror.
This essentially public act therefore responds to the manipulation and
transformation of space that is a contested realm of the political itself.
Spatial practices of the imagination might yet represent, therefore, bearers
of hope through their capacity as persistent 'blind spots' in the war on
terror. They pose the possibility for a unique form of political agitation:
the ability to generate mirrors to every atrocity that is removed from tangi-
ble social consciousness. The ability to challenge sensational media or the
geographical boundaries that make Guantanamo Bay an *other* place, even
a dystopian no-place.

---

[26] Agamben, *Homo Sacer*, p. 20.
[27] Giorgio Agamben, *Means Without End: Notes on Politics*, trans. Vincenzo Binetti
and Cesare Casarino (Minneapolis: University of Minnesota Press, 2000), p. 41.
[28] *Ibid.* p. 45.

The performance of dystopia is a performative critique of the two-dimensional, 'filtered' and fleeting manner in which most political ideas are televised or otherwise mediated. It attempts to challenge a dominant mode of the mediation of political ideas. As a political *practice*, therefore, it comes from a more general tradition of manipulating space (that which is already socially 'integrated' and inscribed with social meanings) and meaning. Consider, for example, the practices of 'subvertising' or 'culture jamming', practices with roots that arguably go as far back as those of carnival. These are acts of altering or subverting existing public messages or official discourse in order to reveal an underlying truth or ideology contained within the message itself. In Saussurian terms we can say that by subvertising a Nike poster the sign's signifier is endowed with negative connotations that then become involved in the consumer's 'sensemaking cycle'.[29] This allows cultural choice to be influenced by political consequences rather than by the branded spectacle. This movement, the ability to draw upon the resources of both graffiti art and fine art, has political consequences. It presumes the explicitly political function of those 'weapons of the weak' described by Scott. Their ability to use existing power structures to their own advantage in a manner that also undermines those very structures. Graffiti that exploits the symbolic power of (ideologically) planned social spaces by hijacking its message, implicit or explicit, with an alternative one, is, to this extent, always political. It contests ownership of the direction of socially produced signs, whether they be billboards, buildings or the installation of art itself.

The rising popularity of stencil graffiti artist Robin Banksy bears testimony to this. In one of his old works, the words 'Designated Riot Zone' are stencilled across the steps of Nelson's column in Trafalgar Square in official typescript.[30] It mimics the disciplining of public spaces through the police imposition of 'designated protest zones' during demonstrations. By doing so it attempts to hijack the publicity of a social monument for a message believed (perhaps) to be a better reflector of social desires. This principle is, in the words of Kalle Lasn, the editor of *Adbusters* magazine, a major motor to the culture jamming movement. It can be called a form of 'political jujitsu', by which the 'momentum of the enemy'[31] is used to undermine its hold on public consciousness. For the French situationists this

---

[29] Dagny Nome, 'Promotional Culture: Seminar in Intercultural Management', *Copenhagen Business School*, www.anthrobase.com/Txt/N/Nome_D_01.htm [accessed 10 January 2006].

[30] Robin Banksy, *Wall and Piece* (London: Century, 2005).

[31] Kalle Lasn, quoted in Naomi Klein, *No Logo* (London: Flamingo, 1981), p. 281.

method was summed up in the term *détournement*. It meant an ability to subvert already existing power relations and the dependence of those relations
on a complex network of spatial symbols and branded signifiers.

Dystopian imagination aims at the heart of what I have attempted to
describe as an inherently *performative* and *spatial* aspect of acts of resistance.
It is what connects the otherwise distinct political practices of graffiti, adver-
tisement alteration and the kind of realist political performance that *This
Is Camp X-Ray* represents. Many will see them as performative critiques of
a hegemony that is inscribed into, and mapped onto, urban design. The
alteration of private and authoritarian messages, perhaps, therefore strive
to undermine, if not destroy, the perceived importance of certain cultural
practices. They can make a claim about the depoliticization of social
spaces precisely by bringing politics back into those spaces and making
them unavoidable. In Chapter 1 I claimed that contemporary neo-liberal
societies increasingly capitalize on the erosion of public spaces of interaction and debate by replacing them with spaces of consumption. Perhaps,
then, the incursion of the performance of politics, whether Utopian or
dystopian, is an attempt to reinsert the function of political imagination in
social practices. In a time of rapid spatial 'development', the implication
is that any space, whether developed or fallow, can become a space of contestation. It can reflect any reality between destitution and gratuitous
affluence. To turn a field into a mirror of a real internment camp is clearly
not a semiotic manipulation of a brand. But it might well manipulate the
public assumption, inscribed as much in empty space as in those filled with
corporate messages, that open spaces aren't *allowed* to do this within the
public transcript.

Conclusion

How do the creative acts of resistance just described function as a contestation of the *new* or an apocalyptic imagination, in opposition to a politics of
fear? It has never been my intention to argue for or against a particular style
of performative protest. The point, rather, is to demonstrate how different
forms of representation are able to attempt to manipulate public space and
bodies in order to confront the depoliticizing effects of fear. Another way of
putting it would be to ask how resistance is able to apply the form of imagination that can break ideological closure, that is able to repoliticize public
space and public imagination into a body that recreates its own world.
I have attempted this by recognizing the persistence of discursive dissent
not only in precedent moments of the imagination of revolt, but as an

integral part of *any* popular contestation of a dominant power. This is evident both in the micropractical tactics of the 'weak' and in the planned orchestration of political demonstration or artistic representation. It appears in the theatricality and creative use of open spaces on many recent public protests against the hegemony of governments, global capitalism or war.

Many acts within this spectrum might be argued to respond directly to the critique made earlier about the 'saturation' of social space by fear or the ubiquity of the social 'text' of permanent war. More importantly, it suggests some ways in which those faith traditions of future orientation mentioned earlier – Utopia, eschatology, and apocalypse – might become more politically engaged in this question of creativity, imagination, and discursive resistance. How might this be the case? The experience, if not the legacy, of practitioners of carnival protest appears to reclaim a sense of imaginative projection of 'another world'. This is as true of the imagination of a Utopian dreamworld as it is of a dystopian rejection of the legitimacy of the present order. And it is in precisely this sense that Jameson maintains a political interest in both the Utopian dreamworlds and dystopian night-mares that constitute the genre of science fiction texts. For even in the emerging tradition of the latter is contained a 'critical dystopia' (which Jameson also calls the 'negative cousin of the Utopian proper'[32]) whose function is to reveal both a warning of the type 'if this goes on . . .' and some affirmation of an originally Utopian human possibility which the dystopia militates against.[33] It is the power of the *expression* of both a Utopian and dystopian future that represents the collective means to liberate political expression from the ideological closure of fear. They do so, moreover, by reorienting a sense of future anticipation as central to political activism – as a site of contestation rather than an ideological given. Participating in the construction of a future is more than a purely symbolic act. It is a transfor-mative and participative process. It challenges, to return to Goodchild's analysis, a certain illusory faith in the future for one that invites the political activist to fill in the blanks. It is to return to the place of political praxis the desire for dreaming and, in Bloch's terminology, the power of the 'not yet'. Thus, against a fatalist reading of history as dialectically 'resolved' in favour of the dominant ideology (capitalism, passivity, fear) performative resis-tance expresses not only a Utopian impulse but an apocalyptic sensibility, in the spirit of perhaps Negri and certainly Derrida's reading of the concept.

---

[32] Jameson, *Archaeologies of the Future*, p. 198.
[33] Ibid. p. 198.

For it is precisely by 'mixing' with the messages and announcements of that which is 'to come', the anticipation of the future, and thus producing a thousand more 'prophets' than those sanctioned by the state, that creative, performative protest resists a culture of fear and fatalism.

This can happen negatively as well as positively. For example, politically motivated art can represent the aesthetic production of fear in order to mirror a social production of fear as *an*aesthetic. As performative, political art, the justification is that such an attempt is cathartic. That is, it emphasizes the transformation of a personal confrontation with politics. It is the critique of ideologically mediated political reality. In so doing, the performance of dystopia has revealed itself to be a lot closer to the interactional element of carnival than commonly thought. Both practices centre on the processes of personal transformation and represent a contestation of spatial power, the subversion of cultural norms. They have the ability to insert imaginary practices in the place of a depoliticized public sphere. The practices outlined above suggest, moreover, that in the pursuit of a culture of hope we need to look to temporal practices that do, in some sense, transcend the boundaries that are given by the 'public transcript'.

If it is *art*, politically conceived, that generates these questions and problematics into public discourse, then this chapter has also opened up a wider exploration of the relationship between discourse and practice itself. It has also consciously opened up opportunities for exploring the greater legacy of thinkers like Foucault and Scott. By blurring the line between *events* of resistance and the social conditions and concepts that make them possible, a wider understanding of the use of space and cultural discourse is introduced to the notion of political imagination.

The emphasis has so far been on the transformative, cathartic experience of creation and performance. However, the acts described in this chapter provoke a further question of participation and the transformation of being public that performative protest alone is unable to answer: namely, what potential do practices of hope generate for the transformation of *collective* movement? What practices of identity and the breaching of boundaries (ideological as well as physical) in public spaces draw out the resources for Utopian imagination and apocalyptic desire introduced above? It is to these concerns that I turn in the next chapter by exploring the mobilization of mass protest.

Chapter 8

How to Be Common

Introduction

This chapter explores the role of collective protest in generating resources for overcoming boundaries of public practice inscribed by a politics of fear. The need for this assessment arises naturally from my previous analysis, because the actions of the multitude are, like public performance and political art, performative, creative and invoke the power of the imagination. An anecdote about the Bread and Puppet Theatre, political artists and puppeteers led by Peter Schumann in America during the 1960s, illustrates the connection between these themes inimically: in which 'population puppets' were used as tools for public performances,

> [the 'population puppets'] never appear alone, but only as masses – grotesque and beautiful at the same time, painted in rough strokes of black on brown papier-mâché. They are vulnerable, targets of the powerful. Yet no matter how decimated – fields and fields of them scattered on the ground, detritus, direct and collateral damage – they always rise up again, protoplasmic, undefeatable. They have the strength and plasticity of the barely formed, the energy of potential. The masses.[1]

Though I use terms such as 'masses', 'people', 'multitude' and 'collectivities' interchangeably throughout this chapter, I am indebted to a recent revival of Spinoza's conception of the 'multitude', principally through thinkers such as Virno, Hardt and Negri. In distinction to European modernity's concept of 'The People', a reflection of Hobbesian sovereignty to bind the people to a singular will (the king's), the post-modern 'multitude' is described as 'a multiplicity, a plane of singularities, an open set of

---

[1] Marc Estrin, *Rehearsing with Gods: Photographs and Essays on the Bread and Puppet Theatre* (Vermont: Chelsea Green Publishing, 2003), p. 82.

relations, which is not homogeneous or identical with itself and bears
an indistinct, inclusive relation to those outside of it'.[2]

In what sense can the actions of a multitude be thought of as 'performance'? As Sidney Tarrow argues, social movements, requiring 'dynamic
symbols' specific to cultures, are forced to produce 'performances' today
because 'they are competing for public space with entertainment, news,
other movements, and the government's attempts to monopolise the
formation of opinion.'[3] The Italian political theorist Paolo Virno also makes
the observation that it is the performative element of these movements
that shatters previously demarcated realms of public and private, political
and aesthetic, action and reflection. In the foreword to *A Grammar of the
Multitude*, Sylvère Lotringer argues to this effect that it is not enough to talk
of a depoliticized public sphere. She asserts, rather, that

> politics itself has changed anyway. Labor, politics and intellect are no
> longer separate, actually they have become interchangeable, and this
> is what gives the multitude a semblance of de-politicization. Everything
> has become 'performative'. [. . .] They are all political because they all
> need an audience, a publicly organized space [. . .]. And they are all per-
> formance because they find in themselves, and not in any end product,
> their own fulfilment.[4]

Virno's critique of the performative element of public political acts provides this chapter with a grounding question. If the crisis of political action
is its subsumption into the 'performance' of capitalist production, what, by
contrast, might a 'nonservile virtuosity'[5] look like, and how might the *masses*
perform it? Who and which processes are controlling or directing the
'score' of public virtuosity? And which ideas of identity and community are
implicit in those processes? Answering these questions also allows me to
suggest how collective protest generates the kind of critique of a politics of
fear that I have identified in the categories of Utopian imagination and
apocalyptic desire. In other words, how does the mobilization of the multitude express itself as a future hope, of that which is 'to come' in opposition

---

[2] Hardt and Negri, *Empire*, p. 103. See also Paolo Virno, *A Grammar of the Multitude*,
trans. Isabella Bertoletti, James Cascaito and Andrea Casson (Los Angeles:
Semiotext(e), 2004), p. 21.

[3] Sidney Tarrow, *Social Movements and Contentious Politics*, 2nd edition (Cambridge:
Cambridge University Press, 1998), p. 107.

[4] Sylvère Lotringer, 'Foreword' in Virno, *A Grammar of the Multitude*, trans. Bertoletti,
Cascaito and Casson, p. 13.

[5] *Ibid.* p. 69.

to a political belief in the perpetual injustices of the present? I shall address these questions by looking at some recent experiments in political expression to emerge from global protest movements: the anti-capitalist movement since the early 1990s, and anti-war mobilizations since 2003. Of particular interest is their experimentation with formulations of new 'universals' and the function of the political concept of a global 'commons'.

Universality and difference

Collective mobilizations of resistance known crudely as anti-capitalist and anti-war both emerge from (while, as I shall show, superseding) a wider, post-Marxist development in protest cultures known as 'New Social Movements'. As Virno puts it,

> the social struggles of the 1960s and 1970s expressed non-socialist demands, indeed anti-socialist demands: radical criticism of labour; an accentuated taste for differences, or, if you prefer, a refining of the 'principle of individuation'; no longer the desire to take possession of the state, but the aptitude (at times violent, certainly) for defending oneself from the state, for dissolving the bondage to the state as such.[6]

Marxist movements from after the Second World War up until the mid-1970s were displaced by the 'Post-Fordist' shift to an increasing concern with lifestyles, informational and 'immaterial' labour, and diversifying products according to 'consumer' identities as opposed to mass production. This period is thus often characterized by the rise of the 'single-issue politics' of feminism, environmentalism, peace, gay rights, animal rights and nationalisms. In more recent times, however, this diversification of political movements has been undermined by broader coalitions that identify a number of local struggles under common targets. These may include global neo-liberalism,[7] or the new militarism subsumed under the war on terror.[8] Mass demonstrations against the invasion of Iraq in 2003 attracted what many are recognizing as one of the most diverse coalitions of campaign groups seen in the peace movement, representing many political, religious

---

[6] *Ibid.* p. 111.

[7] See, for instance, *Confronting Capitalism: Dispatches from a Global Movement*, ed. Eddie Yuen, Daniel Burton-Rose and George Katsiaficas, (New York: Soft Skull Press, 2004); Paul Kingsnorth, *One No, Many Yeses: A Journey to the Heart of the Global Resistance Movement* (London: Free Press, 2003).

[8] See Gary Taylor and Malcolm Todd (eds), *Democracy and Participation: New Social Movements in Liberal Democracies* (London: Merlin Press, 2003).

and class spectrums. The anti-WTO protests in Seattle, 1999 were also symbolically significant to this effect, since it became immediately recognizable
that opposition to neo-liberalism was a foundation of groups as disparate as
Trade Unions, conservationists, anarchists, and religious groups. As Richard
Searle, an anti-war campaigner in Manchester, related these 'new' identifi-
cations, focal points of rupture represented a much deeper convergence of
ideas, of which the anti-war coalitions were a reflection:

> Seattle was important in the sense that it brought together Trade Unions,
> Turtles, and Teamsters. That was new . . . and it was successful . . . the field
> of exchange and ideas were also a response to that dog eat dog mentality
> of the rich get richer . . . that became the point, that all these different
> strands coalesced at one moment and bequeathed us a new language,
> [the] fact that the word 'anti-capitalist' came around . . . when you use
> the words capitalism and anti-capitalism, well, *what is* capitalism? . . . and
> 'another world is possible' . . . what is that world that's possible? Why
> would I use those words?[9]

This move towards subsuming the differences of various political desires
underscores what some are calling the return to a desire for *universals*.
It also, represents I would argue, the clearest attempt of protest movements
to undermine the *homogenizing* effect of a politics of fear. This is because,
as I have argued a key feature of depoliticization within a culture of fear is
its ability to atomize the political experience of 'being public', imposing as
it does a localized 'administration' of control and the erosion of collective
political identity. But what exactly is meant by universals and universality?
These concepts relate to an interpretation of the political that transcends
the particularity of local struggles. An interpretation, in other words, that
provides a foundation for all struggles under new signifiers. It is not without
its problems. The concept is seen as particularly controversial in its association with a politics of universal human nature, Kantian universalizability,
and, more critically, 'the fear [. . .], that what is named as universal is the
parochial property of dominant culture, and that 'universalizability' is indissociable from imperial expansion'.[10] My own appropriation of the term

---

[9] Richard Searle was the Press and Communications Officer for The Greater
Manchester Coalition to Stop the War. I interviewed Richard in Manchester on
15 July 2004.

[10] Judith Butler, 'Restaging the Universal: Hegemony and the Limits of Formalism'
in *Contingency, Hegemony, Universality: Contemporary Dialogues on the Left*, ed. Judith
Butler, Ernesto Laclau and Slavoj Žižek (London: Verso, 2000), pp. 11–43 (p. 15).

bears more resemblance to what Judith Butler refers to as the 'procedural method', which, 'purports to make no substantive claims about what human beings are' and instead 'establishes universalizability as a criterion for justifying the normative claims of any social and political programme'.[11] Many voices of the post-modernist left have also, in relation to even a broad definition of universalism, assumed a cynical stance. Baudrillard, for example, has written that:

> The universal has had its historical chance. But today, confronted with a new world order to which there is no alternative, with an irrevocable globalization on the one hand and the wayward drift or tooth-and-nail revolt of singularities on the other, the concepts of liberty, democracy and human rights cut a very pale figure indeed, being merely the phantoms of a vanished universal. Matters are not, however, finally settled, even if it is now all up with universal values. In the void left by the universal, the stakes have risen, and globalization isn't certain to be the winner. In the face of its homogenizing, solvent power, we can see heterogeneous forces springing up all over, forces which are not only different, but antagonistic and irreducible.[12]

Mass movements like the anti-capitalist and anti-war mobilizations might therefore represent a paradoxical integration of both universalizing and diversifying trends. Two decades ago, in *Hegemony and Socialist Strategy*, Ernesto Laclau and Chantal Mouffe emphasized the importance of this paradox. They saw the unification of struggles as an essentially communicative task. That people and their engagement in social spaces have become politicized is not in doubt. But whereas political struggle used to be conceived in terms of a 'politics of frontiers',[13] political life today is characterized, it seems, by a dispersal of 'antagonisms' and 'frontier effects'[14] between which recognition of common values and universal aims must be *forged* consciously and strategically:

> All these (political) demands can be seen as aiming at particular targets which, once achieved, put an end to the movement. But they can be seen

---

[11] *Ibid.*

[12] Jean Baudrillard, *Screened Out*, trans. Chris Turner (London: Verso, 2002), p. 159.

[13] Ernesto Laclau and Chantal Mouffe, *Hegemony and Socialist Strategy*, 2nd edn (London: Verso, 2001), p. 133.

[14] *Ibid.* p. 137.

in a different way: what the demands aim for is not actually their *concretely* specified targets: those are only the contingent occasion of achieving (in a partial way) something that utterly transcends them.[15]

Universals might yet, therefore, provide a key to understanding what 'new' modes of political practice are capable of contesting contemporary tactics of social control and political fatalism. It is the bold claim of universalism, indeed, that we see traces of the eschatological anticipation of a 'coming community', or in other words that points to a vision of a community of universal values (such as justice, equality). Universals might thus provide a response to a culture of political *defeatism* that has often been associated with the 'retreat' into localized struggles in the last few decades. Laclau and Mouffe wrote *Hegemony and Socialist Strategy* in 1985, a year that has particular resonances for the experience in Britain of the defeat of class-based political struggles (the miners' strike, for instance) and the proliferation of issue-based ones (the anti-roads, animal rights, anti-nuclear, etc.). To Laclau and Mouffe, these developments responded directly to an identity crisis suffered as a consequence of the sense of limit created by the different political ends of social movements. They thus saw that an absence of 'universalizing discourse' leads unavoidably to a cultural sense of failure.[16] In response, Laclau and Mouffe did not favour falling back upon the modernist illusion that the exercise of these universalisms will 'bring about a society reconciled with itself'.[17] Instead, they believe, the new hope should be that universal values will emerge as an ambiguous and dynamic aspect of particular struggles that always points beyond themselves to a Utopian horizon. As Laclau writes, 'the universal emerges out of the particular not as some principle underlying and explaining the particular, but as an incomplete horizon suturing a dislocated particular identity.'[18] The popular attribution of recent protests to coalition-style movements such as the World Social Forum, People's Global Action, Jubilee 2000 or Stop the War Coalition thus present a unique opportunity to read Laclau and Mouffe's thesis anew. What are we to make of their call for hegemonic strategy in the light of these developments? Have their calls been answered? The discourse to emerge from both anti-war and anti-capitalist mobilizations has forced

---

[15] Ernesto Laclau, 'Identity and Hegemony: The Role of Universality in the Constitution of Political Logics' in *Contingency, Hegemony, Universality*, ed. Butler, Laclau and Žižek, p. 84, italics in the original.

[16] Laclau and Mouffe, *Hegemony and Socialist Strategy*, p. 126.

[17] Ernesto Laclau, *Emancipation(s)* (London: Verso, 1996), p. 51.

[18] *Ibid.* p. 28.

some to admit what Laclau had suggested: that without a *strategic* unification of particular struggles, social identities fail to 'constitute themselves' in the political sphere.

The potential for actions of the multitude to oppose a politics of fear (as the inability to imagine political alternatives) reveals itself in the need to think beyond the formation of a mass movement as a purely *quantitative* exercise in registering disaffection or opposition. Actions of the multitude can also provide *qualitative* discursive means for identifying against a certain voice of authority. Clearly, for instance, the moral questions raised by the invasion of Iraq produced its own unified aims (to stop the war), but the production of unified opposition wasn't determined by these aims. Inasmuch as protests normally produce a series of oppositional identities and symbols of resistance, the question of whether new *universals* are sustained becomes relevant once more. This is because, as both protesters and philosophers (such as Laclau) have argued, it is in the ability to communicate new desires abstracted from their particular aims that new possibilities for political life are *imagined*. The unprecedented unification of social groups under the banner of opposition to the Iraq war did not happen by accident. As Richard Searle put it:

> because we were unified, we broke down barriers, but you needed a conscious strategy to do that . . . these things never happen spontaneously. The bigger the numbers, the bigger people are drawn into it, the bigger the process of questioning. And then . . . the people start to question what they generally read in the newspaper.[19]

In a similar way, Laclau and Mouffe want to suggest that the most urgent task of the left is to make connections between political desires and the widening scope of 'civil society', a move initiated by Gramsci. Gramsci sought to widen the task of 'proletarianization' to encompass a wide scope of cultural practices, an 'organic and relational whole, embodied in institutions and apparatuses'[20] as related to class struggle.

How do Laclau and Mouffe's analysis help us to understand actions of the multitude as collective imaginary and potentially 'Utopian' practices? For one thing, the principle of hegemonic articulation is the attempt to define many distinct points of political struggle as contributing to a common revolutionary act through forming a 'chain of equivalences' to a universal

---

[19] Richard Searle, interviewed in Manchester (2004).
[20] Laclau and Mouffe, *Hegemony and Socialist Strategy*, p. 67.

struggle. The application of this theoretical unification might thereby encourage a practical, strategic unification of diverse political desires. Laclau acknowledges the influence of Rosa Luxemburg's concept of the 'overdetermination' of particular struggles in this idea. Of the 1917 Russian Revolution, Luxemburg wrote that 'a revolutionary mass identity is established through overdetermination, over a whole historical period, of a plurality of separate struggles. These traditions fused, at the revolutionary moment, in a ruptural point.'[21] In the context of the anti-war and anti-capitalist movements, it could therefore be argued that consensuses slowly form around key moments which, at least in terms of the domination of certain types of discourse, mark ruptural points in the cultural legitimation of protest identities. Thus, what may appear as simply the accumulation of political unrest in the form of street protest or organized demonstration is often subsequently interpreted as a unified *discourse* of opposition. For example, 2 years after a 'Carnival Against Capital', occupying London's Square Mile while G8 ministers met in Cologne was reported as mindless anarchist thugs without any agenda, *The Financial Times* had this to say: 'the protesters are winning. They are winning on the streets. Before too long they will be winning the argument. Globalisation is fast becoming a cause without credible champions.'[22]

These brief examples of mass protest suggest that the 'protoplasmic' masses mentioned in the introduction to this chapter provide a way out of an isolating and defensive particularism. The implications for a study of collective practices of hope are that, rather than dreaming of the same, universalizable Utopia, actions of the multitude can be seen first and foremost as a process whose participants (organizers, marchers, convenors, etc.) produce new modes of being political. They do this through a reimagination, not of universal human nature, but of *acts* that reclaim commonality. It is to a more detailed analysis of what this desire for a 'commons' might mean, that we must now turn.

How to be common

Laclau's emphasis is on the universal/particular relation as constituting a tension and a paradox. A more recent analysis of the potential of the 'multitude', however, allows a more nuanced interpretation. Michael Hardt

---

[21] Laclau, *Emancipation(s)*, p. 41.
[22] Philip Stevens, 'A Poor Case for Globalisation', *The Financial Times*, 17 August 2001.

and Antonio Negri's *Empire* is useful in this respect. 'Empire' is Hardt and Negri's conceptual tool for describing the new paradigm of sovereign power as a decentred and totalizing global 'order' rather than a regime of conquest.[23] It therefore unites traditional critiques of (for instance) capitalism, globalization and liberalism, but also describes the changed political realities generated by Empire as the source of 'new possibilities to the forces of liberation' through the emergence of alternative 'global flows and exchanges'.[24] It is certainly not without its problems. As some critics have pointed out, Empire can often seem an opportunistic category. That is, it provides the occasion for simply redefining the same political struggles of yesterday in a new light and thereby providing a post-modern rationale for any number of fragmented responses to Empire. It articulates clearly, nevertheless, the new found *liberation* of particular struggles from the confines of the local, the national and the boundaries of modernity. This is made possible by the very fluid nature of new global power structures themselves: 'the concrete universal is what allows the multitude to pass from place to place and make its place its own. This is the common place of nomadism and miscegenation.'[25] This view therefore supplements this chapter's exploration of the new role of universals. It does this by appreciating the increasing adoption by contemporary protest movements of the notion of 'commons'.[26] This can be seen in the ability of protesters to converge, communicate and protest on a number of international causes beyond traditional borders and nationalisms. It can also be seen in the defence of the commons from a variety of perspectives: natural and social habitats; human welfare and genetic organisms; the freedom of information and cultural knowledge. All these developments arguably represent a desire for commonality based on new identified 'crises' of political life. It therefore presents a significant development to our understanding of political responses to an uncertain future. Recently active organizations, such as the No Borders Network;[27] International Solidarity Movement;[28] or symbolic protests like the Camp X-Ray reconstruction in Hulme, can all be seen as attempts at exposing the encroaching borders that are placing all under siege. But they can also be seen as experiments in new political

---

[23] Hardt and Negri, *Empire*, p. xiv.

[24] *Ibid.* p. xv.

[25] *Ibid.* p. 362.

[26] See Eddie Yuen, 'Introduction' in *Confronting Capitalism*, ed. Yuen, p. xxii.

[27] See *No Borders Network*, www.noborders.org [accessed 5 March 2006].

[28] See International Solidarity Movement, www.palsolidarity.org/main [accessed 17 July 2007].

constitutions. That is, they provide new grounds for *being common* against a more dominant mode of being atomized. They protest the construction of identifiable and commodifiable citizens, the subjects of biopolitical control.

Thinkers like Hardt, Negri and Virno all argue that a desire for *new* understandings of commonality is a product of post-Fordist social relations. Post-Fordist culture represents an ability to make 'common' and public new ways of thinking the political. As Virno sees it, the Aristotelian concept of 'the common places' is useful here. It is used to describe the linguistic means of relating universally to others, in distinction to the 'special places' of expertise and contextuality.[29] Virno argues that a condition of today's multitude is to be denied those special places and, instead, in order to escape feeling atomized, to adopt a general intellect, to become a public thinker. How does this analysis of 'being common' reflect a contemporary role for the Utopian imagination? The notion of the commons of the public intellect (which implies ideas, discourses and actions) can be seen as an attempt to reclaim its own imaginative Utopia, in the wide sense in which I defined the word earlier. This is witnessed as a practice of discursive solidarity as much as a desire to 'act as one', in movement. The anti-war and anti-capitalist gathering have, in particular, demonstrated precisely this desire for sharing in a common place, language and identity, for a rich diversity of political dreams and visions. Mass acts of protest can therefore be seen to transcend the boundaries of ideological closure. They are resistances to, as much as anything else, boundaries that may define in advance which language could *normally* be spoken in everyday life. It should thus also be noted that the multitude, comprising the subjects of this 'everyday life' itself, is never entirely free of ideological boundaries either. Virno, always insisting that the multitude is an ambiguous creation, stresses that the sharing of 'linguistic-cognitive talents' in a post-Fordist regime simply means making adaptable labour more ready for new forms of exploitation. The real task of political critique must therefore be to understand the general intellect as the formation of a political 'public sphere' or global commons, where the 'official' public sphere has been demystified and rejected. And it is for this act of demystification that a genuinely 'other' mode of imagination, envisioning and apocalyptic dreaming, becomes a political task. The unification of very concrete and practical political desires presupposes that the necessity of a given political order is transcended

---

[29] Aristotle, *Rhetoric*, I, 2, 1358a, quoted in Virno, *A Grammar of the Multitude*, p. 35.

through the belief in another world, another set or priorities, another way to imagine the future.

But what exactly is this everyday, official mode of commonality that is being rejected? If we can speak of such a thing, how does it relate to the contemporary environment inscribed by a politics of fear? Virno describes fear as having a performative function in the state-run public sphere. In this respect, the critique already given in Part I, of a *normalized* state of emergency and paranoia, also implies an inability to identify with others and their own fears beyond the localized concerns of, for example, nationalism. Public fear is fused with an existentialist form of internalized 'anguish', writes Virno, through the subsumption of interior life into a kind of servile publicness. Hobbes himself had made use of this inside/outside distinction to describe how public fear has the function of actually providing refuge from the feeling of 'uncanniness'.[30] The experience of a dissenting multitude is, however, that it can be confronted by those to whom the inside/outside distinction has been demythologized and blurred.

The experience of the nomadic multitude (referring, once again, to the popular resistance to boundaries and borders) therefore represents a practical and strategic refusal. It refuses the kind of consolation offered its anxieties through a state of guaranteed insecurity, the state of permanent anxiety. That protest movements are once again invoking a language of global citizenship (or the rising popularity of the term 'global civil society') might equally be seen as a response to fear as consolation for the 'empty' universals produced by the state, such as its guarantees of *peace* and *security*. This general movement stands in direct opposition to the escape recommended through a disengaged publicness caught in the 'fantastic' grip of fear. Inasmuch as that illusory form of disengagement was found to be a false economy of the future (a secular eschatology), contemporary practices of the multitude can be seen as alternative modes of imagining the future. What else can explain the explosion of rhetoric, in protest cultures, of spatial resistance, of breaking down fences, windows, barriers,[31] of liberating spaces and commons and proclaiming 'no borders, no frontiers'[32]? Do these expressions not characterize a need to refuse the false 'publicity' of contemporary politics and recreate the meaning of that word? Virno's suggestion is that only the multitude thus conceived, and not the project-oriented

---

[30] Virno, *A Grammar of the Multitude*, p. 34.

[31] See Naomi Klein, *Fences and Windows* (London: Flamingo, 2002).

[32] See, for instance, Vanessa Baird, 'No borders!: Report on No Border Camp in Strasbourg' in *New Internationalist Special Features*, 25 March 2002, www.newint. org/features/strasbourg/250702.htm [accessed 15 March 2006].

concept of 'the people', can achieve a '*non-state public sphere*', a geography of emancipation. This, after all, was his point in highlighting the power of the tactic of 'exit' or 'flight' from capitalist production or national borders as processes of liberation.[33] They are described by Virno as forms of 'radical disobedience' that not only challenge the legitimacy of civil obedience to the state, but constitute an imminent critique of the very nature of post-modern forms of obedience and acquiescence. Refusal, in the form of strikes, blockades, hunger strikes and non-compliance, are as present today in protest culture as they were during the 1930s. All that has changed today is the diversification of modes of state administration and, alongside it, the modes of refusing to obey. Acts that contest physical borders by militarist state policies might therefore also represent the erosion of 'legitimate' publicness. Their aim is the replacement of an ideology of fear and closure with an imaginative reconstruction of 'the common places'.

What evidence is there today for Virno's assessment of the natural propensity of the multitude to find ways of evading duty, of refusing en masse? In the run-up to the invasion of Iraq in 2003, anti-war mobilization had been largely confined to marching, and thus gathering the visibility of its popular base. At the start of the war this popular base turned immediately to acts of civil disobedience. It attempted to disrupt the war effort through road blockades, strikes, sit-ins, occupations and acts of sabotage against military equipment and convoys.[34] A telling example of the increasing social breadth of such response was seen by the participation of children in mass demonstration. Thousands of school children across the country walked out of school, joined in protests and breached police lines.[35] That people of all ages and social groups knew that disrupting the economic order of their own society was also to disrupt the oppression of another nation was also a new discursive victory for mass protests. By civil disobedience and exit of this kind, perhaps, a sense of Virno's analysis, in which the multitude is able to subvert the production of publicness into a virtuoso score, is contextualized. Virno goes so far as to say that civil disobedience is the 'fundamental form of political action of the multitude'.[36] This does not only imply the rejection of incoherent laws within a general system of legitimation, but

---

[33] Virno, *A Grammar of the Multitude*, p. 70.

[34] For an in-depth account of many of the UK protests that fell foul of the mainstream press as soon as war on Iraq had started in 2003, see *Peace de Résistance, SchNEWS Annual 2003*, issues 351–401 (London: Calverts Press, 2003).

[35] See 'Pupils Stage Mass Anti-war Protests', *BBC News*, 19 March 2003, http://news.bbc.co.uk/1/hi/education/2862923.stm [accessed 16 January 2006].

[36] Virno, *A Grammar of the Multitude*, p. 69.

the ability to undermine the State's power over its subjects altogether. It is this form of refusal, strengthened by the power of numbers, which represents the innovative and Utopian dimension of the multitude as the practice of hope:

> Nothing is less passive than the act of fleeing, of exiting. Defection modifies the conditions within which the struggle takes place, rather than presupposing those conditions to be an unalterable horizon; it modifies the context within which a problem has arisen, rather than facing this problem by opting for one or the other of the provided alternatives. In short, exit consists of unrestrained invention which alters the rules of the game and throws the adversary completely off-balance.[37]

Conclusion

What do acts of mass mobilization, the unification of struggles and coordinated acts of disobedience reveal about popular responses to a politics of fear? One particular answer to that question has been attempted from the point of view of the process of building a movement. As a supplement to the Foucauldian view that wherever there is power, there is resistance,[38] this analysis has added a new dimension of critique: without hegemonic unification, these resistances remain too varied, too diverse. As Laclau and Mouffe say, 'only in certain cases do these forms of resistance take on a political character and become struggle directed towards putting an end to relations of subordination.'[39] In the light of my critique of a depoliticized public sphere, the very nature of public, coordinated acts taking on a 'political character' today necessarily involves actions that allow individual political statements, practices and lifestyles to relate to a wide act of political imagination, encompassing many different political desires. One piece of evidence for that process today comes from a proliferation of international meetings. These are groups that attempt to frame a convergence of global political demands and the confluence of different political identities. The World Social Forum, People's Global Action or the International Days of

---

[37] *Ibid.* p. 70.

[38] Michel Foucault, 'Powers and Strategies' in *Power/Knowledge: Selected Interviews and Other Writings 1972–1977*, ed. Colin Gordon, trans. Colin Gordon and others (London: Harvester Press, 1980), pp. 134–145 (p. 142).

[39] Laclau and Mouffe, *Hegemony and Socialist Strategy*, p. 153.

Action against the invasion of Iraq in 2003 are testimony to this global trend in political formation.

Despite the differences in their approach to the subject, an essential element has united the theories of Laclau, Virno, Hardt and Negri. That is a recognition that a new way of conceiving the collective and unified emergence of political desires is needed to counteract the definitions of public participation and values in a consumerist, paranoid society of control. This consensus can be seen in the interpretations of the new 'Post-Fordist' conditions of political constitution, or in the rise in autonomous actions of commonality and social solidarity. Essentially they suggest that today political practices of the multitude also represent a new collectivizing form of the Utopian imagination. In place of the tendency for capitalist society to favour enclosures; restriction of movement; cooperation of all through the correct channels of participation, the *mode* of this imagination has been found to be as much about non-engagement as it is about engaging with power structures. And what united the exploration of Utopian, eschatological and apocalyptic belief earlier was, indeed, a call to constantly transform by lifting and suspending the legitimacy of a given regime. Here Virno's categories of 'radical disobedience' and 'exit' are better equipped than most. They explain effectively how practices of the multitude are – or have the potential to be – the constant actions of lifting borders. Within a politics of fear those borders are simultaneously ideological and physical. To disrupt exploitative production is thus to regain control of modes of living. It is to contest spatial practices, to refuse to be walking advertisements or lines of communication for profit-making. It is also, therefore, to create ways of perceiving the future as a mode of political participation itself. In distinction to a mode of participation that maintains a state of passive acquiescence associated with a politics of fear, the action of collective protest can appear as the re-engagement of future hope with political practices of the present moment, indeed of the everyday.

Finally, the appraisal of multitudes conducted in this study has done nothing to denigrate the experience of individual experiences of this act of the imagination. On the contrary, it introduces a unifying dimension to something unavoidably physical. It necessarily involves elements of the individual confrontation with the effects of fear, atomization and alienation. Hardt and Negri, exemplifying this association, favoured the term 'posse' with regard to the radical multitude. There are metaphysical connotations of the potentiality and power of the subject in this word:

> posse is what a body and what a mind can do [. . .]. The posse produces the chromosomes of its future organisation. Bodies are on the front lines

in this battle, bodies that consolidate in an irreversible way the results of past struggles and incorporate a power that has been gained ontologically.[40]

It is to the physical power of embodied protest, therefore, already witnessed in some of the accounts of disobedience used in this chapter, that I turn next.

---

[40] Hardt and Negri, *Empire*, pp. 408–410.

Chapter 9

Bodies of Resistance

Introduction

The previous chapter responded to the question, 'what can the multitude do?' within a culture of depoliticization. The current chapter asks, 'what can individual bodies do?' This question can once again bridge some of the observations of the experience of control described in the first part of this book, and some of the hopes enunciated in the categories of hope described in the second. For the question of the individual, embodied experience of political resistance today must face the question of the fearful, capitalized requirements of the body. Foucault's suggestion, made in 1980, concerning the relationship of the body to power, that 'one needs to study what kind of body the current society needs',[1] has two implications for this chapter. The first is that a greater understanding is needed of the conditions of the body required by social powers. As Foucault asks again, 'what mode of invest-ment of the body is necessary and adequate for the functioning of a capitalist society like ours?'[2] An erasure of the body from political participation has taken not only a discursive form (a growing inability to identify and describe political reality as effects upon, with, and from flesh and blood life). It also appears as the erasure and disenfranchisement of physical acts, the ability to *be* and *do* politically.

The second implication from Foucault's question is quite simply that it is necessary to look to physical practices themselves. Because it is still bodies that are socialized, in the policing and ordering of the political sphere, it is also physical practices that finally contest that socialization. It is physical acts, finally, that challenge those definitions of the roles, identities and materials assumed in the political constitution of fear:

---

[1] Michel Foucault, 'Body/Power' in *Power/Knowledge*, ed. Gordon, trans. Gordon and others, pp. 55–62 (p. 58).
[2] *Ibid.*

If societies persist and live, that is, if the powers that be are not 'utterly absolute', it is because, behind all the submissions and coercions, beyond the threats, the violence, and the intimidations, there is the possibility of that moment when life can no longer be bought, when the authorities can no longer do anything, and when, facing the gallows and the machine guns, people revolt.[3]

The individual that refuses, from the student standing in front of advancing government tanks, to the fearlessness of the suicide bomber, has not lost any of its symbolic power or controversy. But the body is also central to my interest in the role of the Utopian imagination in challenging a politics of fear. By looking a little deeper than their surface appearance, this chapter aims to uncover what two-way processes of 'biopower'[4] are operative in political life. Reaching further than Foucault's initial analysis, therefore, this chapter proposes seeing physical protest as in some sense a transcending of boundaries. Physical practices of civil disobedience protest against the givenness of political reality. As such they serve as a counterpractice to ideological closure and the institution of certain parameters of appropriate action or behaviour. As acts that affirm the fluidity and freedom of bodies across borders and ideologically imposed boundaries, physical acts of resistance point further to the practice of a Utopian imagination. Particularly in their capacity as acts that express 'solidarity' with the bodies of others, physical acts of protest can, I shall argue, point to an imaginative gesture similar to the expression of universality described in the previous chapter. That is, as bodies engaged in acts of resistance, they can presage and articulate a future that promises an end to the conditions that enslave and dispossess the bodies of the present.

I proceed with this analysis by first uncovering the strategic *disappearance* of bodies and embodied political subjectivity as a condition of a depoliticized and 'fantastic' public sphere generally. This provides a contextual backdrop from which to understand the importance of the physicality of protest. Next I look to the notion of *solidarity* in providing a key to the ability for protest to able to repoliticize the public sphere. The phenomenon of solidarity actions make implicit assumptions about what a body can

---

[3] Michel Foucault, 'Useless to Revolt?' in *Power*, vol. 3, ed. James D. Faubion, trans. Robert Hurley (London: Penguin, 1994), pp. 449–453 (pp. 449–450).

[4] Foucault coined the term 'biopower' to indicate 'technologies' of power that directed the life of the subject towards certain norms, disciplines, regulations and productions, as opposed to the old notion of power over the body by threat of death by the sovereign. See Foucault, *Histoire de la sexualité*, vol. 1, p. 183.

do to force a space of free movement and identity across both theoretical and physical boundaries and borders.

Where are the bodies?

What are the sanctioned and 'illegal' position of bodies in the political sphere? The history of direct action movements suggests a continual reinvention of the embodiment of political participation.[5] From the destruction of genetically modified crops to the occupation of forests, roads or construction sites by blockading their access, these actions have generated a significant discourse surrounding the legitimacy, public acceptability and effectiveness of physical disruption. But they are also significant for their implicit claims about what (almost) *all* bodies are capable of doing, and not only the ones prepared to risk abuse, violence, arrest or death. To immerse one's body in that climate, to imagine oneself *involved* in some of those daily struggles, therefore, is to address the overarching question posed at the beginning of this chapter: *what can bodies do today?* Actions of resistance or disobedience are therefore testimony in many ways to a contestation of body politics and of biopower itself.

In order to better understand the significance of what resistant bodies make possible, it is necessary to evaluate the claim, hinted at in the introduction to this chapter, that contemporary social life is marked by a systematic erasure of the body from the political sphere. It is often stated that political modernity models itself on the notion of 'reincorporation'. This idea likens the state, as 'body politic', to that totalitarian figurehead not dissimilar to the king's head which it purported to cut off with the birth of the enlightenment.[6] Jacob Rogozinski, resurrecting phenomenology's insight into the 'fleshness' of the body, has argued that successive attempts at reinventing modernity, from Rousseau to Marx, in terms of a rejection of absolute power in the 'Total Body' of sovereignty have all resulted in the mangled restructuring of that body in some form of terror, that is, the displacement of one 'body' of power to another.[7] Hence the constant reinvention of the modern 'pseudobody of community'.[8] This reinvention

---

[5] See, for example, April Carter's overview of a history of direct action in *Direct Action and Democracy* (Cambridge: Polity Press, 2005).

[6] Foucault, 'Truth and Power' in *Power/Knowledge*, ed. Gordon, trans. Gordon and others, pp. 109–133 (p. 121).

[7] *Ibid.* p. 32.

[8] *Ibid.*

can be described as an act of violence – an attempted erasure of the radical carnality of plural living individuals. It is therefore a form of disembodiment of the political itself. Rogozinski sees the only alternative to the terrorizing body of the state in the social movements and actions by which flesh-bodies thwart its homogenizing gaze, the 'anarchical and plural flesh' of bodies experiencing themselves as bodies.

In a similar way, the purpose of this chapter is also to examine acts of the body as protest against its disappearance. For what is the use of a reimagination of collective bodies, or the solidarity people must now show to the 'other' bodies that totalitarian systems reject (through asylum procedures and other forms of state racism, for instance), unless to reconfigure experiences of the body? Is not the power of physical protest the ability to move, exit, stay put, deviate and manipulate commands, and thus to transcend the boundaries of 'normal' political, spatial and temporal practices themselves?

The presence of bodies of resistance also takes on a *globalizing* role in which protest transcends localities. By so doing they are able to resist any form of ideological monopoly over the naming, defining, displacing, ignoring and inventing of bodies. Examples such as the success of the *Asociación Madres de Plaza de Mayo* in Argentina serve as a powerful indication of the power of memory and of embodied witness. These women, mothers of an estimated 30,000 children 'disappeared' by the military dictatorship between 1976 and 1983, have congregated every week in Buenos Aires since 1977, holding up placards with names and photographs of the disappeared. Their action has also had some success. Despite continual harassment and the murder of some mothers themselves, ex-members of the military are beginning to admit some of the murders after pressure from its international exposure.[9] Similar examples can be found in the symbols of protest at 'decorporalized' war within the war on terror. This much was clear from the powerful appearance of images and discourses of the hidden victims of the attack on Iraq throughout the conflict. The image of a tortured Iraqi prisoner at Abu Graib prison has become perhaps the most powerful example: a broken, abused body turned into an icon of the brutality of the war through media sensationalism. Conversely, the image of US soldiers' dead bodies were consistently hidden from public view. Since the begin-

[9] 'Mothers of the Plaza de Mayo', *Wikipedia*, http://en.wikipedia.org/wiki/Mothers_of_the_Plaza_de_Mayo, [accessed 5 December 2005].

ning of the US invasion, the Pentagon issued a directive forbidding the media any coverage of returning American coffins.[10]

But the decorporalization of war also justifies looking for those practices that oppose a fantasy of disembodiment with an alternative form of imagination. At stake in the battle over bodies, in other words, is the desire, and the suppression of desire, for 'the Real', as Žižek says, over the fantasy of sanitizing discourse.[11] How then might practices of hope be a politically *imaginative* process, therefore? A desire for the Real reveals a chaos and lawlessness inherent to contemporary politics that is brushed over by the false assumption that as warfare progresses, casualties will diminish. Acts of resistance to a politics of fear in this sense inevitably involve the discursive, symbolic as well as physically manifested reinsertion of the 'flesh' of the oppressed. 'Disembodied discourse' can be considered a common trend in many features of post-structuralism and its inherited suspicion of subjective agency. Charlotte Hooper has pointed out that the 'fantasy of disembodiment' is also a key feature of the contemporary public sphere which

> depends on the apparent invisibility or absence of bodies in social discourse, so that masculine reason could be separate from and untainted by the body. This apparent invisibility has been assisted by a huge investment in the general social sanitization of bodies and bodily functions, particularly in public spaces.[12]

Examples of this depoliticized aspect of post-modern culture can be found in the erasure of bodily needs by replacing public meeting places, social centres or other sites of social care, with those of purely commercial interest.

What do these comments about a decorporalized political sphere say about the *potential* for bodies to constitute practices of hope? How can they radically imagine an alternative public sphere? Foucault's detailed studies of the political significance of bodies is once more of some help here, because he portrays both the oppressive and resistant capacity of 'body politics' as closely integrated into social norms of behaviour. On the one

---

[10] Penny Coleman, 'Veterans' Suicides: A Hidden Cost of Bush's Wars', *Alternet*, November 2007, www.alternet.org/waroniraq/67556.

[11] Žižek, *Welcome to the Desert*, p. 11.

[12] Charlotte Hooper, 'Disembodiment, Embodiment and the Construction of Hegemonic Masculinity' in *Political Economy, Power and the Body*, ed. Gillian Youngs (London: Macmillan Press, 2000), pp. 39–51 (p. 39).

hand, the landscape I have been trying to describe as a politics of fear bears a certain affinity with the world described in *Discipline and Punish*.[13] On the other hand, the power/pleasure relations emerging out the *History of Sexuality* (which describes the 'erotic investment' of disciplining sexual practices[14]) show the principle of power turning on itself. The remaining task of this chapter is therefore to describe what happens when this view of the investment of the body is applied to a more explicit politics of *new* carceral practices in the war on terror.

What possibilities do resistances hold beyond the realm of the family, gender and sexuality, with the ways in which bodies comport themselves? What happens when resistance becomes an art of living? We can begin by considering Foucault's personal encounters with the uses of the body in protest situations: those produced by Iran, where he taught during the popular revolution of 1979. Witnessing the courage by which young people staged demonstrations day after day in which thousands were slaughtered by the military, Foucault was moved by the evidence these acts gave to the existence of a 'collective will'. The Iranian revolts, in their acceptance of certain martyrdom in many cases, presented Foucault with the 'irreducible' and 'inexplicable' nature of the body that would prefer annihilation to subservience.[15] The observation is not confined to martyrdom, however. It demonstrates the persistence of rebellion in general as an irreducible factor of history. The lesson from Iran was that

> an absence of fear and an intensity of courage, or rather the intensity that people were capable of when danger, though still not removed, had already been transcended. In their revolution they had already tran- scended the danger posed by the machine gun that constantly faced all of them.[16]

Solidarity and risk

It is now possible to ask what contemporary understandings of the function of resistant bodies are available to protesters in the context of a politics of

---

[13] Michel Foucault, *Surveiller et Punir: naissance de la prison* (Paris: Gallimard, 1975).

[14] Foucault, *Histoire de la sexualité*, vol. 1.

[15] Foucault, 'Useless to Revolt?', p. 449.

[16] Michel Foucault, 'Iran: The Spirit of a World Without Spirit' in *Politics, Philosophy, Culture: Interviews and Other Writings, 1977–1984*, ed. Lawrence D. Kritzman, trans. Alan Sheridan and others (London: Routledge, 1988), pp. 211–224 (p. 220).

fear. How do people transcend the parameters of possible action dictated by the closure of physical spaces? A useful starting point for answering this question is to consider the ability for physical practices to counterpose an alternative imagination of political practices by redrawing lines of connection, or *solidarity*, between their own and others' bodies. This concept has given new life to a protest movement that is attempting to reinsert the body into the discourses and practices of globalization. A rhetoric of collective bodies, or *universal* bodies, might therefore be suggested. In particular it is present in the rising popularity of crossing national and cultural boundaries to be 'alongside'. It demands travelling long distances, and often risking injury or death, to protest an oppressive or dangerous situation. The International Solidarity Movement (ISM), presents us with a concrete example of this trend. Established in 2001, ISM is one of a number of groups set up under the guidance and invitation of Palestinian peace activists to invite international volunteers to Israel/Palestine. Their intention is to engage in non-violent direct action in order to 'dramatize the terrible conditions under which Palestinians live because of the Occupation, and to protect them from physical violence from Israeli soldiers and settlers'.[17] ISM volunteers from around the world have accompanied Palestinians to harvest olives in occupied territory; acted as human shields against Israeli military or settler attacks; delivered supplies to refugee camps under curfew; participated in peaceful demonstrations; dismantled roadblocks and observed the treatment of Palestinians at checkpoints. One motivation (among many) for inviting internationals is the belief that faced with the presence of foreign bodies, the likelihood of human rights abuses are decreased, and that some kind of media publicity is generated. Within these transformations of political space (and therefore assumptions about 'repoliticization') lies an awareness of the power of bodies to replace a discourse that has become too predictable. Thus, in a manner perhaps radically undermined by most analyses of 'body politics', it is not only the backlash of language, interpellation and subverted identities, as Judith Butler might suggest,[18] that engenders hope where it might not have existed before. It is also a reclamation of bodies themselves in inappropriate social spaces.

The introduction of these political desires to 'be physical' thus adds this possibility: that an imaginative and 'embodied' discourse of hope is one

---

[17] Anonymous, *International Solidarity Movement Information Pack.*

[18] See Judith Butler, *The Psychic Life of Power* (1997); Judith Butler, 'Performativity's Social Magic' in *The Social and Political Body*, ed. Theodore R. Schatzki and Wolfgang Natter (New York: Guilford Press, 1996), pp. 20–47.

that continually rewrites or even *inscribes* places themselves with new presence. This involves questioning the everyday placement of bodies. Why here, and not there? Experiences of the body in 'extreme' situations such as occupied Palestine force a consideration of bodily practices generally and the reasons for considering one's own body, politically, in that way. Some examples of those situations demonstrate, for instance, an underlying surprise with which activists saw that bodily responses to situations became natural, unhesitating, 'in the right place'. The desire to be physically reconnected with the effects of one's actions opens a lot of questions about the motivation to use one's body in certain ways.

The question of physical danger and its usefulness was therefore seen entirely in relation to a concept of empowerment through vulnerability. One ISM activist, Sharon, was shot in the stomach by an Israeli soldier while on a demonstration in Palestine. She insisted that the experience only confirmed her wish to overcome the 'barrier' of physical threat in pursuing her goal:

> This theme of putting your body in the way . . . if you *do* that you're essentially . . . you can be handing over your body to someone who has the power to damage it, and, you know, for some people that's the most fundamentally frightening thing you could come up with, and certainly, because I do think sometimes, OK, so I've been arrested and . . . I've been in prison for a *short* time, and I've been shot . . . which means . . . when all those things are threatened, to stop me doing what I want to do, I can think, well, I can handle that if that's the result of what I want to do, that's not going to stop me.[19]

Accounts of activists in Palestine relate in some sense to the notion of a physical 'limit' to social power's control of bodies spoken of by Foucault. The implication is that there is an irreducibly physical aspect to practices of hope as contesting a politics of fear. Foucault is primarily concerned with the *fact* of courageous protest, and its significance for the defiance of predictable history:

> One does not dictate to those who risk their lives facing a power. Is one right to revolt, or not? Let us leave the question open. People do revolt; that is a fact. And that is how subjectivity (not that of great men, but of anyone) is brought into history, breathing life into it . . . it is because of

---

[19] Sharon (pseudonym), interviewed in Manchester (2004).

such voices that the time of human beings does not have the form of evolution but that of 'history', precisely.[20]

This expression certainly provides a powerful contextual response to the suggestion made earlier that protest must today contain an element of undermining the inherently fatalist view of human history. But in addition it paints a picture of resistance as something one does when one has nothing to lose, as was the case for the Iranian students. We must therefore consider the implications of resistance that chooses physically committed resistance as a tactic of blurring the very definition of what one 'has' to lose. Resisting a disembodied politics of fear, in other words, might also involve a critique of despair as a discipline of the body. This ties it closely to Foucault's sense of the 'care of the self'.[21] In the context of the actions of the ISM, resistance inevitably raises the question of the 'validity' of dying in a place far removed from political responsibility as conceived in Western society.

This proximity of resistance to the possibility of death presents the resister with an ultimate limit. It is interesting to compare this sense of limit with the sense of 'warding off' of death by which capitalized fear was described by Massumi in Part I. In comparison to a secular eschatology of the 'never ending', the proximity of resistance to a 'possible' and meaningful end presents a powerful alternative angle. The subject of *sacrifice* in political direct action, and its relationship with martyrdom, is an area too wide to enter into here. Nevertheless, it can be suggested in passing that perhaps it is only those who *do* relinquish control of their body in this way who come closest to understanding how its use may shape acts of hope. The impression that these actions give is an attempt at re-engaging people with the stubbornness and 'irreducibility' of bodies that can trigger a wide spectrum of actions associated with physically committed resistance.

Conclusion

In this chapter I have focused on the willingness of activists to *be political* in those spaces opened to practices of hope by the body's own resilience and creativity. Bodies that enable a culture of hope have been found to be not

---

[20] Foucault, 'Useless to Revolt?', p. 452.
[21] See Michel Foucault, *Histoire de la sexualité, vol. 3: le souci du soi* (Paris: Gallimard, 1984).

only those who risk arrest, harm or death, but also those who must wait, for hours and days, at checkpoints, houses or hospitals, just to allow others a space for being human in dehumanized spaces. Actions like these demonstrate something unique about the ability to contest the depoliticization of the public sphere. Acts of solidarity are powerful when they expose as illusory the everyday reasons by which people need *not* be in solidarity. One of their functions may be to expose the logic by which people feel 'safer' in a capitalized and militarized society. As another ISM activist, Laura, puts it in relation to her overall experience,

> [for me], it's not being in Palestine which is the difficult bit . . . what's difficult is trying to equate the way we live with what is happening in the rest of the world . . . much harder than standing in front of a tank. To *not* be despairing about that, to *not* be utterly broken by that is really difficult.[22]

A politics of fear is thus essentially a discipline of the body as much as it is expression and communication. It involves the co-option of one's body into an emerging routine of surveillance, discipline and normalization. It is also marked by the experience of being virtual. It is the sense of relating to political reality most clearly through the mediation of fantasy, as the example of war reporting used in this chapter attested to. A politics of fear paradoxically anodizes and veils the apocalyptic sensibility of a body that craves transformation, revelation, a rending of the veil, an exposition of the lies of a given political reality. A politics of fear revels in the very opposite of apocalyptic revelation: a physical presence stripped of flesh, of needs, of suffering, in its production of a decorporalized public sphere.

The findings of this chapter therefore have clear implications for an appraisal of the function of Utopian imagination. Utopian belief operates by suspending the legitimacy of a given ideology. Similarly practices of resistance constitute a form of suspension of the everyday closure of political options. An attempt to break down 'decorporalized' public space is attempted through forms of direct action. While a subject of diverse interpretations in itself (in its relation to non-violence, legality, effectivity, etc.), direct action at its simplest resembles a form of being present, of trespass, of the imaginative placing of the body, and in this sense is a fundamentally transformative and arguably Utopian practice. Analysing the production of broken bodies in the war on terror (such as the torture of suspects), has also raised significantly the political stakes of reconnecting discourse on the

---

[22] Laura (pseudonym), interviewed in Manchester (2004).

body to political events. An aide of General Norman Schwarzkopf once commented during Desert Storm, that 'this is the first war of modern times where every screwdriver, every nail is accounted for', while also admitting, 'I don't think anybody is going to come up with an accurate count of Iraqi dead.'[23] The primary implication of this attitude is in modes of response through acts of resistance. Responding to the body's erasure identifies one more mode by which the political subject is able to be where it shouldn't. Actions of political solidarity and risk therefore recommend paying closer attention to the *experiences* of the body as a language, a physically inscribed text, of Utopian imagination. The French philosopher Jean-Luc Nancy has contributed to this 'language' by expressing an urgent task to 'think the thought of the body'.[24] Today we need, he explains, a way of thinking that transcends discourse itself. This would be a bodily way of thinking body itself, and would thus, perhaps, repoliticize bodily practices. We must recognize two fundamental aspects of bodily resistance that immediately open up the possibility of a body politics both as discourse and praxis. The first is to see the vulnerability of body, or as Nancy simply puts it, 'wound', as representing the irreducibility of suffering. It is that which moves us towards others. The second aspect is to see the body as constant process, flowing and open possibility: 'everything is possible. Bodies resist. The community of bodies resists. The grace of a body offering itself is always possible. The pain of a body suffering is always available. Bodies call again for their creation.'[25] It is from this aspect of the imaginative, fluid capacity of bodies acting in defiance of limits imposed them that we can recognize a Utopian impulse even here, in the operation of bodies in the most inhospitable of places. But there is also arguably an element of apocalyptic imagination in the experience of resistance as the visionary pursuit of another world, an expectation of the new, and a refusal of the 'time' of death and acquiescence in the present. As a practice that invites myriad expressions of this promise of discontinuity and rupture in history, physical resistance bears affinities with at least Derrida's understanding of the apocalyptic refusal of linear history and of the fatalism of the 'end of history' thesis.

---

[23] Quoted by John Pilger, 'The Lies of Old' in *Tell Me Lies: Propaganda and Media Distortion in the Attack on Iraq*, ed. David Miller (London: Pluto Press, 2004), pp. 18–22 (p. 18).

[24] Jean-Luc Nancy, 'Corpus', trans. Claudette Startilio, in *Thinking Bodies*, ed. Juliet Flower McCannell and Laura Zakaria (Stanford: Stanford University Press, 1994), pp. 17–31 (p. 27).

[25] *Ibid.* p. 23.

Reflections on Part III

In Part I of this book Deleuze and Guattari emphasized that desire is not
innocent. On the contrary, it comprises two seemingly opposed 'virtual
poles': on the one side, a fascist-paranoid 'molar-moral drive of Oedipal
desire, works[ing] to fashion society into samenesses of varying scales'. On
the other side, there is 'anarchy-schizophrenia [. . .], anoedipal desire that
respects the partiality of bodies [. . .], their 'perversity'; their difference.'[1]
For to affirm the possibility of resistance is to recognize that neither the
subtlest act of propaganda, nor the most violent campaign of fear and
repression happen within a political vacuum. They involve desires, practices and bodies. As Foucault is famous for insisting, these can never be
relied upon to internalize fear and repression *all* of the time. If we are to
look for ways to untangle the auto-production of fear in society, then desire
must be kept open. We must imagine it searching for and anticipating
'the rupture within causality that forces a rewriting of history on a level with
the real, and produces this strangely polyvocal moment when everything is
possible'.[2] A similar attempt has been made in the last three chapters comprising Part III. The convictions of activists and the accounts of a history of
disobedience have revealed an element of contemporary political desires
that no purely theoretical investigation could have achieved. This is the
desire for reinserting a certain political *style* of the everyday. It is a style of
being political that is denied normal political practice and discourse in a
climate of paranoia and acquiescence. Not only spaces, words, actions or
identities, but a repoliticization of the everyday has been a hallmark of
practices of hope explored here. Insofar as these practices attempt to sus-

---

[1] Massumi, *A User's Guide*, p. 119.
[2] Deleuze and Guattari, *Anti-Oedipus*, p. 378. See also Goodchild, *Deleuze and
Guattari*, p. 82.

pend the given parameters of political participation in the conditions of 'post-democracy' all suggest a radically *imaginative* capacity. They represent, in other words, the ability for political desire to transcend the conditions of ideological closure that define a politics of fear.

A strong theme running through all of these analyses has also been, either implicitly or at times explicitly, to challenge the conclusions of that specifically *future*-oriented aspect of such closure. It revealed a mirror to the fantastic, mediatized representation of politics as war without end. It revealed an alternative imagination of public *dis*engagement based on the creation of a 'non-state public sphere'. And it revealed the positioning of bodies in those spaces of crisis and risk that normally constitute a *paralysing* vision of the future and are therefore 'out of bounds'.

Conclusion

Albert Camus said that the only important question in philosophy was that of suicide, or, more precisely, whether or not life was worth living.[1] My own investigations make it clear that the most important question facing society today is that of *political* suicide, which might also be described as the abandonment of the imagination of the future. A competing fantasy of the future operates today as a dominant security paradigm: a politics of fear. Today we inhabit, in a state of acquiescence, a terrorized present. How then, have these observations been the backdrop for investigating practices of hope? Camus' reasoning proceeded from a kind of curiosity for how it is that the human spirit rebels in the face of the palpable absurdity of the world. This book has been driven by a similar curiosity. Why is it that people, against so much fear and political paralysis, act as if the manipulation of 'terror' had not already crushed them?

Situating contemporary apocalypses

In order to answer this question I have attempted to untangle myriad interpretations of the 'apocalyptic', that cryptic signifier for a host of contemporary attitudes to both hope and fear. To get to this point has entailed uncovering the underlying reality of perpetual crisis and constitution of everyday experience. That everydayness provokes some to name as 'gradual apocalypse'[2] the social and ecological crises facing the planet. Baudrillard, similarly, lamented the inability to imagine the end. It is almost as if we are suffering a kind of collective post-millenarian pathology. Following Derrida, I have also added to this the idea of the 'non-event' of contemporary apocalypse. This is the belief that what makes talking of the end so tragic is

---

[1] 'juger que la vie vaut ou ne vaut pas la peine d'être vécue'. Albert Camus, *Le mythe de Sisyphe* (Paris: Gallimard, 1942), p. 15.

[2] See Andrew McMurry, 'The Slow Apocalypse: A Gradualist Theory of the World's Demise', *Post-Modern Culture*, vol. 6, no. 3 (May 1996), http://muse.jhu.edu/journals/postmodern_culture/v006/6.3mcmurry.html [accessed 21 March 2006].

its non-appearance. Finality never arrives – it is always on the horizon, never experienced.

Thus, my analysis engaged with the 'gradual apocalypse' of contemporary political life and in so doing returned to my original concern with a politics of fear. Fear is, in its myriad manifestations, whether affectively, psychologically, culturally or ideologically, something that strips the political act to a state of abstraction and disengagement. Norman Cohn's celebrated analysis of the influence of social and ecological crisis as motors for social unrest[3] (including radicalized millenarian movements) therefore needs substantial revision. For on the one hand analyses of more recent apocalyptic movements (from Waco to Aum Shinrikyo, but including secular apocalyptics such as the militant phase of the ecological movement Earth First![4]) can indeed be understood as crises of modernity. They are the 'waning of the cultural center' of 'liberal universalist ideologies' and the expectation of an 'ultimate postapocalyptic recentering of culture'.[5] And the war on terror may indeed be a political reality still portrayed in apocalyptic terms of good and evil. On the other hand contemporary apocalypse can be seen as something that tranquilizes rather than agitates. In the preservation of a war without end, today's global management of terror seems to correspond only to Baudrillard's 'excess of reality'.[6] The impossibility of 'punishing' death (such as those from the 9/11 attacks), in other words, when those deaths are a mirror held up to an already violent and terrorizing system (US hegemony), is immediately matched by the *popular* impossibility of imagining alternatives at all, of *being political*. The communication and presentation of terror today invites a response (*we have to do something*) but paralyses the political means of responding in hope (*all action is useless*). It creates, in other words, the impossibility of politics. The logic of terror is a cycle of violence, and this has become successfully integrated into biopolitical governance. The paradigm of governance through hypersecurity signals

---

[3] 'Again and again one finds that a particular outbreak of revolutionary chiliasm took place against a background of disaster: the plagues that preluded the First Crusade and the flagellant movements of 1260, 1348–1349, 1391 and 1400; the famines that preluded the First and Second crusades [. . .]; the spectacular rise in prices that preluded the revolution at Münster.' (Cohn, *Pursuit of the Millennium*, p. 315).

[4] See, for example, Martha F. Lee, *Earth First!: Environmental Apocalypse* (New York: Syracuse University Press, 1995).

[5] Thomas Robbins and Susan J. Palmer, 'Introduction' in *Millennium, Messiahs, and Mayhem: Contemporary Apocalyptic Movements* (London: Routledge, 1997), p. 4.

[6] Baudrillard, *Spirit of Terrorism*, p. 17.

the death of the public sphere. The reality of apocalypse *now* is therefore something simultaneously shocking and banal. It is the anaesthetization of the political, the veiling of death itself. The universalized reality of terror (if you're not scared, you're guilty) has been portrayed as normalized and pacified fear.

The politics of fear described in this book therefore represents a perverted sense of *apokalypsis* or 'revelation'. For a politics of fear is a veiling, rather than an unveiling, of the means to die. If there is a singularity in the way that apocalyptic is announced today it is that no-one any longer bears the prophetic responsibility to *prepare the way* for what is to come. For what is the dominant announcement, the public transcript, to use Scott's term, today? Turning to the dominant media discourse and political rhetoric of war on terror, suspension of liberties and demonization of outsiders, it is in many respects a war with no end. If Negri's lessons on the political constitution of time have taught us anything, it should therefore relate concretely and materially to the way in which we live 'in' suspended time of terror. As Mark C. Taylor writes, mirroring Blanchot, 'the disaster, then, is the non-event in which nothing happens. The eventuality of nothing ruins all presence by interminably delaying the arrival of every present.'[7] Against Heidegger's ecstatic ontology of a being-towards-death, therefore, a culture of perpetual apocalypse has proved death to be the continual deferral of liberation. It is the *never ending* as opposed to the promise of the *yet to come*.

Political eschatology

What has a religious perspective added to these observations? In a sense, this study has shown that theological analyses of future anticipation simply *widen* the crisis that is a politics of fear. An ambiguity of the 'coming' as apocalyptic event for many religious narratives is seen to be an agonizing and indefinite one, precisely in its capacity to provoke yearning in the heart of the believer. The narrative delay of the *parousia* expressed as crisis for the early Christian community therefore bears an uncomfortable affinity with the gradual apocalypse of the war on terror (the crisis that is never resolved). It is only with the help of Derrida's inspired concept of the apocalyptic as an explosion of different messages and acts of resistance that we are offered some way out of this problem. In the light of Derrida's apocalyptic, we are

---

[7] Mark C. Taylor, 'Nothing Ending Nothing' in *Theology at the End of the Century: A Dialogue on the Postmodern*, ed. Robert P. Scharlemann (Charlottesville: University Press of Virginia, 1990), pp. 41–75 (p. 67).

allowed to consider the influence of many different modes, or styles, of that act of deferral. We become enchanted, not paralysed, by the *not yet*, the *to come*, the acting *as if*. And we are invited to consider and reaffirm the enduring power of myth in both the manipulation and the autonomous movement of political imaginaries throughout the ages. Apocalyptic in this broad sense identifies with the expectation of the new event. It is a mythic element arguably denied it by eschatology traditionally conceived. Furthermore, it represents the prophetic function of seeking response and attentiveness. Thus it identifies political hope within the *mythos* of apocalyptic desire. It is the paradox announced by the Hebrew prophet, Isaiah, who declares that an apocalyptic response is a recognition that reality is in some sense already transformed: 'Do not remember the former things, or consider the things of old. I am about to do a new thing; now it springs forth, do you not perceive it?' (Isa. 43.19).

By affirming the power of myth I do not mean to argue for the persistence of specific religious narratives. Appropriating religious fervour as a political orientation towards the future has long been an activity championed by those apocalyptic visionaries that take political power *away* from popular, imaginative use and to the benefit of the power of the state or religious megalomaniacs.[8] I *do* on the other hand wish to affirm myth's positive and transformative power against John Gray's rejection of Utopian myths as the ultimate origins of political violence. My understanding has more in common with Ricoeur's definition of myth: 'a vast field of experimentation, or even of playing with hypotheses'.[9] My own field of experimentation has articulated the possibility for meaningful resistance as protecting a mode of temporal suspension. *Kairòs* time means ruptured time. It is time that suspends the logic of progress from its subsumption into the *exceptional* time of war without end. It is thus a theo-political category of resistance, and by no means implies a philosophy of necessary violence to purify the old world in pursuit of the new. The relevance of theological categories of eschatology and apocalypse are related only to the continued practice of an alternative vision of the future, not to a judgement on how that future might be achieved.

The true 'field of experimentation' in society's pursuit of the future must never rest solely in rhetoric, however. As I claimed in the introduction, this book has been an attempt to open up the meaning of practices of resistance as acts of faith in the future. In light of the experiments articulated in

---

[8] See, for instance, Bruce Lincoln, *Holy Terrors: Thinking about Religion after September 11* (London: University of Chicago Press, 2003).

[9] Paul Ricoeur, quoted in O'Leary, *Arguing the Apocalypse*, p. 21.

Part III, I must conclude that the antagonistic element of protest today also functions as a kind of mythic narrative of the future, though one that allows myriad interpretations and expressions. Actions that express the 'as if' of politics (a notion of open possibility) challenge a presupposition that practices are continually underwritten by fear. They do this in the contexts of the transformation of social space, collective potential and also the movement of the body. And they permit themselves an articulation of the political *to come* without defining in advance what, or whom, they anticipate. This iconoclastic Utopianism, or 'apocalypse without apocalypse' to use Derrida's term, refers to a fragmentation of many apocalyptic imaginaries, monopolized by no religion or ideology:

> Perhaps you will be tempted to call this the disaster, the catastrophe, the apocalypse. Now here, precisely, is announced – as promise or threat – an apocalypse without apocalypse, an apocalypse without vision, without truth, without revelation, *of dispatches* [des envois] (for the 'come' is plural in itself, in oneself), of addresses without message and without destination, without sender or decidable addressee, without last judgement, without any other eschatology than the tone of the 'Come' itself, its very difference, and apocalypse beyond good and evil. 'Come' does not announce this or that apocalypse: already it resounds with a certain tone: it is in itself the apocalypse; '*Come*' is apocalyptic'.[10]

This form of apocalyptic desire describes a dispersed, creative and non-authoritarian form of Utopian resistance. It is an absence of guarantees, blueprints or conditions against which to measure one's hope. We might call it a post-modern style of apocalyptic belief. But if this is so it has not appeared as the face of relativist nihilism or a veiled despair. Commenting on the anti-capitalist demonstrations and riots that took place alongside the G8 summit in Genoa in July 2001, Hardt and Negri commented that 'protest movements, [. . .] do not provide a practical blueprint for how to solve problems, and we should not expect that of them. They seek rather to transform the public agenda by creating political desires for a better future.'[11] And this indeed was also a hallmark of Derrida's own version of Utopian

---

[10] Derrida, 'Apocalyptic Tone', p. 94, italics in the original.

[11] Hardt and Negri, 'What the Protesters in Genoa Want' in *On Fire: The Battle of Genoa and the Anti-capitalist Movement*, ed. Anonymous (London: OneOff Press, 2001), pp. 101–103 (p. 103).

politics, requiring this condition of no guarantee. An '*invincible desire for justice*', writes Derrida,

> is not and ought not to be certain of anything, either through knowledge, conscience, foreseeability or any kind of programme as such. This abstract messianicity belongs from the very beginning to the experience of faith, of believing, of a credit that is irreducible to knowledge.[12]

The lesson of a Utopian reading of protest movements tells a similar story. A stark contrast emerges between two 'future faiths'. If activism is a 'credit' of faith it stands in certain contrast to the illusory faith of capitalism: a culture of perpetual debt and the deferral of the future. *That* faith was characterized by Goodchild as the essence of the God of capital, which might also be recognized as the God of terror, and represents the very opposite of faith in an open, unwritten future.

On the one hand then, there is an assured vision of justice that repeats its power in the strong arm of the politics of fear. On the other hand, there is the uncertain justice of myriad apocalypses claiming alternative voices of the future. As I have tried to argue throughout this book, this contrast revealed itself as a fundamentally *temporal* reorientation. For a politics of fear can also be articulated as a time whose onward march allows no alternatives, no mode of expectation, no promise, no rupture. It only allows pure, commanded synchronicity. How do political practices challenge this command time? Through the creative manipulation of public space; the ability for a multitude to provide alternative universalisms; and the freedom of bodies to traverse boundaries of political, cultural and sexual identities. These practices constitute in their own way the articulation of a desire for anti-capitalist time. It is time outside given time, time of possibility or '*kairòs*'. *Refusal* is a temporal act that unites some of what Paolo Virno recognized in the potential of new politicizing subjects and the refusal implicit to life in the 'time that remains' preached by St Paul. That which unceasingly constructs opportunities for life through negative labour, work without profit, cooperation and freedom of mobility,[13] in fact all of the labours and redefinitions of public and political space that were represented as 'experiments in hope'. All of these styles of repoliticization affirm an imperative for reconstituting the time of politics through acts of imagination. And it is

---

[12] Jacques Derrida, *Acts of Religion*, ed. Gil Anidjar (London: Routledge, 2002), p. 56, italics in the original.
[13] Virno, *A Grammar of the Multitude*, p. 70.

the realm of imagination in *distinction* to the false expectancy of futurist fantasy that appears to be the most 'common' commodity of all. Clearly, the brief examples of acts of resistance looked at in this book do not come close to describing the rich diversity of actions and occupations that we label activism (let alone explore the ambiguity of that term in the first place). But they do, I feel, address specifically the challenge posed to politics from the depoliticizing effects of the war on terror. And they do that in ways that makes dialogue with theology not only possible, but imperative. For they engage with the concept of Utopian imagination that transcends a given reality. They therefore describe an imperative to hope as the contestation of the visible, the known, and the inevitable.

Theo-politics

The greatest challenge to the methodology of this study has been in its attempt to construct an equal dialogue between political, philosophical and theological discourses. It was never my intention to assert the authority of one particular discourse through which to assess the others. Rather, I have tried to listen to, and take seriously, everyday *practices* of both despair and hope through the 'lenses' of all three as distinct modes of speaking of the end. In what sense, then, have I achieved a commentary of contemporary acts of hope in the light of 'political theology'? Some light can be shed on this question by positioning my work within some other currents of contemporary theology. I have, for instance, been motivated by a similar integration of theology and politics exemplified by the Catholic theologian William Cavanaugh. I have tried to reflect his concern to recognize the approach of both theology and politics as 'practices of the imagination'.[14] But I have also tried to identify a motivation to uncover state practices and wider mainstream political culture as false theology (I am indebted to the work of Philip Goodchild also in this respect). It can be seen as a 'secular parody'[15] of certain attributes of divine power. This has been exemplified in the *absolute* limit and ideological closure of apocalyptic terror. Unlike Cavanaugh, however, and in distinction from certain strands of 'Radical Orthodoxy', my task has *not* been to reinscribe religious practices as the

---

[14] William T. Cavanaugh, *Theopolitical Imagination: Discovering the Liturgy as a Political Act in an Age of Consumerism* (London: T&T Clark, 2002).

[15] William T. Cavanaugh, 'The City: Beyond Secular Parodies' in *Radical Orthodoxy: A New Theology*, ed. John Milbank, Catherine Pickstock and Graham Ward (London: Routledge, 1999), pp. 182–200 (p. 193).

necessary remedy to depoliticized public life and state practices. There is
no 'theological framework' unifying my political critique. And I certainly
do not want to suggest a theological input as presenting 'the only non-
nihilistic perspective' available.[16] What my analysis *has* captured, however, is
a sense of urgency in integrating religious concepts and categories for
reconceiving political practices of hope. Theo-political notions of the imagination and the future, play with assumptions about power and time that
are too useful, as descriptive tools, to ignore. More importantly, perhaps,
they are implicit to acts of resistance *already* operative in the social sphere.

Many contemporary writers speak about the 're-enchantment of the
world' only negatively (in order to proclaim the death of scientific authority
and the transfer of anti-intellectualism into superstition[17]). In contrast to
this I have tried to demonstrate that it is also possible to talk more positively
about the discursive *potential* opened up by this fragmented and overlap-
ping geography of the sacred and the secular. Fifty years ago in 'Theology
and Political Theory' Jacob Taubes, echoing George Sorel on the legacy
of the 'spirituality' at the heart of politics in the nineteenth century, commented that 'only myth delivers a criterion for societal action and only
myth can work as a driving force behind the historical process'.[18] For Taubes,
this only highlighted the danger of mythical desire detached from the
ground of authority. Authority, once occupied by religion, subsequently
threatened chaos without the 'rule of reason':

> without the rule of reason [. . .], the mythical energies immediately fall
> prey to such configurations as 'the general strike,' 'blood and soil' or
> 'national honour' because, while myth is innate in the soul, if it is blind
> its power is purely destructive.[19]

Today, however, we should contrast this warning with a suggestion that
what is to be feared is also the *paralysis* of mythical energies themselves.
Without a means to give legitimacy, including a theological legitimacy, to

---

[16] John Milbank, Catherine Pickstock and Graham Ward, 'Introduction: Suspending
the Material: The Turn of Radical Orthodoxy' in *Radical Orthodoxy*, ed. Milbank,
Pickstock and Ward, p. 4.

[17] See Morris Berman, *The Re-enchantment of the World* (Ithaca: Cornell University
Press, 1981).

[18] Jacob Taubes, 'Theologie und politische Theorie' in *Vom Kult zur Kultur: Bausteine
zu einer Kritik der historischen Vernunft*, ed. A. and J. Assmann, W.-D. Hartwich and
W. Menninghaus (München: Wilhelm Fink Verlag, 1996), pp. 257–267. I am
indebted to Paul Fletcher for a translation of this passage.

[19] *Ibid.*

contemporary mythic desires, it is the rule of reason, and particularly political reason, whose power becomes purely destructive, a war without end.

If this study has made any methodological discoveries, it must be to conclude that it is essential to explore ways of *listening*, as opposed to ways of *speaking*, to the voice of protest. We must explore the question of hope through a variety of political, philosophical and theological languages. My own hope is that by increasing a diversity of interpretations of cultural movements it becomes more and more possible to do this. We become better equipped to deliver the fruits of political action as genuine and radical commentaries on political possibility. To reflect on the most obvious example: the originally theological category of eschatology has functioned, not unlike the analyses of Paul Fletcher and Philip Goodchild, to highlight more than its influence on dominant political cultures. It also presents itself as a conceptual resource that might provide alternative world-views and expressions of hope within those cultures. Commenting on the emergence of 'secular eschatologies' is therefore of more than anthropological or sociological interest, though it is *not* able to go as far as to suggest a total reconception of political ontology, as Goodchild does.[20] It serves, nevertheless, to suggest the means for a theological input to political thinking. It does this through a reworking of popular approaches to hope, imagination and the future. These are categories that both act politically and transcend the narrow boundaries of thought often afforded them. Despite this, however, it is the fact that I have chosen *apocalyptic* as the occasion for a confluence between theological and political desires that has presented the greatest challenge. It has also exposed the limits to my search for a useful and responsible political theology. I have wanted, on the one hand, to demonstrate that apocalyptic desire has historically represented the political manipulation of theological symbols and cosmological myth for its own ends. On the other hand, I have also wanted to show how apocalyptic can represent the disentanglement of political energies, motivations and desires from oppression and political paralysis.

To do this I have pursued an assumption whose proper working out has been impossible within the scope of this study: namely, that one of the paradoxes of post-modernity is its simultaneous concern with the 'plane of immanence' (in the sense that society's highest values are inscribed into temporal *processes* and institutions) on the one hand, and its transcendence (breaking its boundaries) on the other. It is my conviction, in fact, that the ubiquity of apocalyptic sensibilities in contemporary life is a prime

---

[20] See Goodchild, 'Capital and Kingdom'.

example of how the notion of the secular as 'this-worldliness' in distinction to the 'other world' is relativized, if not made irrelevant. They are relativized through a movement, sometimes creative, and often destructive, of the fusion of those worlds as at times indissociable political desires. It is interesting to note John Milbank's definition of this immanentist social logic: he sees it as a description of the totality of reality without recourse to the eternal. In other words what is commonly perceived to be *all that there is*. He goes on to argue that such an assumption within political thought does seem strange alongside what he calls a 'Spinozistic twist' to the cultural atheism of neo-Marxists and other contemporary 'secularists'.[21] Invoking the second paradoxical concern of the post-modern, he thus defines the *saeculum* theologically as signifying 'the time before the eschaton'.[22] In other words, what our 'secular' concerns signify is the boundary beyond which we require faith more than we do certainty. Beyond the production of the modern identity stands the post-modern identity, 'a self able to transcend, identify with, and promote, or else refuse, the totality of process in the name of a truer 'life' which is invisible'.[23]

I can only provide an epilogue (or prologue?), then, by way of referring to this shift, this refusal, or 'exit' from the world of paralysing fear on behalf of those who dare to hope. Might it also represent a relativizing, or a throwing off kilter, of the notion of 'time before the eschaton' itself? The products of apocalyptic imagination are a strain on the very distinctions between 'before' and 'after'. That strain reveals itself most lucidly within a political culture that glorifies the *stasis* or 'polar inertia' of the present.[24] That which most generates the need for a theological lens on political practices is its production of an alternative conception of *temporality*. In particular it is the generation of a politically productive and creative 'apocalyptic time'. In the broad terms in which I have examined them, a transition from an eschatological rationality to an apocalyptic strategy emerges. The latter represents an emphasis on the performance of visionary transformation that believes itself capable not only of imagining that 'another world is possible', but also in its description, announcement and embodiment through political practices themselves.

---

[21] John Milbank, 'The Gospel of Affinity' in *The Future of Hope*, ed. Miroslav Wolf and William Keterberg, p. 156.

[22] Milbank, 'Gospel of Affinity', p. 155.

[23] *Ibid.* p. 157.

[24] See Paul Virilio, 'The Last Vehicle' in *Looking Back on the End of the World*, ed. Dietmar Kamper and Christoph Wulf, trans. David Antal (New York: Semiotext(e), 1989), pp. 106–119 (p. 106).

Ultimately, then, Wilhelm Reich's question with which I started is not nearly as appropriate as the parallel one posed by Foucault on the subject of physical resistance. For Foucault's chosen context, the Soviet 'Gulag', read the terrorizing and paralysing effects of fear within the war on terror:

> We must open our eyes . . . to what enables people there, on the spot, to resist the Gulag, what makes it intolerable for them, [. . .]. What is it that sustains them, what gives them their energy, what is the force at work in their resistance, what makes them stand and fight? [. . .]. The leverage against the Gulag is not in our heads, but in their bodies, their energy, what they say, think, and do.[25]

---

[25] Foucault, 'Powers and Strategies', p. 136.

Bibliography

Abercrombie, Nicholas, Stephen Hill and Bryan S. Turner, *The Dominant Ideology Thesis* (London: George Allen and Unwin, 1980).

Addley, Esther, 'High Anxiety', *The Guardian*, 13 February 2003.

Agamben, Giorgio, *Homo Sacer*, trans. Daniel Heller-Rozen (California: Stanford University Press, 1998).

—— *Means Without Ends: Notes on Politics*, trans. Vincenzo Binetti and Cesare Cesarino (Minneapolis: University of Minnesota Press, 2000).

—— *The Time That Remains*, trans. Patricia Dailey (California: Stanford University Press, 2005).

Ali, Tariq, *The Clash of Fundamentalisms* (London: Verso, 2002).

Altheide, David L., *Creating Fear: News and the Construction of Crisis* (New York: Walter de Gruyter, 2002).

Althusser, Louis, *Lenin and Philosophy and Other Essays*, trans. Ben Brewster (New York: Monthly Review Press, 1971).

Anderson, Benedict, *Imagined Communities: Reflections on the Origin and Spread of Nationalism* (London: Verso, 1991).

Anonymous, *On Fire: The Battle of Genoa and the Anti-capitalist Movement* (London: OneOff Press, 2001).

Anonymous, *Peace de Résistance, SchNEWS Annual 2003*, issues 351–401 (London: Calverts Press, 2003).

Arendt, Hannah, *Crises of the Republic* (New York: Harcourt Brace Jovanovich, 1972).

Aristotle, *Physics: Books III and IV*, trans. Edward Hussey (Oxford: Oxford University Press, 1983).

Badiou, Alain, *Saint Paul: The Foundation of Universalism*, trans. Ray Brassier (California: Stanford University Press, 2003).

Baird, Vanessa, 'No borders!: Report on No Border Camp in Strasbourg' in *New Internationalist Special Features*, 25 March 2002, www.newint.org/features/strasbourg/250702.htm [accessed 15 March 2006].

Bakhtin, Michael, *Rabelais and His World*, trans. Hélène Iswolsky (Bloomington: Indiana University Press, 1984).

Banksy, Robin, *Wall and Piece* (London: Century, 2005).

Barber, Benjamin R., *Fear's Empire: War, Terrorism, and Democracy* (London: W. W. Norton and Co., 2003).

Barkun, Michael, 'Politics and Apocalypticism' in *The Encyclopedia of Apocalypticism, vol. 3: Apocalypticism in the Modern Period and the Contemporary Age*, ed. Stephen J. Stein (New York: Continuum, 1999), pp. 442–460.

Barth, Karl, *The Epistle to the Romans*, trans. Edwyn C. Hoskins (Oxford: Oxford University Press, 1933).

────── *Church Dogmatics*, vol. 3, part 2, ed. G. W. Bromiley and T. F. Torrance, trans. Harold Knight and others (Edinburgh: T&T Clark, 1990).

Bauckham, Richard, *The Climax of Prophecy: Studies on the Book of Revelation* (Edinburgh: T&T Clark, 1993).

Baudrillard, Jean, 'The Anorexic Ruins' in *Looking Back on the End of the World*, ed. Dietmar Kamper and Christoph Wulf, trans. David Antal (New York: Semiotext(e), 1989), pp. 29–45.

────── *The Illusion of the End*, trans. Chris Turner (Cambridge: Polity Press, 1994).

────── *Simulacra and Simulacrum*, trans. Shelia Faria Glaser (Ann Arbor: University of Michigan Press, 1994).

────── *The Gulf War Did Not Take Place*, trans. Paul Patton (Sydney: Power Publications, 1995).

────── *Screened Out*, trans. Chris Turner (London: Verso, 2002).

────── *The Spirit of Terrorism*, trans. Chris Turner (London: Verso, 2002).

────── *Passwords*, trans. Chris Turner (London: Verso, 2003).

Baumgarten, Albert (ed.), *Apocalyptic Time* (Leiden: Brill, 2000).

Beardsworth, Richard, *Derrida and the Political* (London: Routledge, 1996).

Beck, Ulrich, *Risk Society*, trans. Mark Ritter (London: Sage, 1992).

────── *World Risk Society* (Cambridge: Polity Press, 1999).

Bentley, James, *Between Marx and Christ: The Dialogue in German-Speaking Europe, 1870–1970* (London: Verso, 1982).

Berman, Morris, *The Re-enchantment of the World* (Ithaca: Cornell University Press, 1981).

Berry, Philippa and Andrew Wernick (eds), *Shadow of Spirit: Postmodernism and Religion* (London: Routledge, 1992).

Blanchot, Maurice, *The Writing of the Disaster*, new edn, trans. Ann Smock (Lincoln: University of Nebraska Press, 1995).

Bleiker, Roland, *Popular Dissent, Human Agency and Global Politics* (Cambridge: Cambridge University Press, 2000).

Bloch, Ernst, *The Principle of Hope*, vol. 1, trans. Neville Plaice, Stephen Plaice and Paul Knight (Oxford: Basil Blackwell, 1986).

────── *The Principle of Hope*, vol. 2, trans. Neville Plaice, Stephen Plaice and Paul Knight (Oxford: Basil Blackwell, 1986).

──────*The Principle of Hope*, vol. 3, trans. Neville Plaice, Stephen Plaice and Paul Knight (Oxford: Basil Blackwell, 1986).

────── *The Spirit of Utopia*, trans. Anthony A. Nassar (Stanford: Stanford University Press, 2000).

Blumenfeld, Bruno, *The Political Paul: Justice, Democracy and Kingship in a Hellenistic Framework* (London: Sheffield Academic Press, 2001).

Boesak, Alan A., *Comfort and Protest: Reflections on the Apocalypse of John of Patmos* (Philadelphia: Westminster Press, 1987).

Borradori, Giovanna, *Philosophy in a Time of Terror: Dialogues with Jürgen Habermas and Jacques Derrida* (London: University of Chicago Press, 2003).

Bourdieu, Pierre, *Acts of Resistance*, trans. Richard Nice (Cambridge: Polity Press, 1998).

Bradstock, Andrew, *Faith in the Revolution: The Political Theologies of Müntzer and Winstanley* (London: SPCK, 1997).

Browning, Michael, 'War Photos That Changed History', *Palm Beach Post*, 12 May 2004, www.palmbeachpost.com/news/content/news/special_reports/war_photos/history.html [accessed 24 February 2006].

Brune, Adrian, 'Terror and Response', *Columbia University Graduate School of Journalism*, 19 September 2001, www.jrn.columbia.edu/studentwork/terror/sep19/vendors.asp [accessed 17 December 2005].

Bull, Malcolm (ed.), *Apocalypse Theory and the Ends of the World* (Oxford: Blackwell, 1995).

Bultmann, Rudolph, *History and Eschatology* (Edinburgh: Edinburgh University Press, 1975).

Burbach, Roger, *Globalization and Postmodern Politics: From Zapatistas to Hi-tech Robber Barons* (London: Pluto Press, 2001).

Burston, Bradley, 'Rachel Corrie and Israel's Army – A Death in Vain?', *Haaretz*, 16 March 2004, quoted in *The Palestine Monitor*, www.palestinemonitor.org/Activism/rachel_corrie_Israel_army_death_in_vain.htm [accessed 8 March 2006].

Bush, George W., 'Address to a Joint Session of Congress', *September 11 News*, 20 September 2001, www.september11news.com/PresidentBushSpeech.htm [accessed 17 December 2005].

——— 'Address to a Joint Session of Congress and the American People', *The White House* (September 2001), www.whitehouse.gov/news/releases/2001/09/20010920-8.html [accessed 10 December 2005].

Butler, Judith, 'Performativity's Social Magic' in *The Social and Political Body*, ed. Theodore R. Schatzki and Wolfgang Natter (New York: Guilford Press, 1996), pp. 20–47.

——— *The Psychic Life of Power* (Stanford: Stanford University Press, 1997).

——— 'Restaging the Universal' in *Contingency, Hegemony, Universality: Contemporary Dialogues on the Left*, ed. Judith Butler, Ernesto Laclau and Slavoj Žižek, (London: Verso, 2000).

Butler, Judith, Ernesto Laclau and Slavoj Žižek, *Contingency, Hegemony, Universality: Contemporary Dialogues on the Left* (London: Verso, 2000).

Camus, Albert, *Le mythe de Sisyphe* (Paris: Gallimard, 1942).

Caputo, John D., *The Prayers and Tears of Jacques Derrida: Religion Without Religion* (Indianapolis: Indiana University Press, 1997).

Caputo, John D., Mark Dooley and Michael J. Scanlon (eds), *Questioning God* (Bloomington: Indiana University Press, 2001).

Carter, April, *Direct Action and Democracy* (Cambridge: Polity Press, 2005).

Castells, Manuel, *The Power of Identity* (Oxford: Blackwell, 1997).

——— *The Rise of the Network Society*, 2nd edn (Oxford: Blackwell, 2000).

Castoriadis, Cornelius, *The Imaginary Institution of Society*, trans. Kathleen Blamey (Cambridge: Polity Press, 1987).

——— *World in Fragments: Writings on Politics, Society, Psychoanalysis, and the Imagination*, trans. and ed. David Ames Curtis (Stanford: Stanford University Press, 1997).

Cavanaugh, William T., 'The City: Beyond Secular Parodies' in *Radical Orthodoxy: A New Theology*, ed. John Milbank, Catherine Pickstock and Graham Ward, (London: Routledge, 1999), pp. 182–200.

———— *Theopolitical Imagination: Discovering the Liturgy as a Political Act in an Age of Consumerism* (London: T&T Clark, 2002).

de Certeau, Michel, *La prise de parole: pour une nouvelle culture* (Paris: Declée de Brower, 1968).

————*The Practice of Everyday Life*, trans. Steven Randall (London: University of California Press, 1984).

———— *La faiblesse de croire* (Paris: Éditions du Seuil, 1987).

———— *L'invention du quotidien 1. Arts de faire*, new edn (Paris: Gallimard, 1990).

———— *La culture au pluriel* (Paris: Éditions du Seuil, 1993).

———— *Capture of Speech and other Political Writings*, trans. Tom Conley (Minneapolis: University of Minnesota Press, 1997).

Chang, Nancy, *Silencing Political Dissent* (New York: Seven Stories Press, 2002).

Chomsky, Noam, 'The Responsibility of Intellectuals', *The New York Review of Books*, vol. 8, no. 3, 23 (February 1967), reproduced in *Chomsky.Info*, www.chomsky. info/articles/19670223.htm. [accessed 21 March 2006].

———— *Deterring Democracy* (London: Vintage, 1992).

———— 'Control of Our Lives' lecture, Kiva Auditorium, Albuquerque, New Mexico, 26 February 2000 in *Zmag*, www.zmag.org/chomskyalbaq.htm [accessed 14 January 2006].

———— 'Collateral Damage', interview by David Barsamian, *Arts and Opinion*, vol. 2, no. 4, 2003, www.artsandopinion.com/2003_v2_n4/chomsky-2.htm [accessed 13 March 2006].

———— Lecture at University of Manchester, Department of Government, 22 May 2004. Souled Out Films [DVD-ROM].

Clandestine Insurgent Rebel Clown Army, www.clownarmy.org/ [accessed 4 January 2008].

Cohen-Cruz, Jan (ed.), *Radical Street Performance: An International Anthology* (London: Routledge, 1998).

Cohen, Stanley and Jock Young (eds), *The Manufacture of News: Social Problems, Deviance, and Mass Media* (London: Constable, 1973).

Cohn, Norman, *The Pursuit of the Millennium: Revolutionary Messianism in Medieval and Reformation Europe and Its Bearing on Modern Totalitarian Movements* (London: Mercury Books, 1962).

———— *Chaos, Cosmos, and the World to Come: The Ancient Roots of Apocalyptic Faith* (London: Yale University Press, 1995).

Coleman, Penny, 'Veterans' Suicides: A Hidden Cost of Bush's Wars', *Alternet*, November 2007, www.alternet.org/waroniraq/67556/ [accessed 12 January 2008].

Collins, Adela Yobra, *Crisis and Catharsis: The Power of the Apocalypse* (Philadelphia: Westminster Press, 1984).

Cox, Harvey, 'The Problem of Continuity' in *The Future of Hope: Theology as Eschatology* (New York: Herder and Herder, 1970), pp. 72–80.

CrimethInc. Workers'Collective, *Days of War, Nights of Love: Crimethink for Beginners* (Atlanta: CrimethInc. Free Press, 2001).

Crouch, Colin, *Post-Democracy* (Cambridge: Polity Press, 2004).

Dark, David, *Everyday Apocalypse: The Sacred Revealed in Radiohead, The Simpsons, and Other Pop Culture Icons* (Grand Rapids: Brazos Press, 2002).

Davis, Creston, John Milbank and Slavoj Žižek (eds), *Theology and the Political: The New Debate* (London: Duke University Press, 2005).

Bibliography

Davis, Mike, *Ecology of Fear: Los Angeles and the Imagination of Disaster* (New York: Vintage Books, 1999).

Debord, Guy, *La société du spectacle* (Paris: Gallimard, 1992).

Deleuze, Gilles, *Negotiations*, trans. Martin Joughin (New York: Columbia University Press, 1995).

Deleuze, Gilles and Felix Guattari, *Anti-Oedipus: Capitalism and Schizophrenia*, trans. Robert Hurley and others (London: Athlone Press, 1984).

—— *A Thousand Plateaus: Capitalism and Schizophrenia*, trans. Brian Massumi (London: Continuum, 2004).

Derrida, Jacques, *Of Grammatology*, trans. Gayatri Chakravorty Spivak (Baltimore: Johns Hopkins University Press, 1976).

—— *Writing and Difference*, trans. Alan Bass (London: Routledge, 1978).

—— 'Of an Apocalyptic Tone Recently Adopted in Philosophy', trans. John P. Leavey, Jr, *Semeia*, no. 23 (1982), 63–98.

—— 'No Apocalypse, Not Now (Full Speed Ahead, Seven Missiles, Seven Missives)' trans. John P. Levy Jr, *Diacritics*, vol. 14, no. 2 (Summer 1984), 20–31.

—— *Positions*, trans. Alan Bass (London: Athlone Press, 1987).

—— *The Post Card*, trans. Alan Bass (Chicago: University of Chicago Press, 1987).

—— *Specters of Marx*, trans. Peggy Kamuf (London: Routledge, 1994).

—— *The Gift of Death*, trans. David Wills (London: University of Chicago Press, 1995).

—— *Acts of Religion*, ed. Gil Anidjar (London: Routledge, 2002).

—— 'For a Justice to Come', interview with Lieven de Cauter, trans. Ortwin de Graef, *Ris Orangis*, 19 February 2004, www.brusselstribunal.org/pdf/ Derrida_EN.pdf [accessed 18 January 2006].

Derrida, Jacques and Elisabeth Roudinesco, *For What Tomorrow: A Dialogue*, trans. Jeff Fort (Stanford: Stanford University Press, 2004).

Doyle, Laura (ed.), *Bodies of Resistance: New Phenomenologies of Politics, Agency, and Culture* (Illinois: Northwestern University Press, 2001).

Dumm, Thomas L., 'Telefear: Watching War News' in *The Politics of Everyday Fear*, ed. Brian Massumi (Minneapolis: University of Minnesota Press, 1993), pp. 307–321.

Eagleton, Terry, Review of *Straw Dogs* by John Gray, *The Guardian*, 7 September 2002.

—— *Figures of Dissent: Critical Essays on Fish, Spivak, Žižek and Others* (London: Verso, 2003).

—— *Holy Terror* (Oxford: Oxford University Press, 2005).

Edwards, David, 'Falling at the Feet of Power: Blair's Sincerity and the Media', *Media Lens*, 21 March 2003, www.medialens.org/ [accessed 10 December 2004].

Eliade, Mercia, *The Myth of the Eternal Return, or, Cosmos and History*, trans. William D. Trask (New York: Princeton, 1954).

Eliot, T. S., *Collected Poems 1909–1962* (London: Faber and Faber, *1974*).

Estrin, Marc, *Rehearsing with Gods: Photographs and Essays on the Bread and Puppet Theatre* (Vermont: Chelsea Green Publishing, 2003).

Ewald, François, 'Two Infinities of Risk' in *The Politics of Everyday Fear*, ed. Brian Massumi (Minneapolis: University of Minnesota Press, 1993), pp. 221–228.

Ferguson, David and Marcel Sarot (eds), *The Future as God's Gift: Explorations in Christian Eschatology* (Edinburgh: T&T Clark, 2000).

Ferguson, Euan, 'One Million. And still They Came', *The Observer*, 16 February 2003.

Fiorenza, Elisabeth Schüssler, *Revelation: Vision of a Just World* (Edinburgh: T&T Clark, 1993).

Fisk, Robert, 'Telling It Like It Isn't', *Znet*, 31 December 2005, www.zmag.org/content/showarticle.cfm?ItemID=9432 [accessed 13 March 2006].

Fletcher, Paul, 'The Political Theology of the Empire to Come', *Cambridge Review of International Affairs*, vol. 17, no. 1 (April 2004), 49–61.

———— 'The Nature of Redemption: Post-Humanity, Post-Romanticism and the Messianic', *Ecotheology*, 9.3 (December 2004), 276–294.

Foucault, Michel, *The Order of Things: An Archaeology of the Human Sciences*, trans. from the French (London: Tavistock/Routledge, 1970).

———— *Madness and Civilization: A History of Insanity in the Age of Reason*, trans. Richard Howard (London: Routledge, 1971).

———— *Surveiller et Punir: naissance de la prison* (Paris: Gallimard, 1975).

———— *Histoire de la sexualité, vol. 1: la volonté de savoir* (Paris: Gallimard, 1976).

———— 'Body/Power' in *Power/Knowledge: Selected Interviews and Other Writings 1972–1977*, ed. Colin Gordon, trans. Colin Gordon and others (London: Harvester Press, 1980), pp. 55–62.

———— 'Powers and Strategies' in *Power/Knowledge: Selected Interviews and Other Writings 1972–1977*, ed. Colin Gordon, trans., Colin Gordon and others (London: Harvester Press, 1980), pp. 134–145.

———— 'Truth and Power' in *Power/Knowledge: Selected Interviews and Other Writings 1972–1977*, ed. by Colin Gordon, trans., by Colin Gordon and others (London: Harvester Press, 1980), pp. 109–133.

———— *Histoire de la sexualité, vol. 3: le souci du soi* (Paris: Gallimard, 1984).

———— 'Iran: The Spirit of a World Without Spirit' in *Politics, Philosophy, Culture: Interviews and Other Writings, 1977–1984*, ed. Lawrence D. Kritzman, trans. Alan Sheridan and others (London: Routledge, 1988), pp. 211–224.

———— 'Useless to Revolt?' in *Power*, vol. 3, ed. James D. Faubion, trans. Robert Hurley (London: Penguin, 1994), pp. 449–453.

Fromm, Erich, *The Fear of Freedom* (London: Routledge and Kegan Paul, 1942).

Fukuyama, Francis, *The End of History and the Last Man* (London: Penguin Books, 1992).

Furedi, Frank, *Culture of Fear: Risk Taking and the Morality of Low Expectation* (London: Cassell, 1997).

———— *Politics of Fear* (London: Continuum, 2005).

Gamble, Andrew, *Politics and Fate* (Cambridge: Polity Press, 2000).

Gilbert, Gustave M., *Nuremberg Diary* (New York: Farrar, Strauss & Co., 1947).

Girard, René and Attilio Scarpellini, 'The Innocent Victim Has a Defender. And He Is in Jerusalem, Conversation with René Girard', *Chiesa*, 23 June 2003, www.chiesa.espressonline.it/dettaglio.jsp?id=6956&eng=y [accessed 17 March 2006].

Goodchild, Philip, *Deleuze and Guattari: An Introduction to the Politics of Desire* (London: Sage, 1996).

———— *Capitalism and Religion: The Price of Piety* (London: Routledge, 2002).

———— 'Debt, Epistemology and Ecotheology', *Ecotheology*, 9.2 (2004), 151–177.

———— 'Capital and Kingdom: An Eschatological Ontology' in *Theology and the Political: The New Debate*, ed. Creston Davis, John Milbank, and Slavoj Žižek, (London: Duke University Press, 2005), pp. 127–159.

———— *The Exceptional Political Theology of Saint Paul*, The Centre of Theology and Philosophy, Nottingham University, www.theologyphilosophycentre.co.uk/papers/Goodchild_Exceptional.doc [accessed 6 June 2008].

Gorringe, Timothy J., *Karl Barth: Against Hegemony* (Oxford: Clarendon Press, 1999).

Gramsci, Antonio, *Selections from the Prison Notebooks*, ed. and trans. Quenton Hoare and Geoffrey Newell-Smith (London: Lawrence and Wishart, 1971).

Gray, John, *Legitimation Crisis*, trans. Thomas McCarthy (Cambridge: Polity Press, 1988).

———— *False Dawn: The Delusions of Global Capitalism* (London: Granta Books, 1998).

———— *Hayek on Liberty*, 3rd edn (London: Routledge, 1998).

———— *Straw Dogs* (London: Granta Books, 2002).

———— *Black Mass: Apocalyptic Religion and the Death of Utopia* (London: Penguin, 2007).

Green, Garret, 'Imagining the Future' in *The Future as God's Gift: Explorations in Christian Eschatology*, ed. David Ferguson and Marcel Sarot (Edinburgh: T&T Clark, 2000), pp. 73–87.

Habermas, Jürgen, *The Structural Transformation of the Public Sphere*, trans. Thomas Burger (Cambridge: Polity Press, 1989).

Hall, Stuart, Chas Chritcher, Tony Jefferson, John Clarke and Brian Roberts, 'The Social Production of News: Mugging in the Media' in *The Manufacture of News: Social Problems, Deviance, and Mass Media*, ed. S. Cohen and J. Young (London: Constable, 1981), pp. 335–367.

Hanson, Anthony Tyrrell, 'Parousia' in *A New Dictionary of Theology*, ed. Alan Richardson and John Bowden (London: SCM Press, 1983), pp. 427–428.

Hardt, Michael and Antonio Negri, *Empire* (London: Harvard University Press, 2000).

———— 'What the Protesters in Genoa Want' in *On Fire: The Battle of Genoa and the Anti-capitalist Movement*, ed. Anonymous (London: OneOff Press, 2001), pp. 101–103.

Harvey, David, *The Condition of Postmodernity: An Enquiry into the Origins of Cultural Change* (Oxford: Basil Blackwell, 1989).

Harvie, David, Keir Milburn, Ben Trott and David Watts, *Shut Them Down! The G8, Gleneagles 2005 and the Movement of Movements* (New York: Autonomedia, 2005).

Havel, Vaclav, *The Art of the Impossible: Politics as Morality in Practice*, trans. Paul Wilson (New York: Knopf, 1997).

Heath, J., and Andrew Potter, *The Rebel Sell: How the Counter Culture Became Consumer Culture* (Oxford: Capstone Press, 2005).

Heidegger, Martin, *Being and Time*, trans. John Macquarrie and Edward Robinson (Oxford: Blackwell, 1962).

———— *The Concept of Time*, trans. William McNeill (Oxford: Blackwell, 1992).

———— *The Phenomenology of Religious Life*, trans. Matthias Fritsch and Jennifer Anna Gosetti-Ferencei (Bloomington: Indiana Univeristy Press, 2004).

Herman, Edward S., and Noam Chomsky, *Manufacturing Consent: The Political Economy of the Mass Media* (London: Vintage, 1994).

Herzog, Don, *Happy Slaves: A Critique of Consent Theory* (London: University of Chicago Press, 1989).

Herzog, Frederick (ed.), *The Future of Hope: Theology as Eschatology* (New York: Herder and Herder, 1970).

Hobbes, Thomas, *Leviathan*, ed. Richard Tuck (Cambridge: Cambridge University Press, 1991).

The Holy Bible, New Revised Standard Version (London: HarperCollins, 1989).

Hooper, Charlotte, 'Disembodiment, Embodiment and the Construction of Hegemonic Masculinity' in *Political Economy, Power and the Body*, ed. Gillian Youngs (London: Macmillan Press, 2000), pp. 31–51.

Howarth, David, Aletta J. Norval and Yannis Stavrakakis, *Discourse Theory and Political Analysis* (Manchester: Manchester University Press, 2000).

Hudson, Wayne, *The Marxist Philosophy of Ernst Bloch* (London: Macmillan Press, 1982).

Hughes, Glenn, *Transcendence and History: The Search for Ultimacy from Ancient Societies to Postmodernity* (Columbia: University of Missouri Press, 2003).

Hunsinger, George (ed.), *Karl Barth and Radical Politics* (Philadelphia: Westminster Press, 1976).

Jameson, Frederic, *The Political Unconscious: Narrative as a Socially Symbolic Act* (London: Routledge, 1981).

———— *Postmodernism: Or, the Cultural Logic of Late Capitalism* (London: Verso, 1991).

———— 'The Politics of Utopia' in *The New Left Review*, 25, 2nd series (January–February, 2004), pp. 35–54.

———— *Archaeologies of the Future: The Desire Called Utopia and Other Science Fictions* (London: Verso, 2005).

Jordan, John and Jennifer Whitney, 'Resistance Is the Secret of Joy' in *The New Internationalist*, 338 (September 2001), www.newint.org/issue338/secret.htm [accessed 21 March 2006].

Kamper, Dietmar and Christoph Wulf (eds), *Looking Back on the End of the World*, trans. David Antal (New York: Semiotext(e), 1989).

Kampfner, John, 'Saving Private Lynch story "flawed"', *BBC News*, 15 May 2003, http://news.bbc.co.uk/1/hi/programmes/correspondent/3028585.stm [accessed 13 March 2006].

Kant, Immanuel, *Critique of Pure Reason*, trans. J. M. D. Meiklejohn, www.marxists.org/reference/subject/ethics/kant/reason/critique-of-pure-reason.htm>.

Katerberg, William, 'History, Hope, and the Redemption of Time' in *The Future of Hope: Christian Tradition Amid Modernity and Postmodernity*, ed. Miroslav Volf and William Katerberg (Cambridge: William B. Eerdmans, 2004), pp. 49–73.

Katz, David S., and Richard H. Popkin, *Messianic Revolution: Radical Religious Politics to the End of the Second Millennium* (New York: Hill and Wang, 1998).

Kaufmann, Walter (ed.), *The Portable Nietzsche* (New York: Penguin Books, 1976).

Keller, Catherine, 'Why Apocalypse, Now?', *Theology Today*, vol. 49, no. 2 (July 1992), 183–195.

Kingsnorth, Paul, *One No, Many Yeses: A Journey into the Heart of the Global Resistance Movement* (London: Free Press, 2003).

Klein, Naomi, *No Logo* (London: Flamingo, 2001).

—— *Fences and Windows* (London: Flamingo, 2002).

Kumar, Krishnan, 'Apocalypse, Millennium and Utopia Today' in *Apocalypse Theory and the Ends of the World*, ed. Malcolm Bull (Oxford: Blackwell, 1995), pp. 200–224.

Laclau, Ernesto, *Emancipation(s)* (London: Verso, 1996).

—— 'Ideology and Hegemony: The Role of Universality in the Constitution of Political Logics' in *Contingency, Hegemony, Universality: Contemporary Dialogues on the Left*, ed. Judith Butler, Ernesto Laclau and Slavoj Žižek (London: Verso, 2000), pp. 44–89.

—— 'Can Immanence Explain Social Struggles?', *Diacritics*, 31.4 (2004), 3–10, http://muse.jhu.edu/journals/diacritics/v031/31.4laclau.pdf [accessed 21 March 2006].

Laclau, Ernesto and Chantal Mouffe, *Hegemony and Socialist Strategy*, 2nd edn (London: Verso, 2001).

La Due, William J., *The Trinity Guide to Eschatology* (London: Continuum, 2004).

Lash, Nicholas, *A Matter of Hope* (London: Darton, Longmann and Todd, 1981).

Lebel, Jean-Jacques, 'Notes on Political Street Theatre, Paris: 1968, 1969' in *Radical Street Performance*, ed. Jan Cohen-Cruz (London: Routledge, 1998), pp. 179–184.

Lebon, Gustave, *The Crowd: A Study of the Popular Mind* (New Jersey: Transaction Publishers, 1995).

Lee, Martha F., *Earth First!: Environmental Apocalypse* (New York: Syracuse University Press, 1995).

Loeb, Paul (ed.), *The Impossible Will Take a Little While: A Citizen's Guide to Hope in a Time of Fear* (New York: Basic Books, 2004).

Lotringer, Sylvère, 'Foreword' in Paolo Virno, *A Grammar of the Multitude*, trans. Isabella Bertoletti, James Cascaito and Andrea Casson (New York: Semiotext(e), 2004).

Ludlow, Morwenna, *Universal Salvation* (Oxford: Oxford University Press, 2005), in *Oxford Scholarship Online*, www.oxfordscholarship.com/oso/public/content/religion/0198270224/toc.html [accessed 20 March 2006].

Lincoln, Bruce, *Holy Terrors: Thinking about Religion after September 11* (London: University of Chicago Press, 2003).

Lynch, William F., *Images of Hope: Imagination as Healer of the Hopeless* (Notre Dame: University of Notre Dame Press, 1965).

Macey, Samuel L. (ed.), *Encyclopedia of Time* (New York: Garland Publishing, 1994).

Machiavelli, Niccolo, *The Prince*, trans. George Bull, new edn (London: Penguin Books, 1999).

Mangan, Lucy, Amy Fleming and Ian Katz, 'This Is My Generation's Equivalent of Living in Fear of the Bomb', *The Guardian*, G2 section, 13 February 2003.

Mannheim, Karl, *Ideology and Utopia*, trans. Louis Wirth and Edward Shils [1936], (London: Routledge, 1960).

Marx, Karl, *Capital*, vol. 1, [1867] abridged edn, ed. David McLellan, trans. Samuel Moore and Edward Aveling [1887] (Oxford: Oxford University Press, 1995).

Marx, Karl and Friedrich Engels, *The Communist Manifesto*, ed. David McLellan, trans. Samuel Moore [1888] (Oxford: Oxford University Press, 1992).

Massumi, Brian, *A User's Guide to Capitalism and Schizophrenia* (London: MIT Press, 1992).

────── 'Everywhere You Want to Be' in *The Politics of Everyday Fear*, ed. Brian Massumi (Minneapolis: University of Minnesota Press, 1993), pp. 3–37.

Massumi, Brian (ed.), *The Politics of Everyday Fear* (Minneapolis: University of Minnesota Press, 1993).

McCannell, Juliet Flower and Laura Zakaria (eds), *Thinking Bodies* (Stanford: Stanford University Press, 1994).

McCutcheon, Russel T., *Religion and the Domestication of Dissent, or How to Live in a Less Than Perfect Nation* (London: Equinox, 2005).

McKee, Alan, *The Public Sphere: An Introduction* (Cambridge: Cambridge University Press, 2005).

McMurray, Andrew, 'The Slow Apocalypse: A Gradualistic Theory of the World's Demise', *Postmodern Culture*, vol. 6, no. 3 (1996), http://muse.jhu.edu/journals/postmodern_culture/v006/6.3mcmurry.html [accessed 21 March 2006].

Michie, David, *The Invisible Persuaders: How Britain's Spin Doctors Manipulate the Media* (London: Bantam Press, 1998).

Milbank, John, 'Problematizing the Secular: The Post-Postmodern Agenda' in *Shadow of Spirit: Postmodernism and Religion*, ed. Philippa Berry and Andrew Wernick (London: Routledge, 1992), pp. 30–44.

────── 'The Gospel of Affinity', in *The Future of Hope: Christian Tradition Amid Modernity and Postmodernity*, ed. Miroslav Volf and William Katerberg (Cambridge: William B. Eerdmans, 2004), pp. 149–169.

Milbank, John, Catherine Pickstock and Graham Ward (eds), *Radical Orthodoxy: A New Theology* (London: Routledge, 1999).

Miller, David (ed.), *Tell Me Lies: Propaganda and Media Distortion in the Attack on Iraq* (London: Pluto Press, 2004).

Moltmann, Jürgen, *The Coming of God*, trans. Margaret Kohl (London: SCM Press, 1996).

────── 'Is the World Coming to an End or Has Its Future Already Begun?' in *The Future as God's Gift: Explorations in Christian Eschatology*, ed. Duncan Fergusson and Marcel Sarot (Edinburgh: T&T Clark, 2000), pp. 129–138.

Motzkin, Gabriel, 'Abnormal and Normal Time: After the Apocalypse' in *Apocalyptic Time*, ed. Albert I. Baumgarten (Leiden: Brill, 2000), pp. 199–214.

Nancy, Jean-Luc, 'Corpus', in *Thinking Bodies*, trans. Claudette Startilio, ed. Juliet Flower McCannell and Laura Zakaria (Stanford: Stanford University Press, 1994), pp. 17–31.

Negri, Antonio, *Time for Revolution*, trans. Matteo Mandarini (London: Continuum, 2003).

Nietzsche, Friedrich, *Twilight of the Idols: Or, How One Philosophizes with a Hammer* in *The Portable Nietzsche*, ed. and trans. Walter Kaufmann (New York: Penguin Books, 1976), pp. 463–563.

────── *The Birth of Tragedy: Out of the Spirit of Music*, trans. Shaun Whiteside, ed. Michael Tanner (London: Penguin Books, 1993).

Nome, Dagny, 'Promotional Culture: Seminar in Intercultural Management', *Copenhagen Business School*, www.anthrobase.com/Txt/N/Nome_D_01.htm [accessed 10 January 2006].

Northcott, Michael, *An Angel Directs the Storm: Apocalyptic Religion and American Empire* (London: I. B. Tauris and Co., 2004).

Notes from Nowhere Collective (eds), *We Are Everywhere: The Irresistible Rise of Global Anti-Capitalism* (London: Verso, 2003).

O'Leary, Stephen D., *Arguing the Apocalypse: A Theory of Millennial Rhetoric* (Oxford: Oxford University Press, 1994).

Palmer, Susan J. (ed.), *Millennium, Messiahs, and Mayhem* (London: Routledge, 1997).

Patterson, Stephen J., 'The End of Apocalypse: Rethinking the Eschatological Jesus', *Theology Today*, vol. 52, no. 1 (April 1995), 29–48.

Péguy, Charles, *Oeuvres Complètes*, vol. 5, (Paris: Nouvelle Revue Française, 1916).

Peters, Ted, 'Eschatological Rationality: Theological Issues in Focus', *Theology Today* (October 1998) reproduced in *Findarticles.com*, www.findarticles.com/p/articles/mi_qa3664/is_199810/ai_n8827206 [accessed 17 March 2006].

Pilger, John, *Hidden Agendas* (London: Vintage, 1998).

―――― 'The Lies of Old' in *Tell Me Lies: Propaganda and Media Distortion in the Attack on Iraq*, ed. David Miller (London: Pluto Press, 2004), pp. 18–37.

Pippin, Tina, *Death and Desire: Rhetoric of Gender in the Apocalypse of John* (Louisville: Westminster/John Knox Press, 1992).

Postel, Danny, 'Gray's Anatomy', *The Nation*, 22 December 2003.

Project for a New American Century, www.newamericancentury.org/index.html [accessed 22 December 2007].

Rahner, Karl, *Theological Investigations*, vol. 4, trans. Kevin Smyth (London: Darton, Longman and Todd, 1966).

―――― *Theological Investigations*, vol. 5, trans. Karl-H. Kruger (London: Darton, Longmann and Todd, 1966).

―――― *Theological Investigations*, vol. 10, trans. David Bourke (London: Darton, Longmann and Todd, 1973).

―――― *Theological Investigations*, vol. 12, trans. David Bourke (London: Darton, Longman and Todd, 1974).

―――― 'Apocalyptic' in *Encyclopedia of Theology: The Concise Sacramentum Mundi*, ed. Karl Rahner, trans. John Griffiths, Francis McDonagh and David Smith (London: Burns and Oates, 1975), pp. 16–20.

―――― 'Eschatology' in *Encyclopedia of Theology: The Concise Sacramentum Mundi*, ed. Karl Rahner, trans. John Griffiths, Francis McDonagh and David Smith (London: Burns and Oates, 1975), pp. 434–439.

Rahner, Karl (ed.), *Encyclopedia of Theology: The Concise Sacramentum Mundi*, trans. John Griffiths, Francis McDonagh and David Smith (London: Burns and Oates, 1975).

Rampton, Sheldon and John Stauber, 'Trading on Fear', *The Guardian*, 12 July 2003.

―――― *Weapons of Mass Deception: The Uses of Propaganda in Bush's War on Iraq* (London: Constable and Robinson, 2003).

Reich, Willhelm, *The Mass Psychology of Fascism*, trans. Vincent R. Carfagno (New York: Farrar, Straus and Giroux, 1970).

Rhythms of Resistance, www.rhythms-of-resistance.org/spip/article.php3?id_article=6 [accessed 16 July 2007].

Richardson, Alan and John Bowden (eds), *A New Dictionary of Theology* (London: SCM Press, 1983).

Ricoeur, Paul, *Du texte à l'action* (Paris: Éditions du Seuil, 1986).

—— *Lectures on Ideology and Utopia*, ed. George H. Taylor (New York: Columbia University Press, 1986).

Riddell, Mary, 'If in Doubt, Go Shopping', *The Observer*, 30 September 2001.

Robbins, Thomas and Susan J. Palmer, *Millennium, Messiahs, and Mayhem: Contemporary Apocalyptic Movements* (London: Routledge, 1997).

Robin, Corey, 'Reason to Panic' in *The Hedgehog Review*, vol. 5, no. 3 (2003), 62–80.

—— *Fear: The History of a Political Idea* (Oxford: Oxford University Press, 2004).

Rogozinski, Jacob, 'Chiasmus in the Polis: The Reversible Flesh of Community in Political Philosophy', in *Bodies of Resistance: New Phenomenologies of Politics, Agency, and Culture*, ed. Laura Doyle (Illinois: Northwestern University Press, 2001), pp. 5–36.

Rosen, Michael, *On Voluntary Servitude: False Consciousness and the Theory of Ideology* (Cambridge: Polity Press, 1996).

Rowland, Christopher, *The Open Heaven: A Study of Apocalyptic in Judaism and Early Christianity* (London: SPCK, 1982).

—— 'Upon Whom the Ends of the Ages Have Come: Apocalyptic and the Interpretation of the New Testament' in *Apocalypse Theory and the Ends of the World*, ed. Malcolm Bull, (Oxford: Blackwell, 1995), pp. 38–57.

Said, Edward, 'Who's in Charge?', *El Ahram*, 6 March 2003, http://weekly.ahram.org.eg/2003/628/op2.htm [accessed 24 March 2006].

Sauter, Gerhard, *Eschatological Rationality* (Michigan: Baker Books, 1996).

—— *What Dare We Hope? Reconsidering Eschatology* (Harrisburg: Trinity Press, 1999).

Schallit, Joel, *The Anti-Capitalism Reader* (New York: Akashic Books, 2002).

Scharlemann, Robert P. (ed.), *Theology at the End of the Century: A Dialogue on the Postmodern* (Charlottesville: University Press of Virginia, 1990).

Schatzki, Theodore R., and Wolfgang Natter (eds), *The Social and Political Body* (New York: Guilford Press, 1996).

Schedler, Andreas (ed.), *The End of Politics? Explorations into Modern Antipolitics* (London: Macmillan Press, 1997).

Schmid, Estella and David Morgan, *A Permanent State of Terror?* (London: Campaign against Criminalising Communities (CAMPACC), 2003).

Schwarz, Regina, *Transcendence: Philosophy, Literature, and Theology Approach the Beyond* (London: Routledge, 2004).

Schwöbel, Christopher, 'Last Things First?' in *The Future as God's Gift: Explorations in Christian Eschatology*, ed. David Ferguson and Marcel Sarot (Edinburgh: T&T Clark, 2000), pp. 217–241.

Scott, James C., *Domination and the Arts of Resistance: Hidden Transcripts* (London: Yale University Press, 1990).

Sim, Stuart, *Derrida and the End of History* (Cambridge: Icon Books, 1999).

Simons, Jon, *Foucault and the Political* (London: Routledge, 1995).

Skrimshire, Stefan 'Anti-G8 Resistance and the State of Exception' in *Shut Them Down! The G8, Gleneagles 2005 and the Movement of Movements*, ed. David Harvie et al (New York: Autonomedia, 2005), pp. 285–290.

Smith, James K. A., 'Determined Hope: A Phenomenology of Christian Expecta-
    tion' in *The Future of Hope: Christian Tradition Amid Modernity and Postmodernity*, ed.
    Miroslav Volf and William Katerberg (Cambridge: William B. Eerdmans, 2004),
    pp. 200–227.
Solnit, Rebecca, *Hope in the Dark: The Untold History of People Power* (Edinburgh:
    Cannongate, 2005).
Sontag, Susan, 'War Without End', *The New Statesman*, 16 September 2002.
―――― *Regarding the Pain of Others* (New York: Farrar, Straus and Giroux, 2003).
―――― 'Regarding the Torture of Others', *The New York Times*, reproduced in
    Truthout, www.truthout.org/cgi-bin/artman/exec/view.cgi/9/4592 [accessed 24
    February 2006].
Stein, Stephen J. (ed.), *The Encyclopedia of Apocalypticism, vol. 3: Apocalypticism in
    the Modern Period and the Contemporary Age* (New York: Continuum, 1999),
    pp. 442–460.
Stevens, Philip, 'A Poor Case for Globalisation', *The Financial Times*, 17 August
    2001.
Tarrow, Sidney, *Social Movements and Contentious Politics*, 2nd edn (Cambridge:
    Cambridge University Press, 1998).
Taubes, Jacob, *Vom Kult zur Kultur: Bausteine zu einer Kritik der historischen Vernunft*, ed.
    A. and J. Assmann, W.-D. Hartwich and W. Menninghaus (München: Wilhelm
    Fink Verlag, 1996).
―――― *The Political Theology of Paul*, trans. Dana Hollander (Stanford: Stanford
    University Press, 2004).
Taylor, Charles, 'A Place for Transcendence?' in *Transcendence: Philosophy, Literature
    and Theology Approach the Beyond*, ed. Regina Schwarz (London: Routledge, 2004),
    pp. 1–11.
Taylor, Gary and Malcolm Todd (eds), *Democracy and Participation: New Social
    Movements in Liberal Democracies* (London: Merlin Press, 2003).
Taylor, Mark C., 'Nothing Ending Nothing' in *Theology at the End of the Century:
    A Dialogue on the Postmodern*, ed. Robert P. Scharlemann (Charlottesville: University
    Press of Virginia, 1990), pp. 41–75.
Tillich, Paul, *The Eternal Now* (London: SCM Press, 2002).
Toole, David, *Waiting for Godot in Sarajevo: Theological Reflections on Nihilism, Tragedy
    and Apocalypse* (London: SCM Press, 2001).
Townsend, Mark and Paul Harris, 'Now the Pentagon Tells Bush: Climate Change
    Will Destroy Us', *The Observer*, 22 February 2004.
Travis, Alan, 'Surge in War Support Confirms Dramatic Shift in Public Opinion',
    The Guardian, 15 April 2003.
Valéry, Paul, *Tel Quel*, 2 (Paris: Gallimard, 1943).
Vaneigem, Raoul, *The Revolution of Everyday Life*, trans. Donald Nicholson-Smith
    (London: Rebel Press, 2001).
Virilio, Paul, 'The Last Vehicle' in *Looking Back on the End of the World*, ed. Dietmar
    Kamper and Christoph Wulf, trans. David Antal (New York: Semiotext(e), 1989),
    pp. 106–119.
―――― 'The Primal Accident' in *The Politics of Everyday Fear*, ed. Brian Massumi
    (Minneapolis: University of Minnesota Press, 1993), pp. 211–218.
―――― *Politics of the Very Worst*, interview by Phillipe Petit, trans. Michael Cavaliere,
    ed. Sylvère Lotringer (New York: Semiotext(e), 1999).

—— *Desert Screen: War at the Speed of Light*, trans. Michael Degener (London: Continuum, 2002).

—— *City of Panic*, trans. Julie Rose (Oxford: Berg, 2005).

Virno, Paolo, *A Grammar of the Multitude*, trans. Isabella Bertoletti, James Cascaito and Andrea Casson (New York: Semiotext(e), 2004).

Volf, Miroslav and William Katerberg, *The Future of Hope: Christian Tradition Amid Modernity and Postmodernity* (Cambridge: William B. Eerdmans, 2004).

Ward, Graham, *Barth, Derrida and the Language of Theology* (Cambridge: Cambridge University Press, 1995).

—— 'Questioning God' in *Questioning God*, ed. John D. Caputo, Mark Dooley and Michael J. Scanlon (Bloomington: Indiana University Press, 2001), pp. 274–290.

White, Eric, 'Kairos' in *Encyclopedia of Time*, ed. Samuel L. Macey (New York: Garland Publishing, 1994), pp. 332–333.

Wigley, Mark, *The Architecture of Deconstruction: Derrida's Haunt* (Massachusetts: MIT Press, 1995).

Wojcik, Daniel, *The End of the World As We Know It* (New York: New York University Press, 1997).

Wolfe, Alan, 'The Snake: A Review of *Empire*', *The New Republic Online*, 4 October 2001, www.powells.com/review/2001_10_04 [accessed 13 March 2006].

Wolfreys, Julian, *Deconstruction – Derrida* (New York: St Martin's Press, 1998).

Youngs, Gillian (ed.), *Political Economy, Power and the Body* (London: Macmillan Press, 2000).

Yuen, Eddie, Daniel Burton-Rose and George Katsiaficas (eds), *The Battle of Seattle: Debating Corporate Globalisation and the WTO* (New York: Soft Skull Press, 2001).

—— *Confronting Capitalism: Dispatches from a Global Movement* (New York: Soft Skull Press, 2004).

Žižek, Slavoj, 'Introduction: The Spectre of Ideology' in *Mapping Ideology*, ed. Slavoj Žižek (1994), pp. 1–33.

Žižek, Slavoj (ed.), *Mapping Ideology* (London: Verso, 1994).

—— *Welcome to the Desert of the Real!* (London: Verso, 2002).

—— *The Puppet and the Dwarf: The Perverse Core of Christianity* (Massachusetts: MIT Press, 2003).

—— *Organs Without Bodies: Deleuze and Consequences* (New York: Routledge, 2004).

Zolberg, Aristide, 'Moments of Madness', *Politics and Society*, 2, (Winter 1972), 183–207.

Zournazi, Mary, *Hope: New Philosophies for Change* (New York: Routledge, 2003).

Films

The Day After Tomorrow. Dir. Roland Emmerich. 20th Century Fox. 2004.

Noam Chomsky. Lecture at University of Manchester, Department of Government. 22 May 2004. Souled Out Films [DVD-ROM].

Index